THE QUEST FOR THE HISTORICAL ISRAEL

Society of Biblical Literature

Archaeology and Biblical Studies

Andrew G. Vaughn, Editor

Number 17

THE QUEST FOR THE HISTORICAL ISRAEL
Debating Archaeology and the History of Early Israel

THE QUEST FOR THE HISTORICAL ISRAEL
Debating Archaeology and the History of Early Israel

Invited Lectures Delivered at the Sixth Biennial
Colloquium of the International Institute for Secular
Humanistic Judaism, Detroit, October 2005

by

Israel Finkelstein

and

Amihai Mazar

edited by

Brian B. Schmidt

Society of Biblical Literature
Atlanta

THE QUEST FOR THE HISTORICAL ISRAEL
Debating Archaeology and the History of Early Israel

Library of Congress Cataloging-in-Publication Data

Finkelstein, Israel.
  The quest for the historical Israel : debating archaeology and the history of early Israel : lectures delivered at the Annual Colloquium of the Institute for Secular Humanistic Judaism, Detroit, October 2005 / by Israel Finkelstein and Amihai Mazar ; edited by Brian B. Schmidt.
      p. cm. — (Society of Biblical Literature Archaeology and Biblical Studies ; 17)
  Includes bibliographical references and index.
  ISBN 978-1-58983-277-0 (paper binding : alk. paper)
  1. Bible. O.T.—Antiquities—Congresses. 2. Bible. O.T.—Criticism, interpretation, etc.—Congresses. 3. Bible O.T.—Evidences, authority, etc.—Congresses. 4. Excavations (Archaeology)—Israel—Congresses. 5. Israel—Antiquities—Congresses. 6. Archaeology and religion—Congresses. I. Mazar, Amihay, 1942- II. Schmidt, Brian B. III. International Institute for Secular Humanistic Judaism. Colloquium (Detroit : 2005) IV. Title.

BS621.F567 2007b
221.9'5—dc22

2007010913

CONTENTS

LIST OF FIGURES AND TABLES

Preface

This book contains the papers that were delivered at an important event. That event was the Sixth Biennial Colloquium of the International Institute for Secular Humanistic Judaism in Detroit. The Institute is the intellectual arm of the worldwide movement of Secular Humanistic Judaism.

Humanistic Judaism depends on science for the story of the Jewish people. With regard to the early history of the Jews it depends on archaeology. It was our great desire to bring together two of the most famous Israeli archaeologists to thrill our audience with the revelation of their recent discoveries. We were not looking for final answers to our questions. We were looking for believable answers.

With the help of Professor Brian Schmidt of the University of Michigan, we were able to bring together Israel Finkelstein and Amihai Mazar to dialogue before an English-speaking lay audience for the first time. The results of the 2005 colloquium lectures entitled "Digging for Truth" were spectacular. This book is the consequence of a quite wonderful weekend.

Sherwin T. Wine, Provost
International Institute for Secular Humanistic Judaism

Note from the Authors and Editor

Rabbi Sherwin Wine was tragically killed on July 21, 2007 in an automobile accident while in Essaouira, Morocco, just as this volume was approaching the final stages of preparation for publication. We, the authors and editor, dedicate this volume to his lasting memory. Neither these essays, nor the Colloquium in which this book has its roots, would have seen the light of day without his tremendous support and unwavering encouragement.

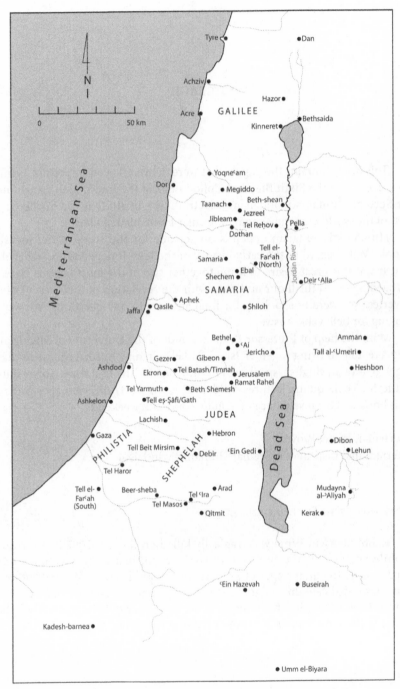

Map of Iron Age sites.

INTRODUCTION

Brian B. Schmidt

Several factors made the lectures presented by Professors Israel Finkel-stein and Amihai Mazar, and their publication here, a reality. First was the urgent need for new syntheses of Israel's early history. Second was the exceptional opportunity to convey the current state of affairs within the field of early Israelite history to an informed and highly receptive public as well as to fellow historians, and to do so from what is self described herein as two centrist perspectives. Third was Rabbi Sherwin Wine's invitation to propose a theme topic for the Biennial Colloquium sponsored by the International Institute for Secular Humanistic Judaism of Detroit. Fourth was the immediate interest expressed by Professors Finkelstein and Mazar in serving as the 2005 Colloquium plenary speakers. Last, but by no means least, were the many months of unswerving support, both leading up to and following the event, freely offered by the members of the colloquium organizing committee.

The timing of the presentation and publication of these lectures by two of the leading archaeologists of the southern Levant could not be more opportune. These lectures follow three decades of dialogue, discussion, and debate within the interrelated disciplines of Syro-Palestinian archaeology, Israelite history, and Hebrew Bible. As each of these fields enters a period of synthesis and re-articulation, even renewed cross-fertilization, following an elongated phase of reassessment and, at times, polarization, a balanced articulation of the issues and their resolution has become a desideratum. The occasional extremist tendencies of recent years—whether of a "radical" minimalist or of a "radical" maximalist orientation—are here complemented by alternative historical reconstructions emanating from a re-emergent, yet transformed, perspective. The essays contained here represent two moderating perspectives and have as their common ground the position that the material cultural data, the biblical traditions, and ancient Near Eastern written sources are all significantly relevant to the historical quest for ancient Israel of the Iron age (if not earlier). Yet, our authors articulate distinct views of Israelite history. Each gives different weight to these three lines of evidence as they bear on the interpretation and historical relevance of a particular epoch, event, or person of the past.

For ease of access, each set of lectures has, more or less, been organized according to the major epochs portrayed in the biblical narratives and within that general framework, both authors explore the controversial topics and issues that have come to the fore over the past two or three decades. Accompanying and introducing both presenters' lectures, I have added a summary in an attempt to highlight the solutions, methods or approaches, and supporting data offered by Professors Finkelstein and Mazar and to initiate further engagement with their proposals.

Part 1

Archaeology and the Quest for Historical Israel in the Hebrew Bible

A SUMMARY ASSESSMENT FOR PART 1

Brian B. Schmidt

Professor Israel Finkelstein initiates his introductory essay with a précis on the relationship between archaeology and the biblical text in modern scholarship. He begins with the nineteenth-century higher-biblical critic Julius Wellhausen and continues well into the twentieth century with what he views as the two dominant opposing schools that emerged, the German and the Anglo-American traditions. Finkelstein adopts as his general starting point that of the higher-critical approach along with some important recent revisions, while he sums up the Anglo-American school as essentially a conservative approach. In the latter case, archaeology has played only a supportive role to the sequential straightforward reading of the biblical text, or, as Finkelstein describes it, "a modern, almost word-for-word rewriting of the biblical story." He then suggests that this in turn explains, at least in part, why biblical archaeology "stalled" in terms of its contributions to the wider field of archaeology. He ends his survey with a summary and critique of a third, more-recent school, that of the so-called minimalists. He describes the minimalist position as follows: "Biblical history totally lacks an historical basis and its character as a largely fictional composition or wholly imaginative history is motivated by the theology of the time of its compilation in the Persian or Hellenistic periods, centuries after the alleged events took place. At best, it contains only vague and quite unreliable information about early Israel. Yet, the continuing power of the biblical narrative is testimony to the literary skill of the authors as they produced a compelling propagandistic work to a highly receptive public."

Finkelstein, however, notes that archaeological surveys, settlement studies, and extra-biblical historical records converge with the biblical traditions at numerous points having to do with geographical and historical matters pertaining to the Iron Age. He asks rhetorically whether or not this is mere coincidence and then goes on to describe such a possibility as "amazing" and the extensive administrative details in the Deuteronomistic History (Deuteronomy or Joshua through 2 Kings) "unnecessary," that is, if it is purely a

Fig. 1. The Tel Dan inscription. Photo courtesy of Zev Radovan.

mythic history. Among other arguments supporting the convergence of these otherwise independent lines of historical information, Finkelstein invokes the Iron II-period reference to the occurrence of the name (and dynasty) of David, "the House of David" or *bytdwd* in the Tel Dan inscription (fig. 1), a fragment of a larger commemorative stele erected most probably by Hazael, king of Damascus, following his conquest of the Galilee. This datum strikes a serious blow to the minimalist position he described earlier on the non-historicity of the biblical character that goes by the same name.

Finkelstein boldly claims that archaeology is the only real-time witness to events described in the biblical text, particularly those relating to the formative phases of early Israelite history. This is so because the biblical text is dominated by theological and ideological themes of the authors and their times. Finkelstein cites three examples of archaeology's contribution to the quest for the early historical Israel. First, he cites the archaeological evidence for the importance of Shiloh in the late-eleventh to the early-tenth centuries B.C.E. and its insignificance during the following Iron II period. Then he refers to the evidence for a society in the Iron I period that included bands of migratory peoples wandering along the margins of urban developments while the same areas in the Iron II period were densely settled and migratory bands no longer existed. Finally, Finkelstein invokes the material cultural data documenting the prominence of the Philistine city of Gath (Tell eṣ-Ṣâfi) in the ninth century B.C.E. and earlier, as well as its demise over the course of the following two centuries.

These he concludes, affirm the antiquity of portions of the stories about David and his times in 1 Samuel, and specifically those traditions concerning Shiloh's importance, those about David and his band of renegades wandering along the southern reaches of Judah, and the references to Philistine Gath's prominence in the David stories. For Finkelstein, all three also allow him to generalize in the following fashion; preserved in biblical traditions are older myths, tales, and memories that served as the nuclei for the stories composed by biblical authors. Although older stories can on occasion and in exceptional cases be detected in the biblical texts, more typically they are preserved in such a manner that reflect multiple layers and multiple realities from an earlier past and are at other times too well integrated into the ideology of the later biblical authors to be isolated in any meaningful way. Thus, as his own methodological starting point, Finkelstein proposes that biblical history should be read through the filter of its point of departure, which for him is the period of its compilation in late-monarchic times, most likely during the reign of King Josiah—not the later Persian or Hellenistic periods as the minimilists have proposed, or, for that matter, the earlier tenth century as Anglo-American scholarship has traditionally upheld. As the archaeological evidence seems to indicate, this is the period of Judah's dramatic growth toward full statehood and widespread literacy and, more to the point, it is from this period of Israel's early history that the biblical traditions can provide the modern historian with the most amount of socio-historical information.

Professor Amihai Mazar introduces his essay by surveying the modern history of archaeology in Israel as well as some of the major changes and new directions that biblical archaeology has undergone in terms of its methods and goals. He defends the concept of a "biblical archaeology" as referring to archaeological activity that pertains to the world of the Bible and as upholding what he views as the essential relationship between artifact and text. He then turns to the question of the historical relevance of the biblical text for reconstructing early Israel's history. For Mazar, this issue lies at the heart of the current controversy over the modern quest for the historical Israel. One means of productively pursuing that question is to employ the findings of archaeology as an independent, if not the primary, witness to the ancient historical reality and as a litmus test for assessing the historical relevance of any given biblical text. Archaeology, for Mazar, remains invaluable in spite of the subjective aspects of the enterprise. Mazar's provisional conclusion regarding the historical relevance of the biblical texts is that, in spite of the literary creativity and ideological biases of the writers as well as the presence of textual complexities resulting from other mediating influences, blocks of biblical materials may have historical relevance and may even preserve ancient pre-Israelite local memories. He lists as examples of what he deems as earlier materials and sources the following: archives in Jerusalem's temple library, palace archives, public commemorative inscriptions (on the analogy provided by the Mesha and Tel Dan inscriptions), oral transmission of ancient poetry (for example, Gen 49, Deut 32, and Judg 5), folk and aetiological stories rooted in the remote past (for example, portions of the Exodus and Conquest narratives, the deeds of the Judges, and biographical information on Saul, David, and Solomon), and historiographic writings explicitly mentioned by the biblical writers (for example, "the books of the chronicles of the kings of Israel").

For Mazar, accepted historical methods, external written sources and archaeological finds enable us to extract reliable historical information embedded in the biblical texts with archaeology functioning as a control tool offering increased objectivity. Mazar cites as an example of this the convergence of historical data from the Assyrian royal inscriptions, the Mesha inscription, the Tel Dan inscription, and the biblical text. Mazar concludes that these written sources, when taken together, confirm that the general historical framework of the Deuteronomistic History relating to the ninth century B.C.E. was based on reliable knowledge of that time period. Even so, Mazar remains more skeptical about the modern enterprise of writing an accurate history of early Israel and especially when it comes to the earliest stages of her past. He imagines the historical perspective preserved in the Bible as a telescope looking back in time. The farther back one goes from what Mazar views as the pivotal period of biblical composition, that is, the eighth to seventh centuries B.C.E., the more imaginative, symbolic, distorted, and "foggier" that past becomes. In addition, one must take into account the impact that such factors as distortion, selectivity, memory loss, censorship, and ideological or personal bias might have brought to bear on the composition of the resultant biblical traditions.

Digging for the Truth: Archaeology and the Bible

Israel Finkelstein

The question of the historicity of the biblical narrative as it pertains to ancient Israel and the ability of archaeology to contribute toward a better understanding of the text have hovered like black clouds over both academic research and public discussion for decades. The debates have been shaped not only by academic research in the fields of archaeology and biblical studies, but also by the cultural and historical processes in our own society. In recent years, we have seen a new "high tide" in the discussion, this time focusing on the problem of the United Monarchy and, in a way, on the question of the validity of the *entire* historical narrative in the Bible.

In the early days of scholarship, the battle over the history of early Israel was fought between a conservative school of thought, including the classical biblical archaeologists, and the higher-critical biblical scholars. A minimalist school, which rejected altogether the value of biblical history for the study of the history of Canaan/Israel in the Iron Age, joined this debate in the 1990s. Without engaging in a detailed survey of the history of research, I wish first to deal with the pros and cons of these two camps—the conservative and the minimalist—and then to turn to my own point of view, representing what I would describe as the voice of the center.

The major proposals of the higher-critical scholars of the nineteenth to twentieth centuries have, in my opinion, withstood the test of time. Admittedly, the assault of the last few decades on the Documentary Hypothesis and the model of a Deuteronomistic History have required that some revisions be made to these theories, but no convincing paradigms have been offered that can replace these models. In my view, they still provide a coherent historical and literary approach to the questions of structure, time, and *Sitz im Leben* as these pertain to the biblical text.

THE RISE AND FALL OF THE CONSERVATIVE CAMP

Scholars in the conservative camp follow the biblical text on the history of Israel in the way the ancient writers wanted us to read it, that is, as a reliable record of Israel's history, narrated in sequential chronological order, from earlier to later periods. Conservative scholars agree that the biblical materials—be they the Pentateuch or the Deuteronomistic History—reached their final shape relatively late in the history of Israel. Nevertheless, others would still claim a tenth- to ninth-century date for the crystallization of much of the material in the Pentateuch and would argue that, in both literary works, the later redactors incorporated early traditions, and even older written sources. While it may be true that only a few in the conservative camp would still try to identify a "Period of the Patriarchs" in the second millennium B.C.E., or explain the destruction of a major Late Bronze Age city as the result of the Israelite conquest of Canaan, many would still read the description of the Exodus on an Egyptian New Kingdom background. Moreover, all scholars in this camp would stand behind the biblical portrayal of a glorious United Monarchy.

In the early days, conservative scholars deployed archaeology to help defeat the higher criticism of scholars such as Julius Wellhausen. William F. Albright, followed by his students (and their disciples in our own days), promoted the idea that archaeology can prove the Bible correct and the critical scholars wrong. Two main case studies were put to the test: the Conquest of Canaan and the great United Monarchy of King Solomon. But the truth of the matter is that archaeology was not given center stage in the debate. It was used only in order to support a preconceived theory. Archaeology played the role of supplying decorative evidence for a history that was a modern, almost word-for-word rewriting of the biblical story. By doing that, scholars of the conservative school promoted historical and archaeological reconstructions that had no actual support in the finds, or were trapped in circular argumentation.

One of the best examples for the first case is the search for biblical Ezion-geber. In the late 1930s, the search for the great Solomon led the archaeologist Nelson Glueck to excavate Tell el-Kheleifeh, a small mound at the northern tip of the Gulf of Aqaba located on the modern border between Israel and Jordan. Glueck identified the site with Ezion-geber, the port from which, so the Bible says, King Solomon launched trade expeditions to exotic lands afar. Glueck uncovered much of the site, separated the remains into five periods of activity, dated them from the tenth to the fifth centuries B.C.E., and identified each according to the biblical references to Ezion-geber and Eilat. Every monarch who was mentioned in the Bible in relation to activities in the Gulf of Aqaba was granted an archaeological stratum. Glueck interpreted the remains of the first period—including what he described as flue holes, air channels, hand bellows, clay crucibles, and furnace rooms—as evidence for a huge copper-smelting industry in the days of King Solomon. Glueck went so far as to dub Ezion-geber the "Pittsburgh of Palestine" and King Solomon "a copper king, a shipping magnate, a merchant prince, and a great builder."

This romantic image later proved to be a fantasy, a wishful illusion based on the biblical text rather than on actual archaeological evidence. A thorough study of the finds has found no evidence whatsoever for smelting activity at the site. The "crucibles" proved to be sherds of locally produced, handmade pottery vessels; the "flue holes" were no more than holes for wooden beams that had rotted away; and there were only a few metallic finds—certainly no evidence of an active smelting industry. No less important, it became clear that the site was established only in the late-eighth or early-seventh century B.C.E. The elaborate stratigraphy of successive kings and their industrial center simply did not exist. In fact, at the time of the historical Solomon in the tenth century B.C.E., this place near the shore of the Gulf of Aqaba was no more than a sand dune.

A good case for demonstrating the second problem—that of circular argumentation—can be found at Gezer. William G. Dever, the excavator of the site and an outspoken student of the Albrightian, or conservative, school of thought, argued that the reconstruction of a great Solomonic United Monarchy is based on solid archaeological evidence, which is based, in turn, on meticulous study of Iron Age pottery: "The pottery from this destruction layer [at Gezer—I.F.] included distinctive forms of red-slipped and slipped and hand burnished (polished) pottery, which have always been dated to the late tenth century. . . . Thus, on commonly accepted *ceramic* grounds—not on naive acceptance of the Bible's stories . . .—we dated the Gezer Field III city walls and gates to the mid–late tenth century." Dever refers here to one of the highlights of the Gezer excavations, the notion that red-slipped and burnished pottery can be used as a peg for dating tenth-century strata. But red-slipped and burnished pottery does not carry a date label. So how was it dated to the tenth century B.C.E.? It was so dated on the basis of its find spot—in a layer linked to a gate that was associated with King Solomon on the basis of a single biblical verse, 1 Kgs 9:15; this is a clear case of circular reasoning.

The same holds true for the idea that some of the great compositions in biblical history took place in the tenth century B.C.E. Scholars argued that one of the sources of the Pentateuch (the J source) and much of the story of the early days of the Davidic dynasty in the books of Samuel were put in writing in Jerusalem in the days of the United Monarchy or immediately thereafter. According to them, this was a time of great enlightenment and composition of literary works. They based their theory on the biblical description of the glamorous kingdom of Solomon, including the mention of the office of scribe in his court—another clear case of circular reasoning. As I have argued time and again, archaeology shows that meaningful scribal activity appeared in Jerusalem only with the rise of Judah to full statehood in the late-eighth century B.C.E., over two centuries after the supposed days of the United Monarchy.

In short, conservative scholars, even the archaeologists among them, reconstructed the history of Israel according to the biblical text. Archaeology played only a supportive role, and this, I suppose, is the reason—contrary to statements by some of its own followers—that "classical" biblical archaeology stalled relative to world archaeology in almost every field of research, for example, in understanding the importance of environmental archaeology, in accepting the value of anthropological and ethnographic comparisons in archaeology, and in introducing studies from the exact sciences. And this is also the reason why the great thinkers of modern world archaeology did not come from the discipline of biblical archaeology. I have in mind such great American and British scholars as Flannery, Binford, Adams, Renfrew, and Braidwood.

THE RISE AND FALL OF THE MINIMALIST SCHOOL

According to a recent group of biblical scholars described as minimalists or deconstructionists, the historical material in the Bible that pertains to the Iron Age is a late composition dating to the Persian or even Hellenistic periods, that is, the fifth to second centuries B.C.E. It is a largely fictional composition motivated by the theology of the time of its compilation, which occurred centuries after the alleged events took place. Thus, it contains only vague and quite unreliable information about the origins and early history of Israel. According to these scholars, the continuing power of the biblical narratives is testimony to the literary skill of the authors, who stitched together old myths, folktales, imaginary records, legendary narratives, and a few memories of historical facts (about the ninth to early sixth centuries B.C.E.) into a single saga of apostasy and redemption.

Philip Davies, for example, saw the compilation of biblical history as a long process in the Persian and Hellenistic periods, with the final form of the narrative probably being created in Hasmonean Judea of the second century B.C.E. Davies depicted the authors of the biblical text as ideologues in service to the temple elite. He traced their ideology back to the political goals of the Judean priests who had returned from exile in the Persian period. As a Persian-appointed elite that ousted the local leadership of Judah, they needed to "create" a history to legitimate their role. The Jerusalem scribes of the post-exilic period collected folktales and vague memories and skillfully wove them into a wholly imaginary history that stressed the centrality of Jerusalem, its temple, its cult, and its priests. This would have been a complete innovation, designed to establish a "national" myth of origin. According to this premise, biblical "history" was not only historically baseless, but powerful, focused propaganda that delivered an essentially made-up story of the Patriarchs, Exodus, Conquest, and the glorious golden age of David and Solomon to a credulous public.

The biblical scholar Thomas Thompson accepted the idea of a very late and almost entirely fictional "history of Israel." He reinterpreted the archaeological evidence in order to reconstruct a multi-ethnic society in Iron Age Palestine, with no distinctive religion or ethnic identity at all. It was a heterogeneous population that was split between the regional centers at Jerusalem, Samaria, Megiddo, Lachish, and other cities. These peoples cherished their own local heroes and worshipped a large pantheon of ancient Near Eastern deities. Biblical scribes falsified that reality with its uncompromising theology of national sin and redemption. That was why, the minimalists argue, there can be no archaeological evidence of the United Monarchy, much less evidence of an historical personality like David, since both were part of a religious mythology wholly made-up by Judean scribes in the Persian and Hellenistic periods.

This revisionist theory of the Bible's utter lack of historical value had its own logical and archaeological inconsistencies. First of all, as the biblical scholar William Schniedewind has indicated, literacy and extensive scribal activity in Jerusalem in the Persian and early-Hellenistic periods were much less influential than in the seventh century B.C.E. The assumption is inconceivable that in the fifth, or fourth, or even second centuries B.C.E., the scribes of a small, out-of-the-way temple town in the Judean mountains authored an extraordinarily long and detailed composition about the history, personalities, and events of an imaginary Iron Age "Israel" without using ancient sources.

The sheer number of name lists and details of royal administrative organization in the kingdom of Judah that are included in the Deuteronomistic History seems unnecessary for a purely mythic history. In any event, if they are all contrived or artificial, their coincidence with earlier realities is amazing. Archaeological excavations and surveys have confirmed that many of the Bible's geographical listings—for example, of the boundaries of the tribes and the districts of the kingdom—closely match settlement patterns and historical realities in the eighth and seventh centuries B.C.E. Equally important, the biblical scholar Baruch Halpern showed that a relatively large number of extra-biblical historical records—mainly Assyrian—verify ninth- to seventh-century B.C.E. events described in the Bible: the mention of Omri in the Mesha stele, those of Ahab and Jehu in the Shalmaneser III inscriptions, Hezekiah in the inscriptions of Sennacherib, Manasseh in the records of Esarhaddon and Ashurbanipal, and so on. No less significant is the fact, as indicated by the linguist, Avi Hurwitz, that much of the Deuteronomistic History is written in late-monarchic Hebrew, which is different from the Hebrew of post-exilic times.

Much of the minimalist effort has been invested in the claim that David and Solomon—the founders of the Jerusalem dynasty—are not historical figures. They argued that, like Abraham, Moses, Joshua, David, and Solomon are not mentioned in any extra-biblical texts and should therefore be seen as legendary personalities. This argument suffered a major blow when the Tel Dan basalt stele was discovered in the mid-1990s. It comprises several fragments of a triumphal inscription written in Aramaic. The king it honored was most probably Hazael, king of Aram-Damascus, who was portrayed in both the Bible and Assyrian records as an important international player in the late-ninth century B.C.E. His battles against Israel are recorded in the books of Kings.

Though fragmentary, this inscription offered a unique perspective on the turbulent politics of the region in the ninth century B.C.E. It describes, from the Aramean perspective, the territorial conflict between Israel and Damascus in the ninth century B.C.E. and records how an Aramean king (Hazael) launched a punishing offensive against his southern enemies (ca. 840 B.C.E.), in which—so he claimed—he killed the king of Israel and his ally, the king of the "House of David" (or *bytdwd*). This was the first time that the name "David" was found in any contemporary source outside the Bible, in this case only about a century after his own supposed lifetime. Moreover, it most probably specified the names of the two later kings—Joram of Israel and Ahaziah of Judah—both of whom are mentioned in the biblical text. Most significantly, Hazael employed a common idiom of his time by naming a state (Judah) after the founder of its ruling (or dominant) dynasty, *bytdwd*—just as the Assyrians labeled the Northern Kingdom as "the House of Omri" or *bit omri*.

THE VIEW FROM THE CENTER

The third camp—to which I belong and which is positioned in the center, is far from either of the other two poles I have treated above. Scholars in this camp adopt a late-monarchic (or exilic) date for a large portion of the Pentateuch and much of the Deuteronomistic History. Hence, they acknowledge the value of these texts in preserving reliable evidence on the history of Israel in monarchic times. However, they see the stories—in the way they are presented in the text—as highly ideological and adapted to the needs of the community during the time of their compilation. Hence, the most meaningful difference from the conservative camp is that the adherents of the centrist camp tend to read the texts in the reverse direction of their canonical order, beginning with the safe anchor of the period of their compilation and reading back—*histoire regressive* as the great French historian of the *Annales* school Marc Bloch called this method. This does not mean that the texts have no historical value. It does imply, however, that in many cases, mainly regarding the formative periods in the history of ancient Israel, they provide us with far more historical information about the society and politics of the writers than about the times described in them.

This means that I would see large portions of both the Pentateuch and the Deuteronomistic History as supplying the ideological platform for the political program of Judah in later, monarchic times. I refer to the pan-Israelite idea, which, to the best of my understanding, first surfaced in full-blown shape at that time. It argued that the Davidic kings are the only legitimate heirs to the territories of vanquished Israel and to the leadership over the Israelites still living in these territories, and that the cult of all Israelites should be centralized in the temple in Jerusalem. As such, the texts are highly ideological on both the political and theological levels. They represent the point of view of one elite faction of Judahite society (we have no idea if it ever formed the majority in late-monarchic times); they certainly do not represent the Northern Kingdom or what Morton Smith years ago called the "syncretistic" party in Judah. We can only imagine how different a history of Israel written by scribes from the Northern Kingdom or by other factions of Judahite society would be had it survived.

As highly ideological texts, even the treatment of periods close in date to the time of the compilation cannot be read uncritically. A good example—emphasized long ago by the biblical historian Nadav Na'aman—can be found in the biblical treatment of the "Assyrian century" in the history of Judah. In most of this period, Judah was ruled by three kings: father, son, and grandson. The first, Ahaz, is depicted as a sinner and as one who cooperated with the Assyrians and compromised Judah's independence. His son Hezekiah is described as the second-most-righteous king from the lineage of David and as a hero who stood firmly and courageously against Assyria. The Deuteronomistic Historian even makes a special effort to hide the fact that Judah remained under Assyrian domination many years after the "miraculous" rescue of Jerusalem from Sennacherib. The grandson, Manasseh, who ruled in Jerusalem for over half a century, is described as the most evil of all apostates and head of all villains. The Exilic redactor of the Deuteronomistic History flatly puts the responsibility for the fall of Jerusalem on his head.

Archaeology has given us a completely different story—or at least a completely different perspective on Judahite affairs. Ahaz saved Judah from the bitter fate of the Northern Kingdom and incorporated it into the Assyrian economy. His policy led Judah to unprecedented prosperity in which Jerusalem and Judah experienced dramatic demographic growth. This was the time when Jerusalem expanded to the Western Hill. Judah apparently participated in the Assyrian-led Arabian trade and as a result, the Beer-sheba Valley flourished. In contrast, Hezekiah made a reckless decision to rebel against Assyria and was therefore responsible for the events that led to the utter devastation of Judah. Archaeology demonstrates the extent of the catastrophe. Almost every site excavated in the Shephelah and the Beer-sheba Valley revealed evidence for destruction. The Shephelah—the breadbasket of Judah—never recovered from the shock. Surveys reveal the dramatic decrease in the number of settlements there in the seventh century B.C.E.

Archaeology also shows us that Manasseh saved Judah from annihilation. Under his *Realpolitik* of cooperation with Assyria, the Southern Kingdom emerged from the ashes, was reincorporated into the Assyrian economy, and reached unprecedented prosperity. Judah increased its role in the Assyrian-led southern trade and the Beer-sheba Valley experienced a record settlement density. Judah must have been the main supplier of olives for the extensive Assyrian oil industry at Ekron (Tel Miqne). As a result, the Shephelah at least partially recovered. Ostraca, seals and seal impressions, weights and other finds indicate that in Manasseh's days, Judah enjoyed an impressive literacy rate.

The lesson here is clear and simple. If a period so close to the compilation of the text shows such a great gap between the heavy ideological construct of the biblical text and the more nuanced economic and social construct of the finds, one should be even more cautious when dealing with the description of earlier periods. The Deuteronomistic Historian could have been even more free to advance his ideology in those cases where the memory of the real events was increasingly more vague.

Once we become aware of the fact that the texts are relatively late in date, and that they preserve the stories from the subjective point of view of the needs of the writers, then we can acknowledge the tremendous power of archaeology as the real-time witness to the events. A good example is Israel's formative period, where archaeology is the only source of information. The Conquest and Judges stories, even if containing a few vague memories of heroic events, mythological or real, are almost complete expressions of the political and theological ideology of Josianic times. The Bible, then, provides only those impressions of the rise of early Israel that the late-monarchic writers wanted to—or could—give us. Only archaeology can inform us about the material culture of the Iron I sites in the highlands, about the dispersal of their settlements, about their economy, and about their relationship with their neighbors. Archaeology also gives us the long-term perspective on the demographic history of the highlands, which reveals the origin of the settlers in the Iron I sites. And, as I will outline below, archaeology is the sole witness for the tenth century B.C.E. In short, archaeology is the "queen of the battle" when it comes to the history of early Israel—especially the formative periods.

The findings from archaeology actually go far beyond this. They can also significantly inform us about the texts themselves, for example, by providing information about their possible date of compilation. As I have already noted, many biblical scholars date two of the three main sources of the Pentateuch, J and E, to early monarchic times, in the tenth century or immediately thereafter. Many more argue that the Deuteronomistic History, even if compiled in the seventh or sixth century B.C.E., incorporated *written* material from the tenth century B.C.E. Archaeology demonstrates, however, that both of these literary theories are highly unlikely.

It is quite clear that both literary works, the Pentateuch and the Deuteronomistic History, were meant to convey theological, cultural, and political messages. As such, they were probably directed at a wider public far beyond the circles of the writers. They were meant to be read by (or to) both the people in the capital and in the countryside of Judah. I would argue therefore that the "standardized" literary works narrating the history of Israel (in contrast to scattered, contradictory, and partial oral traditions) must have been written in an urban society, one with a high level of knowledge, sophistication, and literacy among the elite and the circles around it. They must have been written when the community was already quite advanced from the socio-political point of view and they must have been written in a period when literacy spread not only in the capital, but also to the countryside of the kingdom. As I will demonstrate below, these conditions did not materialize in Judah and Jerusalem before the late-eighth century B.C.E.

As I have already mentioned, though the Pentateuch and the Deuteronomistic History were put in writing relatively late in Israelite history, most biblical scholars would accept that they include materials that originate from times prior to that of their written compilation. The problem is that in most cases the old memories are so vague, or so manipulated by the later writers, that the early realities in them are beyond recovery. Only archaeology can assist scholars in identifying such earlier traditions, but even then, it can do so only in part and in isolated cases. I wish briefly to demonstrate this with three examples, all from the Deuteronomistic History.

The excavations at Shiloh in the 1980s have shown beyond doubt that the site reached its peak of activity in the mid-Iron I, in the late-eleventh century

B.C.E. Throughout most of the lengthy Iron II period, there was only meager activity at the site. Shiloh seems to have been deserted. It is clear therefore that the stories in 1 Samuel about the importance of Shiloh in pre-monarchic times cannot reflect late-monarchic realities. Rather, they must represent some memories concerning the importance of the site in earlier times.

The same holds true for the cycle of stories regarding the wandering of David and his men along the southern fringe of Judah. These narratives clearly fit the description of a band of Apiru—uprooted people who lived on the margins of the society—moving in a sparsely settled region and far from the control of any central authority. This kind of background does not fit the late-monarchic period, when the area was densely settled and lacked any trace of a remaining Apiru reality. Therefore, I see no alternative but to argue that the stories reflect what I would label a continuous, "Amarna-like" social development in the Judahite hill country prior to the great demographic growth of Judah in the late-eighth century B.C.E.

The third example relates to Philistine Gath. Recent excavations at Tell eṣ-Ṣâfi, the location of this biblical city, proved that it reached its zenith in the ninth century B.C.E. At that time it may have been the largest city in Philistia, one of the most important cities in the entire country. Then, in the late-ninth century, it was besieged and put to the torch, seemingly by Hazael of Damascus. Gath never recovered from this shock. Sargon II mentions it in the late-eighth century as a dependent of Ashdod. Assyrian and biblical records from the seventh century B.C.E. list only four Philistine cities—Gath is absent. It is clear therefore that the biblical stories about the time of David, which describe Gath as the most prominent Philistine city, must preserve an early- or middle-ninth-century reality.

But there is much more than old memories in the late-monarchic composition labeled the Deuteronomistic History. It is unthinkable that the biblical authors invented stories only in order to serve their aims. Had they done that they would have lost their credibility among the people of Judah, their target population. It is more reasonable to assume that the authors collected myths, folktales, popular heroic tales, and shreds of memories known to the population of Judah and employed them in their cause. Needless to say, not everything was incorporated into the text. The authors included those stories that suited their theological and ideological agenda.

But collecting stories is one thing and preserving their older meanings and contexts is another. The underlying idea in many biblical studies of the conservative camp, that old memories were orally transmitted, unchanged through the centuries, is unrealistic and somewhat naive. Old stories must have absorbed different layers of realities on their way down through the centuries until they were put in writing. Therefore, as Neil Asher Silberman and

I have shown elsewhere, in the stories of David's rise to power and the succession of Solomon in the books of Samuel, one can identify several horizons representing different realities of the tenth to seventh centuries B.C.E.: heroic stories that may have preserved original tenth-century memories; stories about the prominence of Gath and the conquests of David that best fit the ninth century; the idea of a central Temple in Jerusalem, which may represent the period immediately following the fall of the Northern Kingdom in the late-eighth century; and stories revealing Greek influence that best fit the late-seventh century (such as the description of Goliath dressed in hoplite armor). From the ideological point of view, there is no question that the most influential social context for the composition of biblical history is that of the time of its compilation, in the late-seventh century B.C.E.

Yet, recognizing the possible historical value of isolated elements is something very different from accepting as reliable the entire story of the rise of a United Monarchy in much earlier times. Should we consider the biblical materials on the *formative* stages in the history of Israel as ahistorical and therefore useless as a source for the study of the rise of ancient Israel? The answer is both positive and negative. Positive, because the biblical materials cannot help us to reconstruct fully these early days. Negative, because they preserve much about the society and realities of the time of their writing. This is the point that I have tried to emphasize—that the main contribution of the "view from the center" is to demonstrate that these texts should not be read as a sequential history, from ancient to later times, but in reverse—from the time of the writing back to the more remote periods of history.

I would summarize by listing the following guidelines for a viable reconstruction of the early history of Israel:

1. Archaeology is the only real-time witness to many of the events described in the biblical text, mainly for the pre-ninth-century B.C.E. formative periods.

2. Biblical history cannot be read as a modern chronicle. It is dominated by the theological and ideological themes of the authors.

3. Biblical history cannot be read in a simplistic way, from early to late. Rather, the point of departure must be a thorough knowledge of the social, economic, and geopolitical realities of the composition period in late-monarchic times (and later, in some cases).

4. There are many old stories in the text, but they are described in a way that fits the ideology of the later authors.

5. Many of the texts are comprised of several layers; only archaeology and extra-biblical sources can help identify and separate them.

6. The starting point for the compilation of the biblical text is the sudden growth of Judah to full statehood as a direct outcome of the fall of

the Northern Kingdom and the integration of Judah into the global economy of the Assyrian Empire.

Had such guidelines been applied from the outset of the modern biblical-historical enterprise, we would not have wasted a century on futile research.

On Archaeology, Biblical History, and Biblical Archaeology

Amihai Mazar

The aim of these essays is to examine some of the currently debated issues pertaining to the relationship between the Hebrew Bible, archaeology, and recent historical reconstructions of the history of ancient Israel. For example, to what extent can the biblical narratives on the early history of Israel be utilized in writing a history of early Israel? Are they historically reliable or are they national sagas created with little or no historical basis, centuries later than the assumed historical time of the events that they describe? Such questions have been raised by scholars for the entire biblical narrative; from the Patriarchal stories, to Israel's slavery in Egypt, the Exodus, the Conquest, the period of the Judges and, more recently, the time of the first three kings—Saul, David, and Solomon. Even the period of the divided monarchy is debated. When did Israel and Judah emerge as states? What did the historical and cultural developments of these states look like?

Questions have also been raised concerning the history of Israel's religion. When did Israelite belief in Yahweh as one god emerge? Was the belief in this particular god identical with the emergence of monotheism? Such subjects, and many related ones, have been central turning points in biblical-historical scholarship as well as topics of immense interest to the general public for over a century and a half. Over the course of a generation, we have seen a new wave of debate among scholars worldwide concerning these issues. This has been followed by a growing interest on the part of the public and the media. In the more recent stages of this debate, archaeology has been playing an ever-increasing role. The opportunity to present these essays are but another expression of the increased interest in these subjects in which the main question to be addressed is to what extent archaeology can contribute to the resolution of the issues at hand.

The branch of archaeology that relates to the Hebrew Bible has been traditionally coined "biblical archaeology." Yet, this term has become increasingly problematic. Is it a legitimate designation, or, as some would pose the question, is it the aim of archaeology to "excavate" the Bible? Can this aspect of archaeology be better defined as an independent branch of scholarship? If we continue to use this term, how should we qualify it? Let us first examine very briefly the two components of the term, namely, "archaeology" and "Bible."

ARCHAEOLOGY

Archaeology is one of the fields of research that emerged during the nineteenth century, and during the twentieth century it developed into a mature, full-blown social-scientific discipline with its own research methods and theoretical frameworks. The goal of modern archaeology is to study various aspects of past societies by reconstructing spatial and temporal social changes as well as a wide range of economic, technological, political, and religious phenomena. Archaeological research is undertaken internationally using a variety of methods developed for fieldwork and for the accurate processing and interpretation of recovered data. The scope of this field of research is wide scale and relates to every aspect of human activity that can be recovered by the spade. The questions asked and the answers given are sometimes complicated and often interpretations of the same body of archaeological phenomena may differ and thereby become the subjects for extended scholarly debate.

The first task of the archaeologist is to locate ancient settlement sites. The study of the spatial distribution of sites over time is essential for reconstructing transformations in settlement patterns, for establishing hierarchic relationships between types of settlements, for evaluating the settlement areas in the various periods, and for estimating the resultant demographic changes over time. This is achieved through the use of field surveys combined with the study of ancient geographic, ecological, and environmental factors. Modern research tools like the computerized Geographical Information System (GIS) help in analyzing the settlement map in relation to the topography, geology, soil types, land uses, water resources, ancient roads, and so on. When such studies are combined with the results of excavations at various sites, archaeologists can reconstruct an integrated picture of the ancient settlement system. Detailed settlement maps, tables, and graphs enable them to follow changes in settlement and demography through time in a given region and to gather information about such topics as the response of human societies to environmental challenges. As we will see, this aspect of the archaeological endeavor is essential for the study of the emergence or origin of early Israel.

In the land of Israel, this aspect of ancient settlement is closely related to the research field known as the historical geography of the Bible, an independent area of research that can be defined as part of the broader field of biblical archaeology. Its goal is to explore the vast geographical data in the Bible and in other ancient written sources such as Egyptian and Assyrian texts, as well as epigraphic documents from the southern Levant. The identification of place-names preserved in written sources with actual archaeological sites was the first major achievement of this field following the exploration of the Holy Land by various pioneers over the centuries. I have in mind such notable figures as Eusebius, the head of the Christian church of Caesarea during the fourth century C.E., Ashtori Haparchi, the Jewish scholar who lived at Beth-shean in the fourteenth century, and nineteenth century scholars like the noted American Edward Robinson who, in 1838 and 1852, carried out the first extensive pioneering exploration of the country in modern times.

All these scholars were aware of the remarkable preservation of ancient biblical names in the place-names of their own times and in particular, in the Arabic names used throughout the region. Some examples include Beth-shean (Arabic Beisan), Bethel (Arabic Beitin), Shiloh (Arabic Sailun), Gibeon (Arabic Jib), and so forth. Historical geography also deals with many other aspects of ancient geography, such as biblical lists of tribal plots and tribal borders, administrative divisions like those of the kingdom of Solomon, political and cultural boundaries, road systems, and much more. Thus, the combined efforts of field surveys and analytical historical geography enables the archaeologist to draw important conclusions regarding the ancient settlement systems and demography in the Holy Land and to relate various ancient texts to the available geographical and archaeological realia.

Archeological excavations explore the inner structures and developments of various types of settlements over time—from small hamlets of desert dwellers to well-planned, fortified cities. The larger sites of the ancient Near East are buried in ancient mounds, which are commonly known as "tells." These sites were located in the most suitable locations for human habitation and were settled and resettled over hundreds or even thousands of years, and thus they often preserve dozens of occupation levels, which archaeologists refer to as "strata." The exploration of a single tell or mound might require long-term and large-scale planned projects that may take several years to complete and even then only small, randomly selected areas can be excavated. In many cases, only the uppermost occupation levels can easily be approached, while deeper levels can only be examined in deep probes or in step trenches along slopes of mounds, and thus remain largely unknown. Furthermore, each excavator has to address what might seem to be an endless number of questions regarding his or her site. What were the environmental resources, such as water and land, available to the site? When exactly was the site settled? Was the population of the site stable or were there population changes or fluctuations? How many occupation phases do the various "strata" reflect and can we define gaps in the occupation? Which part of the site was settled in each period? What reasons brought an end to each occupation phase? What was the town plan in each of those occupation periods? What were the building materials and techniques used? What kind of subsistence strategy was employed in each settlement period? If there were violent destructions—who or what caused them? Can we relate such destructions to historical events known from other sources? These are only a few of the many questions that the archaeologist might ask.

Reliable answers to such questions can be achieved only by methodical, well-controlled excavation methods and a thorough understanding of many phenomena and features in each excavation. The decipherment of depositional processes and the stratigraphy of a site are the most challenging tasks of the field archaeologist. The depositional processes are the result of diverse and sometimes unexpected human decisions and activities of a distant past. The image of a tell as a cake composed of horizontal layers (or "strata") that can be peeled off, one by one, by the archaeologist was a common one in the early stages of research, but the reality proved to be much more complicated. The correct understanding and documentation of complex, multilayered sites both mentioned in the Bible and archaeologically attested, such as Hazor, Megiddo, Beth-shean, Lachish, as well as many others, are absolutely crucial to an accurate interpretation of Israel's early history.

Less complex, yet no less informative, are many other types of sites reflective of human activity, such as isolated farms, hamlets, citadels, agricultural and industrial installations, cemeteries, ancient roads, and ports. Many of these sites have been recovered by chance during salvage operations related to intense development in modern times, and others have been explored within the framework of more formalized research projects. Desert archaeology and underwater archaeology are two specialized branches of archaeological investigation. Both contribute unique types of data to the archaeological enterprise. For example, cultic sites in the deserts of Sinai and the Negev have informed us immensely about the origin of the biblical "standing stones" or *masseboth*. The Phoenician merchant shipwrecks discovered just a few years ago at great depths below the surface of the Mediterranean Sea have provided us with our first archaeological encounter with an actual Phoenician ship that probably looked like the Tyrian ship described in Ezek 27.

The combined evidence from these diverse sites provides archaeologists with a panoramic view of various modes of human life. In my career over the past thirty years, I have excavated two multilayered medium-sized towns (Tell Qasile and Tel Batash [Timnah]), two multilayered major cities (Beth-shean and Tel Reḥov), as well as a series of smaller, single-period sites: an early-Israelite village settlement, a citadel, a watchtower, a cultic site, and a desert farm or road station. Each of these sites had a different story to tell about ancient Israel's material culture, society, and life ways.

Returning to the excavation process itself, the finds that archaeologists typically recover include pottery vessels, various artifacts made of metal, stone, bone, and other materials, seals, inscriptions, art objects, and cult objects of various kinds, burial remains and funerary goods, and, in rare cases, we may also find organic materials like wood and textile items. Detailed study of these objects is essential for defining temporal and spatial changes in the material culture. We can define regional cultures as well as study the origins and diffusion of cultural features. We can detect foreign influences, local and international trade networks, processes of colonization, and immigration. Such detailed research provides the basis not only for relative dating, but, together with the aid of firmly dated objects, for absolute dating and chronology.

There are many examples of the successful results of such meticulous studies in biblical archaeology. For example, the study of the Philistine culture as a culture of immigrant peoples became possible only thanks to precise analysis of pottery and other artifacts and comparative study with artifacts from Greece and Cyprus. Moreover, the identification of what is thought to be Israelite material culture in the period of the Judges became possible only with the meticulous comparison of that cultural data with the Canaanite culture known from the lowlands.

Another important aspect of modern archaeology is the wide-scale cooperation with scientists from various fields such as botany, zoology, physical anthropology, geology, geomorphology, chemistry, physics, geography, metallurgy, computer science, statistics, remote sensing, and more. This kind of cooperation has opened many new horizons of research as exemplified by recent published studies. By way of example, in the summer of 2005 at Tel Reḥov, we uncovered the remains of several beehives from the tenth century B.C.E., the only ones so far discovered from any site in our region. After we suggested the identification of the hives, a scientist from the Weizmann Institute analyzed their clay walls and indeed identified the remains as beeswax residue.

The use of radiometric dating, that is, measuring the isotope ^{14}C in organic materials, particularly in seeds, has become a very important tool for dating. For example, at Tel Reḥov, we managed to gain a precise series of dates from seeds spanning the twelfth to ninth centuries B.C.E., which have become an important factor in the current debate over Iron Age chronology.

Archaeological projects require much technical work, including drafting and drawing of architectural plans and artifacts, spread photography, restoration, and conservation of objects and structures. Wide use of computer software is needed in order to handle ever-growing databases, to process

quantitative analyses of various kinds, to help in creating typological seria-
tions, and to create three-dimensional images, just to mention a few of the
applications now used in field archaeology.

The collection, processing, integration, interpretation, and publication of
these numerous data are not simple tasks, and the integration of finds from
various individual sites into a comprehensive regional picture can be compared to the assembling of a huge jigsaw puzzle. It is a complex and expensive
enterprise. As an excavation director, I imagine myself sometimes standing
in the center of a huge intersection, surrounded by radiating branches of
study and research. And although archaeological fieldwork has its glamor and
great moments of discovery, the daily routine involves lengthy, tiring stages of
documentation, processing of finds, integrating results, and preparing final
publications. The actual work of the archaeologist extends well beyond the
popular image of Indiana Jones, the treasure hunter.

A higher level of the archaeological enterprise is that of interpretation,
synthesis, and explanation. This so-called armchair stage of archaeology deals
with the reconstruction of the broader aspects of social, political, economic,
and ethnic changes in a given region or country. The subjects of research and
interpretation cover all aspects of life, several of which I mentioned above: the
human response to the environment; agricultural and industrial technologies;
demography; comparative studies of architecture and domestic artifacts; warfare; daily life, including diet, cooking, baking, spinning, and weaving, as well
as metallurgy; religious practices and beliefs; art; iconography and symbolism; paleography; transportation and trade; and burial customs. This is only
a partial list of the many subjects that constitute human activity. The goal is
to reconstruct as much as possible a complete portrait of ancient society, from
the life of the poorest peasant to that of the king or priest.

As such, various questions emerge as to the modes of life within the
society explored. Were the people nomadic, semi-nomadic, or sedentary?
Were they ranked or egalitarian? Was it a tribal society with family lineage
as a major component? Archaeologists try to reconstruct the emergence of
social and political systems such as states and empires in order to understand
colonization, immigration, assimilation, and symbiosis of different groups.
The ancient economy is reconstructed by studying modes of agricultural
and industrial production, ancient technologies and evidence for short- and
long-range trade systems. Gender archaeology attempts to study the roles of
women in society; religious beliefs and cult practices are reconstructed on the
basis of temples, cult objects, and burial practices; cognitive aspects of life that
may be deduced from the finds are also addressed in modern research. Most
of these subjects concern long-term social and technological changes. Yet,
in many cases we can detect certain events, typically those that are the more

dramatic or crisis-oriented events for ancient peoples like earthquakes and military conquests. Such events, though tragic for an ancient population, are rewarding for the archaeologist who excavates them, since they "freeze" certain moments in the life of a society and can yield abundant finds. Examples from my own experience are the destruction layers dated to the Iron II period, which I excavated at three sites, Tel Reḥov, Beth-shean, and Timnah (Tel Batash). These could be attributed to certain Aramean, Assyrian, and Babylonian military conquests between the ninth and late-seventh centuries B.C.E. The specific evidence for such conquests is thick, burnt conflagration layers in which whole households were buried. Such "time capsules" enabled my team to reconstruct rather extensively the material culture of a certain site during a particular time period.

A variety of theoretical frameworks have been developed over the past few decades in archaeological interpretation. One of the best-known trends is the so-called processualist archaeology or "New Archaeology," which dominated scholarship from the 1960s to the 1980s. This approach emphasized ecological and environmental determinism and gave less weight to human decisions and actions. Since the early 1990s, post-modern modes of thinking have inspired archaeological interpretation; "post-processualist" archaeology, as it is known today, has opened the door for much more varied and flexible interpretation; various possible explanations for the same archaeological phenomena are acceptable, and the role of human decisions and of the individual in history is taken into consideration more than in the previous period. These trends have direct implications on our subject. They can, for example, offer alternative solutions to the debate over the historicity of David and Solomon.

In sum, archaeology is a much more complex discipline than most people think. Its methods of analytical research and deduction provide the only way to reconstruct an outline of historical periods and lost cultures where there are no written records, while for periods where we have written sources, archaeology gains significant importance as a complementary tool for historical reconstruction, even counter-balancing texts that may be biased or loaded with propaganda and ideology.

Because it is the Holy Land, the land of Israel has continuously been the focus of archaeological research from the beginning of the modern era. In the nineteenth century, it suffered from the infancy of the new discipline. In fact, early archaeologists inflicted much damage on sites like Jerusalem in the early years, that is, prior to World War I. Yet in those years, pioneers like Sir Flinders Petrie developed new concepts and methods that laid the foundation for later advances in research. Between the two world wars, American and European expeditions conducted large-scale excavations at major sites and laid the foundation for the systematic archaeological research of the Holy

Land. These were the years when the concept of biblical archaeology took shape under the leadership of the American scholar William F. Albright. His unique personality and wide-ranging knowledge of all aspects of ancient Near Eastern studies inspired a whole generation of scholars; among them are some of the founders of biblical archaeology in Israel, like Benjamin Mazar and Yigael Yadin. This school strived for the integration of archaeology with biblical history, historical geography, paleography, Near Eastern history, philology, and art history into a comprehensive field of knowledge.

After 1948, archaeology in Israel and Jordan developed rapidly. The large-scale excavations at Hazor led by Yadin served as the training ground for a new generation of Israeli archaeologists, who later developed their own projects and methods of research. American, European, Australian, Japanese, and Jordanian teams have continued exploration in Israel and Jordan, and now these countries have become some of the most intensively and dynamically explored in the entire world. But how can this vast amount of ever-accumulating data serve to reconstruct biblical history? To this question, we now turn.

On the Historicity of the Bible

As mentioned previously, our concern in these essays is mainly the questions, to what extent can we extract history from the biblical text? and, what are the methodological problems involved in relating archaeological research to the study of biblical history? After all, the title of the colloquium from which this volume derives was "Digging for Truth." But can we discover the absolute truth for our field? My answer is "yes" concerning certain matters, but I have serious doubts regarding many others.

A wide spectrum of views exists concerning the process and stages of writing and redaction of the Hebrew Bible, and the evaluation of the biblical text in reconstructing a history of Israel. In particular, the biblical stories from the times of the Patriarchs to the kingships of David and Solomon are the subjects of serious debates. There are those who accept the biblical narrative as true history; they are mostly scholars or authors of religious backgrounds, either Jewish or Christian, who believe in the truth of the Bible and are not ready to give up the biblical stories either as the Word of God or at least as straightforward true history writing. A recent example is the six-hundred-page book by Kenneth Kitchen *On the Reliability of the Old Testament*, in which the author vigorously defends the historicity of the details of the Bible using extensive material from the ancient Near East. His concluding sentence is:

> The Old Testament comes out remarkably well, so long as its writings and writers are treated fairly and evenhandedly, in line with independent data.

On the other side of the spectrum stand scholars who all but negate the historicity of the entire Hebrew Bible and claim that it was written during the fourth to third centuries B.C.E. as total fiction, reflecting *in toto*, the intellectual and theological world of the much later writers. Philip Davies, for example, defines biblical Israel as a modern invention of scholars. Niels Peter Lemche, one of the main authors in this group writes,

> the Israelite nation as explained by the biblical writers has little in the way of a historical background. It is a highly ideological construct created by ancient scholars of Jewish tradition in order to legitimize their own religious community and its religio-political claims on land and religious exclusivity. (*The Israelites in History and Tradition* [Louisville, Ky.: Westminster John Knox, 1998], 165–66.)

This group of scholars has been dubbed "revisionist," "minimalist," or even "nihilist," though they themselves decline any common general term for their school or "movement" so to speak. In between these two extremes there is wide space for various views that may collectively be defined as "middle-of-the-road" or moderate. Professor Finkelstein and I stand at two different points on the centrist continuum. Our views differ on certain important issues, but we share more in common than we do with either of the two extreme groups described above.

An archaeologist like me, who is an outsider to textual research, must make a choice between divergent views when trying to relate archaeological data and interpretation to the biblical sources. My own choice is to follow those who claim that the initial writing of the Torah (the Pentateuch or Tetrateuch), of the Deuteronomistic History and large parts of the prophetic and wisdom literature took place during the late monarchy (eighth to early-sixth centuries B.C.E.), while during the exilic and post-exilic periods they underwent further stages of editing, expansion, and change. Yet, I also accept the view of many scholars that the late-monarchic authors utilized earlier materials and sources. These may include:

1. The archives of the Jerusalem Temple library.
2. Palace archives (though the existence of such archives remains disputed).
3. Public commemorative inscriptions, perhaps centuries old (no Israelite ones have been preserved, but potential analogues include those of Mesha of Moab and Hazael of Damascus, two of Israel's major opponents in the ninth century).
4. The oral transmission of ancient poetry. This may include the Song of Miriam, the Song of Deborah, the Blessings of Jacob, and other ancient poetic texts.

5. Folk stories and aetiological stories rooted in a remote historical past. These include many of the stories in the biblical literature, such as portions of the Exodus and Conquest accounts, stories about the deeds of the Judges, the biographies of Saul, David, and Solomon, the Elijah and Elisha cycles, and so on.

6. Earlier historiographic writings that are referred to in the Hebrew Bible as the "Book of the Chronicles of the Kings of Israel" and the "Book of the Chronicles of the Kings of Israel" cited in the books of Kings:

> Now the rest of the acts of Ahab: and all that he did, and the ivory house which he built, and all the cities that he built, are they not written in the Book of the Chronicles of the Kings of Israel? (1 Kgs 2:39; NRSV).

This sounds as if the author had in front of him some earlier form of written history.

It is generally accepted that many of the stories incorporated in the Deuteronomistic History, though based on folk stories and traditions, were reworked under the influence of late-Judean (that is, southern) theology, ideology, and editorial processes. Nevertheless, such stories may retain valuable historical information that can be accessed with the help of accepted historical methods coupled with external written sources and archaeological finds. As modern interpreters, our task is to extract any reliable historical information embedded in these literary texts, using archaeology as a tool of control and heightened objectivity.

Both Assyrian inscriptions and local inscriptions like the stelae of Mesha, king of Moab, and of Hazael, king of Damascus (better known as the Tel Dan inscription), confirm that the general historical framework of the Deuteronomistic narrative relating to the ninth century was based on reliable knowledge of the historical outline of that century. Our understanding of the periods *preceding* the ninth century is of course foggier. Israel is not mentioned in any external source following its lone reference in the inscription of the Egyptian pharaoh Merneptah, which dates to 1206 B.C.E., that is, until we come to the mid- to late-ninth-century Mesha inscription 350 years or so later.

I imagine the historical perspective in the Hebrew Bible as a telescope looking back in time: the farther in time we go back, the more dim the picture becomes. Considering that the supposed telescope stood somewhere in the late-eighth or seventh centuries B.C.E., it gives us a more accurate picture when we look at the ninth century than when we view the tenth century, and so forth. Oral traditions and stories embedded in the biblical historiography might preserve more extensive authentic details concerning events or phenomena closer to the time of writing, while the farther away we get from the supposed events, the stories become more imaginative and symbolic, and are perhaps accompanied by greater distortion of earlier information. We also have to recall selective memory and memory loss, censorship, and biases due to ideological, theological, personal, or other motivations. This is true with any history, even of the last century, not just ancient history. Allow me to cite a well known example from the history of Israel's 1948 War of Independence. There is the official history, produced by the Department of History in the Israel Defense Forces, and there are various other versions, among them postmodern narratives that deconstruct various aspects of the official history of this war. When dealing with a period long past and with almost no direct written sources, like the early biblical period, it is extremely difficult to assess the biblical data and so one may ask whether it is possible at all to write an accurate history of early Israel.

In spite of these dangers, the working hypothesis of the view that I represent is that information in the Deuteronomistic History and other biblical texts may have historical value, in spite of the distortions, exaggerations, theological disposition, and literary creativity of the biblical authors and editors.

The Role of Archaeology and the Definition of "Biblical Archaeology"

The correlation of archaeological finds and texts is only one aspect of the archaeologist's work—perhaps one of the most difficult—yet it is a challenge that must be faced. In light of the conflicting views concerning early biblical history, archaeology can provide external, presumably objective, data on realia related to the issues currently under debate. It also has the potential to provide independent judgment of biblical sources by allowing us to examine in certain cases their historical reliability. In addition, it provides numerous observations on many aspects of early-Israelite society that cannot be extracted from the biblical text itself.

However, the interpretation of archaeological data and its association with the biblical text may in many cases be a matter of subjective judgment, since it is often inspired by the scholar's personal values, beliefs, ideology, and attitude toward the text or an artifact. In many cases, when archaeological discoveries are utilized in order to prove one historical paradigm or another, we are confronted with arguments that are, at their core, circular. This was true for William F. Albright and his followers, and is still true today, and thus it should be recalled that many archaeological conclusions are not certifiably factual, no matter when or by whom they were proposed.

Despite this, the role of archaeology as an invaluable tool for examining various aspects of biblical historiography and of the early periods of Israelite history—the Late Bronze through the Iron age—remains firmly intact. Investigations have shown that there are both many correlations between archaeology and biblical references, as well as many contradictions. This situation is only natural in light of the Bible's complex process of transmission described above.

But the role of archaeology is well beyond confirming or denying certain biblical events or other references. Archaeology is in fact the main tool for reconstructing many aspects of Israelite society, economy, daily life, and religion, as well as those of Israel's neighbors. It offers a unique perspective on the Israelites as part of the wider context of the Levant and the entire ancient Near East.

Nevertheless, after more than 150 years of research in this field, there are still debates and discussions concerning the definition of biblical archaeology as a concept and field of research. During the last generation, the term received some bad publicity. It was considered by many as a field of study loaded with theological and ideological agendas, reflecting the religious beliefs of Christianity or Judaism. We often hear that biblical archaeology's main goal is "to prove the Bible" so to speak. William G. Dever preached for many years that we needed to redefine our field of research as "Syro-Palestinian Archaeology," thus relocating it in the wider context of Near Eastern archaeology, unrelated to biblical studies. A few years ago, the American Schools of Oriental Research, a nondenominational academic organization, decided after a long debate to change the name of its popular magazine, *Biblical Archaeologist*, to *Near Eastern Archaeology*. The change reflected the desire of American archaeologists working in our field to liberate the discipline from any religious framework.

At the background of this change stood the dichotomy between American archaeologists of our region who are faculty members of theological seminaries, divinity schools, or departments of biblical, Jewish, or religious studies, and those in the forefront of American archaeological theory and practice who hold appointments in departments of anthropology and history. In America, the term biblical archaeology continues to be used by conservative Christian researchers, as evidenced in a new book entitled *The Future of Biblical Archaeology* (edited by J. K. Hoffmeier and A. Millard), which appeared in 2004. Similarly, the Biblical Archaeology Society and its magazine *Biblical Archaeology Review*, though private and nondenominational, reflect in their names a well-defined targeted public, much of it composed of conservative Christians who are interested in the Bible and its world. There is a broad gap between this approach and the professional approach to archaeology as part of the larger fields of anthropology and history, and this has resulted in the refutation of the term biblical archaeology by many scholars in the United States. Strangely enough, Dever himself calls now for a return to the old term and proposes that we just add the qualifying word "New"—this "New Biblical Archeology" remains the same old woman, but wearing the new dress of current archaeological methodology and more "anthropological" ways of thinking.

In Israel, the term biblical archaeology has been accepted in a more simplistic way as a means of referring to all archaeological activity related to the Bible and its world. In my view, the term biblical archaeology should continue to be used as a generic or broad term, defining all aspects of archaeological research that are related to the world of the Bible. This is a broad definition that includes vast geographical regions from Iran to Greece and from Turkey to Egypt, that is, the entire Middle East and eastern Mediterranean. The archaeology of each of these regions contributes in some degree to our understanding of the biblical world, and as such it contributes to biblical archaeology. According to this definition, biblical archaeology is not an independent scientific discipline, but rather the "shopping cart" that collects data from the various branches of Near Eastern archaeology and utilizes them in studying the Bible in its world.

Though written in what was at the time one of the smallest and most negligible states of the ancient Near East, the Bible is perhaps the most profound product of the ancient Near Eastern world. Many of the achievements of this cultural world, rooted in the third, second, and first millennia B.C.E. are embedded in it. Many ancient local memories can be identified in the biblical text; some of them even seem to be pre-Israelite and adapted by the Israelites as part of their heritage. Archaeology may provide us with a clue to such cases. In this wider framework, the archaeology of the land of Israel has a central role in providing the most direct access to the society that created the biblical text.

Such a "Bible-centered" orientation is criticized by various kinds of scholars: on the one hand there are the "minimalists" who would not accept the Bible as related to the Iron Age, and on the other hand there are the archaeologists who claim that archaeology should be treated as a self-contained discipline and that professional archaeologists should not intervene in the study of biblical history or culture. Yet, to me and many others it appears that removing the connection between archaeology and the Bible would strip our field from its flesh and leave just the dry bones. The relationship between the text and the artifact is the essence of biblical archaeology; it remains for us to cope with the questions that are raised, avoiding on the one hand a naive and fundamentalist approach to the text and, on the other, any excessively manipulative, uncritical, or imaginative interpretations.

PART 2

USING ARCHAEOLOGY TO ASSESS THE BIBLE'S TRADITIONS ABOUT "THE EARLIEST TIMES"

Summary Assessment for Part 2

Brian B. Schmidt

Professor Finkelstein isolates the Patriarchal stories as a litmus test for what we can presently know about the historical relevance of the biblical traditions since (1) these stories with their compelling literary artistry and canonical status hold a special place in the Judeo-Christian tradition to which much of earlier scholarship was so closely attached, and (2) there is a long history of that scholarship, predominantly German and Anglo-American in origin, that can be invoked as a means of avoiding the repetition of past errors. He then reviews some failed attempts of the past at identifying the historical Abraham in the late-third to early-second millennia B.C.E. These include the now well-known proposals that Abraham was a nomad-immigrant-invader-donkey caravaneer of Amorite origin whose contemporaries instigated the sudden collapse of the Early Bronze Age urban system of the Levant, or that Abraham was a tent dweller who situated himself near major cities of the Middle Bronze period as portrayed in the Mari texts, or that Abraham and his relatives observed such social and legal practices as the provision of surrogate mothers and adopted slaves for childless parents that are preserved in the second-millennium tablets from Nuzi in northern Iraq. In these and other instances of an extraordinary claim on the part of some earlier scholars, Finkelstein reviews the subsequent scholarly critiques that followed, and that neutralized such claims.

Finkelstein then reverses direction somewhat by noting that other scholars long ago identified telling anachronisms in the Patriarchal stories that point to their much later compositional setting in the eighth to seventh centuries B.C.E.; the time of the late Judahite monarchy. He lists the late domestication of camels, the first-millennium prominence of the city of Gerar, the frequent mention of neighboring peoples and polities that did not exist as distinct political entities until the first millennium, such as the Arameans and Transjordanian groups like the Edomites, Moabites, and Ammonites, and references to cities and places that are attested or only existed within the context of the Assyrian and Babylonian empires of the first millennium. All these and more indicate for Finkelstein that a seventh-century background is the most likely one for the compilation of the early version of the Patriarchal narratives. These and similar details cannot be dismissed as mere incidentals and later editorial additions since they are central elements in the narrative plots and point to the date and message of the text as well as to its implied audience. For Finkelstein, the message is essentially one advocating Judah's preeminence over the northern territories as articulated by seventh-century B.C.E. scribes. These writers produced the Bible's historiographic narratives under the impetus of a Josianic ideological agenda of expansionism.

Having established the Patriarchal stories as his guiding model, Finkelstein then turns to the Exodus and Conquest stories. Here he notes that the geography and place-names mentioned in the Exodus and wanderings stories fit best within the seventh to sixth centuries B.C.E. or the Saite period in Egypt. The Conquest accounts in Joshua and Judges cannot be interpreted in a straightforward fashion from archaeological data that were invoked by scholars in the early- to mid-twentieth century in support of a military invasion of Israelites at the end of the Late Bronze Age. It now appears that (1) several sites mentioned in the Bible's Conquest story described as being inhabited were not, or else were insignificant villages in the Late Bronze Age, (2) at the end of the Late Bronze period, Canaan's urban system did not suddenly collapse, and, in any case, the elongated process was part of a much wider Mediterranean urban demise, (3) Egypt continued to control and dominate Canaan throughout the second half of the twelfth century, and, finally, (4) surveys indicate the peoples who (re-)emerged in Canaan in the early-twelfth century B.C.E. were indigenous groups transitioning once again, just as their ancestors had repeatedly done, from a nomadic mode of subsistence to a sedentary mode and back again. In summary, for Finkelstein, while some older traditions may have been preserved in the stories about the Patriarchs, the Exodus, the Conquest, and the Settlement, their overall themes, lessons, and realities have as their historical context for compilation, Judah of the seventh century.

When it comes to the biblical text's historical relevance for reconstructing Israel's earliest stages of history in the second millennium B.C.E., whether on the basis of the Patriarchal stories, the Exodus story, or the Conquest and Settlement stories, Professor Mazar articulates a position in which old traditions from the second millennium were initially passed down orally and then written down in the first millennium. To be sure, many aspects of the accounts have been lost, distorted, or changed over time, and in other cases only generally coincide with what we know of the period. Furthermore, while some important elements evince direct correlations with the biblical traditions, others stand in direct contradiction to isolated biblical accounts. In any case,

Mazar does not assume that the biblical stories themselves are necessarily historically accurate or that the human characters in them are historical figures.

Some of the older traditions that previous scholarship identified as having survived in the biblical traditions include the land of Canaan as an early, prosperous urban culture with pastoral clans living in between fortified cities, a shared Amorite stock of personal names, and the accessibility of international routes along the entirety of the Fertile Crescent. From his survey of proposals offered by previous scholars in support of second-millennium or Middle Bronze Age parallels with the Patriarchal stories, Mazar does not identify which of these specifically he would endorse. Instead, he turns to the Exodus, Conquest, and Settlement stories in the Hebrew Bible to illustrate the validity of his approach. For example, the West Semitic or Hyksos dynastic rule over Egypt, the major building projects of Pharaoh Ramesses II, and the migration of slaves from Egypt are all attested in the archaeological and historical record. Mazar would also argue that all three of these find their analogues in the biblical traditions of the book of Exodus. Furthermore, the mention of a people "Israel" in the land of Canaan preserved in Pharaoh Merneptah's stele from the end of the thirteenth century B.C.E. most likely points to the waves of peoples attested in the archaeological record who settled in the hill country and in Transjordan at this time.

The Conquest narratives likewise preserve ancient memories of events that actually occurred, such as the conquest of populated sites like 'Ai and Hazor in the book of Joshua. While the archaeological and historical evidence suggests a rather complicated process underlying these particular biblical traditions, for Mazar in the final analysis, they too represent memories of second-millennium events that were preserved orally for centuries and only subsequently written down and revised in later times. Nevertheless, Mazar recognizes that in some other cases, archaeology and the biblical traditions evince outright conflict. For example, several cities are described as having been destroyed or attacked in the Bible, but archaeology demonstrates that, in a number of cases, such cities either did not exist in the transitional phase between the end of the Late Bronze Age and the beginning of Iron I (for example, Heshbon and Arad), or they remained intact and inhabited during this period never having suffered destruction (for example, Lachish). For Mazar, the conclusion to be drawn is that, while archaeology negates the Bible's Conquest story as an historical event, it can shed some light on how ancient memories and their equally ancient oral interpretations found their way into the much later written work we know now as the book of Joshua. Various events and traditions about the distant past spanning this lengthy period of transition and turmoil have survived. These events and traditions are reflective of ancient local destructions and conflicts between Canaanite tribes and clans or between urban Canaanites and Israelites. They found their way into the collective memory of the later Israelites in the form of a telescoped reflection on that ancient past.

Patriarchs, Exodus, Conquest: Fact or Fiction?*

Israel Finkelstein

This essay deals with the formative periods in the history of biblical Israel, and, as such, is at the same time easier and more complicated. Easier, because most of us agree that the biblical description of this era in the history of ancient Israel does not deal with actual events in the second millennium B.C.E. It is more complicated because much of the evidence is negative and therefore difficult to present. In addition, we are dealing with two different compilations—the Pentateuch and the Deuteronomistic History—which many scholars have understood as representing different phases in the authorship process.

The source in the Pentateuch that preserves most of the "historical" material in Genesis—the J source—was traditionally dated to the tenth century B.C.E., while it has always been clear that the story of the Conquest of Canaan in the Deuteronomistic History was put in writing much later. In recent years this view has gradually changed, mainly as a result of higher-critical research. Today many scholars identify a close relationship between the J source and the Deuteronomistic History and I would vigorously argue that both reflect late-monarchic realities. Both locate late-monarchic Judah in the center of their narratives, which in turn serve their ideological and theological goals. Needless to say, Genesis and Exodus also portray some later, Persian-period concerns.

I will first discuss—somewhat at length—the story of the Patriarchs as a case-study for the "historical" part in the Pentateuch. Then, in light of the treatment of the Patriarchal narratives, I will briefly comment on the Exodus and Conquest narratives.

---

*This chapter is adapted from the Patriarchs chapter in Neil Asher Silberman and Israel Finkelstein's book, *The Bible Unearthed: Archaeology's New Vision of Ancient Israel and the Origin of its Sacred Texts* (New York: Free Press, 2001).

THE PATRIARCHS

The story of the Patriarchs—how a family transforms into a nation—is the first great saga of the Bible. The biblical account of the life of the Patriarchs is a typical family story with all its joy and sadness, love and hatred, deceit and cunning, famine and prosperity. It is also a universal, philosophical story about devotion and obedience, faith and piety. But is it a historically reliable description of the birth of the people of Israel?

THE FAILED SEARCH FOR THE HISTORICAL ABRAHAM

Many of the early biblical archaeologists had also been trained as theologians. It was therefore essential for them to accept that God's promise to Abraham, Isaac, and Jacob was given to actual people who represented the earliest history of ancient Israel. The biblical scholar and archaeologist Roland de Vaux noted that "if the historical faith of Israel is not founded in history, such faith is erroneous, and therefore, our faith is also." And William F. Albright, the doyen of biblical archaeology, echoed the same sentiment, insisting that "as a whole, the picture in Genesis is historical, and there is no reason to doubt the general accuracy of the biographical details." Indeed, from the early decades of the twentieth century, with the great discoveries in Mesopotamia and the intensification of archaeological activity in Palestine, many biblical historians and archaeologists were convinced that the new discoveries would prove that the Patriarchs were historical figures. They argued that the biblical narratives, even if compiled at a relatively late date (in their view in the period of the United Monarchy), nonetheless preserved at least the main outlines of an authentic, ancient historical reality.

Albright argued that certain details such as personal names and land-purchase laws in the stories in Genesis may be found in the records of second-millennium B.C.E. Mesopotamian societies from which the Patriarchs ostensibly originated. No less important, the Patriarchs are described as conducting a bedouin way of life moving with their flocks through the hill country of Canaan. These elements convinced Albright that the age of the Patriarchs was an historical reality. He thus began to search for evidence for the presence of pastoral groups of Mesopotamian origin in Canaan around 2000 B.C.E.—a date that seemed to fit the biblical chronology of the Patriarchs.

Albright's hypothesis was the most influential of all attempts to locate the Patriarchs on historical and archaeological grounds. Canaan of the third millennium B.C.E.—the Early Bronze Age—was characterized by full blown urban life. Large cities developed in the lowlands; they were surrounded by formidable fortifications and accommodated palaces and temples. Then, in the late-third millennium B.C.E., this flourishing urban system collapsed.

The cities were destroyed or abandoned and many of them never recovered from the aftershock. In addition, many of the rural settlements around them were abandoned. What followed was a period covering a few centuries that reflected a very different culture with no large cities, when most of the population—at least as believed by archaeologists in the 1950s and 1960s—was practicing a pastoral nomadic mode of subsistence before urban life gradually recovered, and when Canaan entered a second urban period, that of the Middle Bronze Age in the early-second millennium B.C.E.

Albright placed the spotlight on the period between the two urban phases, the Intermediate Bronze Age (which he labeled "Middle Bronze I"). He and other scholars of the time argued that the collapse of the Early Bronze urban culture was sudden, and that it was the outcome of an invasion of pastoral nomads from the fringe of the desert in the northeast. He identified the invaders with the Amorites (or Amurru) of the Mesopotamian texts. Albright and his followers dated the Abraham episode in the Genesis stories to this phase in the history of Canaan. Albright suggested that Abraham, "a caravaneer of high repute," took part in the great trade network of the nineteenth century B.C.E. Texts of that time found at Kültepe near the city of Kayseri in central Turkey attest to prosperous trade relations between Mesopotamia and Anatolia, thus paralleling the Ur to Haran movement of Abraham in Gen 11. A contemporary tomb painting from Beni Hasan in Egypt provides evidence for caravan trade between Transjordan and Egypt as described in the Joseph story in Genesis. In both cases, donkeys were used as the beasts of burden. Nelson Glueck supplied apparent archaeological substantiation for this latter theory. His surveys in Transjordan and the Negev desert revealed hundreds of Intermediate Bronze Age sites, which for Albright provided the background for the stories about Abraham's activity in the south.

Yet the "Amorite Hypothesis" did not last long. With additional excavations, most scholars came to the conclusion that the Early Bronze urban system did not collapse overnight, but declined gradually over many decades due more to local economic and social upheavals within Canaan than to a wave of outside invaders. In addition, it became clear that the term Amorite was not restricted to pastoral people, but also included village communities of the early-second millennium.

The theorized similarity between the pastoral way of life in the Intermediate Bronze Age and the descriptions of Abraham's nomadic lifestyle also came under attack. It is now clear that the late-third millennium was not a completely nomadic period. It is true that there were no large cities at that time and the ratio of the pastoral nomads to the general population grew significantly. Yet, much of the population remained sedentary, living in villages and hamlets. Furthermore, in sharp contradiction to the theory of a great migration of nomads from the north, the continuity of architecture, pottery styles, and settlement patterns suggests that the population of Canaan in this inter-urban phase was predominantly indigenous. The same people would reestablish urban life in Canaan in the cities of the Middle Bronze Age. In short, the ups and downs in Canaan, from urban life to collapse into a more rural-pastoral society and back to a second urban phase are not understood today as reflecting mass migrations and changing populations, but rather as phases in the ages-long, repeated cycle of urban growth, collapse, and then regrowth of the same indigenous population of Canaan.

From the chronological point of view, it became apparent that the recovery of urban life started at least a century before the date given by Albright for Abraham's activity as a donkey caravaneer in the south. Finally, important biblical sites that are mentioned in the Abraham stories, such as Shechem, Beer-sheba, and Hebron, did not yield finds from the Intermediate Bronze Age. These sites were simply not inhabited at that time.

Another theory proposed identifying the age of the Patriarchs as the Middle Bronze Age, the peak of urban life in the first half of the second millennium B.C.E. Scholars advocating this view, such as Roland deVaux, argued that the nature of the Middle Bronze Age, as known from both text and archaeology, better fits the biblical description, mainly because the Patriarchs are depicted as living in tents next to cities. Archaeologically, all the major sites mentioned in Genesis—Shechem, Bethel, Hebron, and Gerar—were fortified strongholds in the Middle Bronze Age. Textually, this tent-city relationship is well attested in the archive found in the early-second-millennium city of Mari on the Euphrates River in Syria. In addition, the supporters of a Middle Bronze date for the Patriarchal period argued that the personal names of the Patriarchs resemble names known from the early-second millennium B.C.E.

Scholars like Cyrus Gordon and Ephraim Speiser referred to similarities between social and legal practices in the biblical description of the Patriarchs and social and legal practices in second-millennium B.C.E. Near Eastern texts. The most important of these texts are the Nuzi tablets from northern Iraq, which date to the fifteenth century B.C.E. To cite just a few examples, in Nuzi a barren wife is required to provide a slave woman for her husband to bear his children—a clear parallel to the biblical story of Sarai and Hagar in Gen 16. At Nuzi, slaves were adopted by childless couples. This is similar to the adoption of Eliezer by Abraham as his heir in Gen 15:2–3. In order to bridge the time gap, Gordon and Speiser argued that the Nuzi tablets also reflect earlier, Middle Bronze practices.

But soon the Middle Bronze/Nuzi solution also disintegrated. From the point of view of archaeology, the difficulty came mainly from what we do not see in the biblical text. The Middle Bronze Age was a period of advanced urban life. Canaan was dominated by a group of powerful city-states ruled from such capitals as Hazor and Megiddo. These cities were strongly fortified by huge earthen ramparts with massive gates. They had great palaces and towering temples. But in the biblical texts we do not see this at all. True, a few cities are mentioned, but not necessarily the most important ones. Neither Shechem nor Jerusalem is there—both were massive Middle Bronze strongholds. In the lowlands we should have heard about Hazor, Megiddo, and Gezer, but not Gerar. To make a long story short, the biblical story of the Patriarchs is not the story of Middle Bronze Canaan. And the phenomenon of nomads living near city dwellers was not restricted to the Middle Bronze period. Peoples had lived in this manner previously and continued to do so at least until quite late in the first millennium B.C.E. As for the names of the Patriarchs, they were common in later periods as well, both in the Late Bronze Age and in the Iron Age.

Regarding the Nuzi texts, later studies have proven that the social and legal practices that show similarities to the biblical narratives cannot be restricted to a single period. They were common in the ancient Near East throughout the second and first millennia B.C.E. For instance, the responsibility of a barren wife to provide her husband with a servant to bear him children appears in later periods, such as a seventh-century marriage contract from Assyria.

Just when a second-millennium solution seemed to be a lost cause, the biblical scholar Benjamin Mazar inserted archaeological data into the late-nineteenth century idea of Julius Wellhausen; that the description of the age of the Patriarchs should be studied against the background of the Iron Age. He pointed to the "anachronisms" in the text, such as the mention of Philistines and the Arameans. Needless to say, there were no Philistines in Canaan in the Middle Bronze Age. Both Egyptian texts and archaeology proved beyond doubt that they settled on the southern coast of Palestine in the twelfth century B.C.E. Instead of seeing their appearance here as a late insertion from the time of the compilation into a tradition about earlier times, Benjamin Mazar argued that the text reflects an intimate knowledge of the Philistine city-states in a period prior to the establishment of the monarchy in Israel. The Arameans also figure prominently in the Patriarchal stories. But they too did not appear on the actual ancient Near Eastern stage of history before the early Iron Age and their early states emerged even later, mainly in the ninth century B.C.E. Yet, Mazar thought that the description of the Arameans as a pastoral people reflects an earlier phase in their history, before they organized their first states.

Mazar was at the same time both right and wrong. He was right in his claim that the reality behind the stories in the book of Genesis should be traced back to the situation in the Iron Age. He was wrong because he opted for too early a date in the Iron Age.

There was one element that united all these theories: their promoters accepted that the Patriarchal age must be viewed, one way or the other, as the earliest phase in a sequential history of Israel. I would argue differently: the stories represent the ideology and needs of the period when the stories were set down in writing, that is, in late-monarchic and post-exilic times.

More Anachronisms

The biblical scholar Julius Wellhausen proposed over a century ago that the stories of the Patriarchs reflected the concerns of the Israelite monarchy, which were projected onto the lives of legendary fathers in a mythical past. In more recent decades, the biblical scholars John Van Seters and Thomas Thompson argued that even if the later texts contained some early traditions, the selection and arrangement of stories expressed a clear message by the biblical editors at the time of compilation, rather than preserving a reliable historical account of earlier times. But when did that compilation take place? The biblical text provides some clear clues.

First, the stories of the Patriarchs are "packed" with camels: usually herds of camels, but, as in the story of Joseph's sale by his brothers into slavery, camels are also described as beasts of burden used in caravan trade. We know that camels were not domesticated as beasts of burden earlier than the early-first millennium; in other words, they were not widely used in that capacity in the ancient Near East until well after 1000 B.C.E. The account of the camel caravan carrying "gum, balm, and myrrh" in the Joseph story reveals an obvious familiarity with the main products of the lucrative Arabian trade that flourished under Assyrian domination in the eighth to seventh centuries B.C.E. Indeed, excavations at the site of Tell Jemmeh in the southern coastal plain of Israel—an important trade entrepot on the main caravan route between Arabia and the Mediterranean—revealed a dramatic increase in the number of camel bones in the seventh century.

The mention of Gerar in Genesis as a Philistine city suggests that it was widely known at the time of the composition of the Patriarchal narratives. Gerar is identified with Tel Haror northwest of Beer-sheba and excavations there have shown that in the Iron Age I—the early phase of Philistine history—it was no more than a small, quite insignificant village. But by the late-eighth and seventh centuries B.C.E., it had become a strong, heavily fortified Assyrian administrative stronghold—an obvious landmark.

Many scholars, particularly those who supported the idea of the "historical" Patriarchs, considered these details to be incidental insertions into an earlier composition. But as Thomas Thompson put it as early as the 1970s, the specific references in the text to cities, neighboring peoples, and familiar places are precisely those aspects that distinguish the Patriarchal stories from completely mythical folktales. In other words, they are crucially important for identifying the date and message of the text.

JUDAH AND ITS NEIGHBORS

The Patriarchal stories offer a colorful human map of the ancient Near East from the unmistakable viewpoint of the kingdoms of Israel and Judah. The Arameans, who dominate the Jacob stories, became an important political factor on the northern borders of the Israelites in the early-ninth century B.C.E. when a number of their kingdoms emerged in the area of modern Syria. Among them, Aram-Damascus was a sometime ally, sometime rival with the Northern Kingdom. The cycle of stories about Jacob and Laban metaphorically express the complex and often stormy relations between Iron II Israel and Aram. On the one hand, they were frequent military rivals. On the other hand, much of the population of the northern territories of the kingdom of Israel seems to have been Aramean in origin. Indeed, the stories of the relations between the individual Patriarchs and their Aramean cousins clearly express the consciousness of shared origins. The biblical description of the tensions between Jacob and Laban and their eventual establishment of a boundary stone east of the Jordan to mark the border between their peoples (Gen 31:51–54, significantly an "E" or "northern" story) seems to reflect the territorial partition between Aram and Israel in the ninth to eighth centuries B.C.E.

The contacts Israelites had with their eastern neighbors are also reflected in the Patriarchal narratives. Through the eighth and seventh centuries B.C.E., the relations of Israel and Judah with the kingdoms of Ammon and Moab had often been hostile. It is therefore highly significant, and amusing, how the neighbors to the east are mocked in the Patriarchal stories. Genesis 19:30–38 (significantly a "J" or "southern" text) informs us that those nations were born from an incestuous union of the two daughters of Lot with their father.

The biblical stories of the two brothers Jacob and Esau provide a clear case of seventh century perceptions presented in more ancient costume. The description of the two brothers, the fathers of Israel and Edom, serves as a divine legitimacy for the political relationship between the two nations in late-monarchic times. Jacob-Israel is sensitive and cultured, while Esau-Edom is a more primitive hunter and man of the outdoors. But Edom did not exist as a distinct political entity until a relatively late period. From the Assyrian sources we know that Edom emerged as a fully developed state only in the late-eighth century B.C.E. It became a serious rival to Judah only with the beginning of the lucrative Arabian trade under Assyrian domination. The archaeological evidence is clear: the first large-scale wave of settlement in Edom accompanied by the establishment of significantly large settlements and fortresses may have started in the late-eighth century B.C.E., but reached its peak only in the seventh and early-sixth centuries B.C.E. Before then, the area was sparsely populated. Excavations at Bosrah (Buseirah), the capital of late-Iron II Edom, revealed that it grew to become a large city only in the Assyrian period.

During the eighth and seventh centuries, the lucrative Arabian cara-van trade in spices and rare incense was a significant factor in the region's economic life. For Judah, a number of nomadic peoples were crucial to this long-range trade system. Several of the genealogies included in the Patriar-chal stories offer a detailed picture of the peoples of the southern and eastern deserts during late-monarchic times. I refer to the Qedarites and others who are mentioned for the first time in Assyrian records of the late-eighth century B.C.E. The biblical city of Tema (Gen 25:15) is probably to be linked with the great caravan oasis of Tayma in northwest Arabia, mentioned in Assyrian and Babylonian sources of the eighth and sixth centuries B.C.E. Though these lists belong to the "P" source in Genesis, which is dated, in the main, to post-exilic times, they may have originated in an earlier time.

Other place-names mentioned in the Patriarchal narratives relating to the surrounding wilderness further confirm this date of the composition. Genesis 14, the story of the war waged by invaders from the north with the kings of the cities of the plain, is a unique source, which may also be dated to exilic or post-exilic times. But, it provides geographical information relevant only to the seventh century B.C.E. "En-mishpat that is, Kadesh" is most likely a refer-ence to Kadesh-barnea, the great oasis in the south, safely identified with ʿEin el Qudeirat in the eastern Sinai, a site that has been excavated and shown to have been occupied primarily in the seventh and early-sixth centuries B.C.E. Likewise, the site referred to as Tamar in the same biblical verse should be identified with ʿEin Hazevah south of the Dead Sea where excavations have uncovered a large fortress that also functioned in the late Iron Age. Thus, the geography and even the basic situation of frightening conflict with a Mesopo-tamian invader would have seemed ominously familiar to the people of Judah in the seventh century B.C.E.

The Genesis narratives also reveal unmistakable familiarity with the loca-tion and reputation of the Assyrian and Babylonian empires of the ninth to sixth centuries B.C.E. Assyria and its two capitals—Nineveh and Calah—are specifically mentioned in the text. The city of Haran, which plays a domi-nant role in the Patriarchal stories, prospered in the early-second millennium B.C.E. and again in the Neo-Assyrian period. Finally, Assyrian texts mention towns in the area of Haran that bear names resembling those of Abraham's forefathers Terah, Nahor, and Serug. It is possible that these were the ancestors after whom these towns were named.

JUDAH'S IDEOLOGY

The biblical scholar Martin Noth theorized that originally the Patriarchal stories were separate regional traditions that were assembled into a unified narrative to serve the purpose of politically unifying a heterogeneous Israelite population. In his opinion, the geographical focus of each of the Patriarchal stories offers an important clue as to where each of the traditions came from. Many of the stories connected with Abraham are set in the southern part of the hill country, specifically the region of Hebron. Isaac is associated with the southern desert fringe of Judah, and in particular, the Beer-sheba region. In contrast, Jacob's activities take place for the most part in the northern hill country and Transjordan—areas that were part of the Northern Kingdom, or Israel. Noth therefore suggested that the Patriarchs were originally separate regional ancestors who were eventually brought together in a single genealogy in an effort to create a unified history. Indeed, it is evident that the selection of Abraham, with his close connection to Hebron, Judah's earliest royal city, and to Jerusalem (or "Salem" in Gen 14:18) was meant to emphasize the primacy of Judah even in the earliest eras of Israel's history.

Prior to the late-eighth century B.C.E., Judah was a rather isolated and sparsely populated kingdom. It was hardly comparable in territory, wealth, and military might to the kingdom of Israel in the north. Literacy was very limited and its capital Jerusalem was a small, remote hill-country town. Yet, after the Northern Kingdom was liquidated by the Assyrian Empire in 720 B.C.E., Judah grew enormously in population, developed complex state institutions, and emerged as a meaningful power in the region. Hence, from the late-eighth century and into the seventh century, Judah developed a unique sense of its own importance and divine destiny. It saw its very survival as evidence of God's intentions from the time of the Patriarchs, namely, that Judah should rule over all the land of Israel. What was needed was a powerful way to express this understanding both to the people of Judah and to the scattered Israelite communities under Assyrian rule.

So, even though the Genesis stories revolve around Judah, they do not neglect to honor northern Israelite traditions. In that respect, it is significant that Abraham builds altars to Yahweh at Shechem and Bethel (Gen 12:7–8), the two most important cult centers of the Northern Kingdom—as well as at Hebron (Gen 13:18), the most important center of Judah after Jerusalem. The figure of Abraham therefore functions as the great unifier of northern and southern traditions, as bridging north and south. While it is possible that the individual episodes in the Patriarchal narratives are based on ancient local folk traditions, the use to which they are put and the order in which they are arranged transform them into a powerful expression of seventh-century Judahite dreams.

The Patriarchal traditions therefore must be considered as a sort of pious "prehistory" of Israel in which Judah played a decisive role. They describe the very early history of the nation, delineate ethnic boundaries, embrace the traditions of both the north and the south, and in the end emphasize the superiority of Judah from the early beginnings. The pre-exilic sources of the Patriarchal narratives should therefore be regarded primarily as a literary attempt to redefine the unity of the people of Israel in the late Iron II period rather than as an accurate record of the lives of historical characters living more than a millennium earlier.

Refashioning Israel's History

Nevertheless, the compilation of Genesis did not end in the seventh century B.C.E. There can be no doubt that its compositional history continued into the Persian period, until at least the fifth century B.C.E.

Scholars have long noted that the Priestly source (or "P") in the Pentateuch is, in the main, post-exilic in date. It is related to the rise of the priests to prominence in the temple community in Jerusalem. The final redaction of the Pentateuch also dates to this period. The biblical scholar Richard Friedman went one step further and suggested that the redactor, the one who gave the final shape to the five books of Moses, was Ezra, who is specifically described as "the scribe of the law of the God of heaven" (Ezra 7:12).

The post-exilic writers needed to reunite the community of Yehud around the Jerusalem Temple in order to give the people hope for a better future; to address the problem of their relationship with neighboring groups, especially in the north and south, and to deal with questions related to domestic problems in the community. With all the differences between them, many of the needs of the post-exilic Yehud community were quite similar to those of the late-monarchic Judahite state. Both were small communities inhabiting a limited territory and acknowledging the fact that they dominated only a small part of the "Promised Land," but also sensing their great importance as the only territorial centers of the Israelite nation.

Both were surrounded by hostile neighbors. Both claimed nearby territories that were outside their realm and both faced problems with "foreigners" from within and without. Hence, much of the ideology of Judah in the late-monarchic period was not alien to the ears of the people in Jerusalem in post-exilic times. The idea of the centrality of Judah and its superiority over its neighbors certainly rang a bell in the consciousness of the people of the late-sixth and fifth centuries B.C.E. But at the same time, other circumstances—such as the disappearance of the House of David and life under an empire—forced the early post-exilic writers to reshape the old ideas in order to fit them to new realities and new needs.

The story of Abraham migrating from a far-away foreign place to the promised land of Canaan to become a great man and to establish a prosperous nation there undoubtedly appealed to the people of Exilic and post-exilic times. In addition, the strong message of separation of the Israelites from the "Canaanites" in the Patriarchal narratives also fits the people of post-exilic Yehud. From both the political and ethnic points of view, the most severe problem lay in the south. After the destruction of Judah, Edomites settled in the southern parts of the vanquished state, in the Beer-sheba Valley and in the Hebron hills. Ethnic boundary-making between the "we" (the post-exilic community in the province of Yehud) and the "they" (the Edomites in the southern hill country) was of utmost importance. Demonstrating, in the story of Jacob and Esau, that Judah is the center and superior, and that Edom is inferior and uncivilized was therefore essential.

The tradition of the tombs of the Patriarchs in Hebron (a "P" story) should also be understood against this background. In post-exilic times, the southern border of Yehud ran between the towns of Beth-zur and Hebron. Remembering the importance of Hebron in the time of the monarchy, the people of Yehud must have mourned the fact that in their own days it lay outside their borders. A tradition placing the tombs of the Patriarchs, the founders of the nation, at Hebron, would therefore serve their goal of establishing a strong attachment to the southern hill country.

No less important, the latest editors of Genesis were eager to show how the origins of the people of Israel lay at the very heart of the civilized world. Thus, unlike the "lesser" peoples who emerged from the undeveloped, uncultured regions around them, they boasted that the great father of the people of Israel came from the cosmopolitan, famed city of Ur. Not only was Ur renowned as a place of extreme antiquity and learning, it gained great prestige throughout the ancient Near East during the period of its reestablishment as a religious center by the Babylonian, or Chaldean, king Nebuchadnezzar. Thus, the reference to Abraham's origin in "Ur of the Chaldeans" would have offered the Jewish people a distinguished and ancient cultural pedigree.

THE EXODUS

This treatment of the Patriarchal stories can serve as a model for the reading of Exodus. In this case too, the attempts to locate the events in the thirteenth century B.C.E., in the time of Pharaoh Ramesses II, have faced insurmountable difficulties. There is no mention of such an event in any New Kingdom Egyptian source, and there is no trace of the early Hebrews in Egypt. The northern coast of Sinai was protected by formidable Egyptian forts that could have easily prevented an escaping people from crossing the desert; there is no trace of Late Bronze remains in the rest of the Sinai peninsula, not even in a place like Kadesh-barnea, where the Israelites are supposed to have camped for a long time; and Canaan of that time was an Egyptian province, administered by Egyptian garrisons where fifty Egyptian soldiers were enough to pacify an area according to the Amarna letters. Finally, many of the places mentioned in the story of Exodus and the wandering in the desert were not inhabited before the eighth or even seventh century B.C.E.

Indeed, the Egyptologist Donald Redford has convincingly shown that both the geography of the Exodus in the eastern Delta and the personal names in the story best fit the Saite period in the history of Egypt, in the seventh and sixth centuries B.C.E., that is, close to the time of the compilation of the biblical texts. A late-date compilation would also fit most of the place-names mentioned in regard to the wandering in the desert. At the same time, Redford did not discard the possibility that Exodus preserves an ancient memory of great events that took place centuries earlier—possibly the expulsion of Canaanite populations known as the Hyksos from the Delta of the Nile in the sixteenth century B.C.E.

Is it possible that the story of a great confrontation between the Israelites and an Egyptian pharaoh was used to send a powerful message to the Judahites of late-monarchic times? In the late-seventh century B.C.E., with the withdrawal of Assyria from the Levant, two great revival programs collided: on the one hand, Judah's dream (under King Josiah) of "reconquering" the lost territories of the ex-Northern Kingdom and "reactivating" the Golden Age of King Solomon, and, on the other, Egypt's plan (under the Saite Dynasty) to revive its great empire in the Levant. Is it possible that an old story on how a great pharaoh was humiliated and defeated by the God of Israel was used in order to send a message of hope to the people of Judah in the time of the authors?

There is no doubt that the Exodus story also had a strong—possibly stronger—impact in exilic and post-exilic times. To put it in the words of the biblical scholar David Clines, "the bondage in Egypt is their own bondage in Babylon, and the exodus past becomes the exodus that is yet to be." Later on, the similarity between the story of the Exodus from Egypt and the memories of the return from exile influenced each other in a reciprocal way. Having read or heard Exodus, the returnees found a mirror to their own plight. According to the biblical scholar Yair Hoffman, both stories tell us how the Israelites left their land for a foreign country; how after a rough period in exile the

Hebrews/Judahites came back to their homeland; how on the way back the returnees had to cross a dangerous desert; how the return to the homeland evoked conflicts with the local population; how the returnees managed to settle only part of their promised homeland; and how measures were taken by the leaders of the returnees to avoid assimilation between the Israelites and the population of the land.

THE CONQUEST

A series of excavations carried out from the late 1920s through the 1950s revealed data that were interpreted as supporting the biblical narrative of the Conquest of Canaan. At many sites, the Late Bronze II cities were destroyed in large conflagrations that were dated to the late-thirteenth century B.C.E. and associated with the invading Israelites. These data were fixed according to the conventional chronology of the Aegean pottery sequence, but this in turn was influenced by the Conquest stories in the Bible; another clear case of circular reasoning.

From the outset, this paradigm, advanced by William F. Albright and, later, by Yigael Yadin, faced strong opposition from German biblical scholars who proposed a completely different paradigm for the rise of early Israel. The progress in archaeological and anthropological research between the 1960s and the 1980s brought about the total demise of the military conquest theory.

First, excavations at key sites mentioned in the Conquest narratives of the Bible, such as Jericho, ʿAi, Gibeon, Heshbon, and Arad, showed that they were either not inhabited in the Late Bronze Age or else were insignificant villages. Second, new finds at Lachish and Aphek and the reevaluation of finds from the older digs at Megiddo and Hazor indicated that the collapse of the Late Bronze Canaanite city-state system was a long process that took at least several decades. Third, historical and archaeological studies have shown the strength of the Egyptian grip on Canaan as lasting well into the second half of the twelfth century B.C.E.; Egypt could easily have prevented an invasion of Canaan by a rag-tag army. Fourth, it has become clear that the collapse of Late Bronze Canaan was part of a wider phenomenon that encompassed the entire eastern Mediterranean. Fifth, the large-scale surveys that were conducted in the central hill country in the 1980s indicated that the rise of ancient Israel was just one phase in a long-term, repeated, and cyclic process of sedentarization and nomadization of autochthonous groups.

Nevertheless, it is inconceivable that the Conquest stories were invented by the late-monarchic writers. The Deuteronomistic Historian must have taken old folktales and fragmented memories and incorporated them in his compilation. Some of these, like the huge piles of stones at ʿAi, could have been the reason for the development of aetiological legends (in this case, explaining the demise of a very old city) connected with specific locales, while others could have preserved vague memories of the collapse of the Old World at the end of the Bronze Age.

But the overall outline of the Conquest narrative reflects late-monarchic realities. Central to deuteronomistic thinking was the idea that all Israelite territories and people should be ruled by a Davidic king and that all Israelite cults should be centralized in the Temple in Jerusalem. This ideology probably emerged after the fall of the Northern Kingdom, but could not have been fulfilled as long as Assyria dominated the region. When the Assyrians pulled out around 630 B.C.E., it seemed possible to accomplish. Thus, at the time when possession of the Land was of great concern, the book of Joshua offered an unforgettable epic with a clear lesson—creating a vivid, unified narrative and demonstrating that when the people of Israel did follow the covenant with their God, no victory could be denied to them. That point was narrated against a highly familiar seventh century background and played out in places of the greatest concern to the deuteronomistic ideology.

So, as noted by the biblical scholar Richard Nelson, the towering figure of Joshua is used to paint a metaphorical portrait of Josiah, the eighth-century would-be savior of all the people of Israel. Josiah is the new Joshua, and the past, mythical Conquest of Canaan is the battle plan for the present fight and the conquest to be. The first two battles—at Jericho and ʿAi (that is, the area of Bethel)—were pitched in territories that were the first targets of the Josianic expansion after the withdrawal of Assyria. Likewise, the story of the Gibeonites who had "come from a far country" to make a covenant with the invading Israelites has a basis in the historical reality of the seventh century B.C.E. Expanding northward, into the area of Bethel, Judah faced the problem of how to integrate the descendents of the deportees brought by the Assyrians from afar who had been settled there a few decades earlier. The very old story of the Gibeonites could provide an "historical" context in which the Deuteronomists explained how it was possible to integrate these people though they were not Israelites by origin.

Next was the conquest of the Shephelah, probably symbolizing the renewed Judahite expansion into this important, fertile region; an expansion that is evident from the distribution of late-monarchic Judahite finds. This area—the traditional breadbasket of the Southern Kingdom—had been seized from Judah by Sennacherib a few decades earlier and given to the cities of the coastal plain. It seems to have been reincorporated into the territory of Judah in the course of the seventh century B.C.E.—either in the days of Manasseh, or in the reign of Josiah, after the Assyrian withdrawal. Finally, the biblical story turns to the north and this time the conquest of the past becomes a utopic conquest for the future. The reference to Hazor calls to mind not only its reputation in the distant past as the most prominent of the Canaanite city-states, but certainly the realities of more recent times when it was the most important center of the kingdom of Israel in the north. Likewise, the territories described in relation to the war in the north perfectly match the Galilee territories of the vanquished Northern Kingdom or Israel. These were the territories that were viewed in seventh-century Judah as lawfully and divinely belonging to the Davidic kings in Jerusalem.

The Conquest stories, then, should be read against the geographical and ideological background of late-seventh century Judah, in the time of King Josiah.

Summary

The Patriarchal, Exodus, and Conquest narratives, which describe the formative history of the people of Israel, cannot be read as straightforward historical accounts. It is conceivable that many of the stories preserve old memories, folk tales, myths, and aetiological anecdotes. Yet, in the way they are portrayed in the Bible, they are wrapped in late-monarchic (and in the case of the Patriarchal and Exodus narratives, also exilic and post-exilic) realities. Moreover, the way in which they were compiled discloses that they serve the ideological aims of their late-Iron II period authors. These stories should not be read therefore in a sequential order, from early to late; rather, they must be understood from late to early—beginning from the perspective of the period when they were set down in writing.

THE PATRIARCHS, EXODUS, AND CONQUEST NARRATIVES IN LIGHT OF ARCHAEOLOGY

Amihai Mazar

The origins of Israel and its crystallization as an ethnic or geopolitical entity are today among the most controversial topics in biblical history. Prior to the 1970s, it was a common practice to identify the Patriarchal period, the route of the Exodus, and the Israelite Conquest of Canaan in direct relation to archaeological finds. This was a dominant agenda among leading scholars like William F. Albright and his followers, Roland de Vaux, and the founders of biblical archaeology in Israel, which included Benjamin Mazar, Yigael Yadin, and others. This approach has been criticized severely over the last thirty years, and, today, many scholars regard these stories as late literary creations with distinct theological and ideological messages and little or no historical value. Others assert that these stories reflect and preserve certain components that are rooted in second-millennium B.C.E. realia, while some conservative scholars still claim that many of these stories reflect true historical events. It is today accepted by almost all scholars that the stories as they have come down to us are a product of Israelite literary work of the late monarchy or later. The questions, to what extent are these literary works preserved ancient stories that passed orally through generations? and, to what extent can we identify any second-millennium B.C.E. realia in these biblical narratives in light of the vast archaeological research conducted in the region? can still be asked.

THE PATRIARCHAL TRADITION

In the years leading up to the 1970s, many scholars shared the common belief that the cultural environment of the Middle Bronze II period (ca.1800/1750–1550 B.C.E.) provided the most suitable background for the Patriarchal stories in the book of Genesis. The land of Canaan appears in these stories as having a prosperous urban culture with pastoral clans living in between fortified cities, and indeed this was the case during the Middle

Bronze II period. Most of the cities mentioned in the Patriarchal stories—for example, Shechem, Bethel, Jerusalem, and Hebron—were settled and fortified during the Middle Bronze period. The second-millennium setting conformed to that of the Patriarchal narratives: the personal names in these narratives are mostly of the "Amorite" type known from the second millennium B.C.E.; thus the name of Jacob appears as a component in the name of one of the Hyksos rulers in Egypt as well as of a place-name in Thutmosis III's list of captured cities in Canaan, but the name is unknown in the first millennium B.C.E. The archives of cuneiform documents from Mari on the middle Euphrates (eighteenth or seventeenth century B.C.E.), Nuzi (fifteenth century B.C.E.), and Emar (thirteenth century B.C.E.) have yielded abundant information concerning the social structure, daily customs, ritual, and laws of the time. Some of these find parallels in the book of Genesis and in other books of the Pentateuch; the wanderings of Abraham from Ur to Haran and from there to Canaan have been explained as reflecting the international connections along the Fertile Crescent during the Middle Bronze II period. The high position of Joseph in Egypt has been viewed as fitting well with the Hyksos period when Semitic princes ruled Lower Egypt and established the Fifteenth Dynasty there in the mid-sixteenth to mid-fifteenth centuries B.C.E. Various other phenomena in the book of Genesis that apply to later periods, such as the extensive use of camels and the appearance of Arameans and Philistines in the Patriarchal stories, have been considered as anachronisms introduced by later editors and compilers of the old oral traditions. Nevertheless, the kernels of these stories were generally considered to be rooted in the Middle Bronze II period. A variation on this hypothesis has been suggested by scholars such as Manfred Weippert who, in a paper published in 1979, proposed that the Patriarchs may have been actual pastoralists who lived as Shasu or nomadic people who are mentioned in Egyptian texts of the Late Bronze age, the time of the Egyptian New Kingdom of the mid-sixteenth to twelfth centuries B.C.E., which parallels most of the Late Bronze Age.

This approach has been opposed by scholars who propose that the stories were created in a much later period closer to the time of their written compilation. Benjamin Mazar had suggested in 1963 that Genesis was compiled in the court of David and Solomon, and that it reflects the reality of their times or of the slightly earlier period of the Judges. During the 1970s, John Van Seters and Thomas Thompson suggested, in two detailed monographs, exilic or post-exilic dates for the entirety of the Patriarchal traditions, and argued against their affinity to any second-millennium B.C.E. backgrounds. Their views became influential, and today most scholars indeed define the Patriarchal tradition as a late invention with no historical validity.

Yet, the questions of when and with whom these stories originated and what is the background to their creation can still be asked. I continue to believe that some of the parallels between the second-millennium B.C.E. culture of the Levant and the cultural background portrayed in the Patriarchal stories as mentioned above are too close to be ignored, indicating that perhaps certain components in the biblical stories are recollections of memories rooted in the second millennium and preserved through common memory and oral traditions. Such stories and traditions could have been transmitted orally over many generations until they were inserted into the biblical narrative sometime during the first millennium B.C.E. To be sure, in the process of oral transmission, many features had been lost, expanded upon, distorted, or changed over the ages, and still others, reflecting much later historical situations, added. This does not mean that the stories should be taken at face value as reflecting the deeds of actual people, nor should they be taken literally as reflecting actual Israelite ancestral history. On the contrary, this aspect of the stories may indeed be a late innovation. I merely wish to claim that some elements of the second-millennium B.C.E. milieu mentioned above, such as private names, place-names, and the status of a Semitic prince in the Egyptian court, may suggest that the stories contain kernels of old traditions and stories rooted in second-millennium B.C.E. realia. As we will see below, this line of thought can be applied to the Exodus and Conquest traditions.

THE EXODUS

No direct evidence on the Israelite sojourn in Egypt and the Exodus can be extracted from archaeology. The only evidence that one might seriously consider is circumstantial. The biblical story of the Hebrews living in the Land of Goshen (the eastern Delta of Egypt) during the time of the Egyptian New Kingdom can be understood in the context of the rich evidence for West Semitic populations living in this area through most of the second millennium B.C.E. As is now well known, these West Semites founded the Fifteenth, or Hyksos, Dynasty in Egypt. During the thirteenth century, Ramesses II, the mighty pharaoh of the Nineteenth Dynasty, built a new city called Pi-Ramesse very close to the location of the older capital of the Hyksos at Avaris. It was a huge city built of mudbrick in an area where large West Semitic populations lived for centuries. The story in the book of Exodus where the Hebrews are portrayed as building the city of Ramesses may reflect this huge building operation of the thirteenth century.

The theme of escape to the Sinai desert is also something that was not unknown during this period. Papyri describe small groups of slaves escaping to the Sinai through the eastern fortification system of Egypt, which corresponds more or less to the line of the modern Suez Canal. The "road of the land of the Philistines" mentioned in Exod 13:17 is probably a term relating the well-known road named by the Egyptians "the road of Horus," leading from the easternmost branch of the Nile Delta (the Pelusiac branch, which is dry today) to Gaza, the main stronghold of the Egyptians in Canaan. One of the earliest roadmaps in the historical records, a wall relief carved on the outer wall of the temple of Amun at Karnak during the time of Seti I (ca. 1300 B.C.E.), depicts over twenty stations along this northern Sinai desert route, each having a small fort and a water reservoir. Archaeological investigations in the northern Sinai and south of Gaza have indeed revealed some of these fortresses. The road was thus well known to the biblical authors, who, however, named it after the Philistines who occupied the southwestern coast of Palestine at the time of writing. The Israelites are said to have avoided this fortified road through northern Sinai, as would have slaves escaping from Egypt, like those mentioned in papyri dating to the end of the Egyptian New Kingdom. Such references to runaway slaves may be taken as typological parallels to the genesis of the Exodus narrative.

In spite of the late-second-millennium B.C.E. relics in the biblical narrative and the few geographical features in the story that may be identified, the Exodus story, one of the most prominent traditions in Israelite common memory, cannot be accepted as an historical event and must be defined as a national saga. We cannot perceive a whole nation wondering through the desert for forty years under the leadership of Moses, as presented in the biblical tradition. And yet it may be conjectured that the tradition is rooted in the experience of a certain group of West Semitic slaves who fled from the northeastern Delta region into the Sinai during the late-thirteenth century, as paralleled by events recorded on papyri from the late New Kingdom in Egypt. Such a group might have joined what would become the Israelite confederacy and have brought with them both the Exodus story as well as new religious ideas. As archaeologists, however, we cannot provide any clues to the Exodus as an event that indeed happened. We cannot identify Mount Sinai and many other place-names in the story; nor were any remains from this period found anywhere in the Sinai, including at the oasis of Kadesh-barnea, which plays such an important role in the story.

Yet, the Exodus story reflects a good knowledge of the geography and natural conditions of the eastern Delta, the Sinai peninsula, the Negev, and Transjordan. This has led various scholars to try and identify specific geographical features related to the Exodus route, such as the location of Mount Sinai. The search for this mountain has gone on since the Byzantine era and at least five candidates in various parts of the Sinai, the Negev, and northwest Arabia have been suggested, with no convincing solution. The biblical "Red

Sea" should be translated from the Hebrew as the Sea of Reeds, and thus the term probably refers to a sweet-water lake. James Hoffmeier recently explored this issue and suggested identifying this sea with an ancient sweet-water lake, which he located close to the northern end of the Suez canal. Yet, even if this identification is correct, it would only corroborate the geographic and environmental background to the story, but it cannot verify its historicity as a major founding event in Israel's history. All that can be said is that the Exodus story is based on some remote memories rooted in the reality of the thirteenth century B.C.E. and on a rather good knowledge of the geographical and environmental conditions of the territories included in the narrative.

Other components of the Exodus tradition relating to the Negev and Transjordan refer to later features not established before the time of the Israelite monarchy (such as the kingdom of Edom) or entirely unknown from actual history (such the Amorite kingdom of Sihon). Thus, the few details that are rooted in thirteenth-century realia still cannot corroborate the historicity of the Exodus, but they may provide a hint as to the earliest date of the emergence of this story. Eventually, the story was transmitted and adapted as a major pan-Israelite narrative. During several centuries of transmission, it was constantly changed and elaborated on until it received the form known to us from the Hebrew Bible.

THE CONQUEST TRADITION

The Conquest narrative in the book of Joshua and other conquest stories in the books of Numbers and Judges have long attracted archaeologists. Destroyed cities are something that archaeologists should be able to discover, and if indeed Israel destroyed many Canaanite cities as described in various conquest narratives (in particular, but not only, in the book of Joshua), then archaeologists should be able to uncover those ruined cities. In the early years of biblical archaeology, historians and archaeologists tended to accept the conquest narrative at face value. Archaeologists like John Garstang, William F. Albright, Yigael Yadin, and others presented the Israelite conquest of the country as a short-lived event that could be identified archaeologically. Yadin was perhaps the last to present Joshua as a real military hero who conquered city after city in Canaan in line with the biblical narrative.

Since the 1960s, however, it has become obvious that this was not the historical reality. Archaeological investigations have shown that many of the sites mentioned in these conquest stories turned out to be uninhabited during the assumed time of the Conquest, ca. 1200 B.C.E. This is the case with Arad, Heshbon, ʿAi, and Yarmuth. At other sites, there was only a small and unimportant settlement at the time, as at Jericho, and perhaps Hebron. Others, like

Lachish and Hazor, were indeed important Canaanite cities, yet they were not destroyed as part of the same military undertaking since approximately one hundred years separate the destruction of Hazor (in the mid-thirteenth century B.C.E.) from that of Lachish (in the mid-twelfth century B.C.E.). At other sites, the archaeological evidence is even more meager.

It is thus now accepted by all that archaeology in fact contradicts the biblical account of the Israelite Conquest as a discreet historical event led by one leader. Most scholars of the last generation regard the Conquest narratives as a literary work of a much later time, designed to create a pan-Israelite, national saga. Nonetheless, even this latter view does not exclude the possibility that certain conquest stories echo isolated, individual historical events that may have occurred during the late-second millennium B.C.E., though perhaps not specifically in relation to Israel as a nation or to Joshua as a military leader. Other stories seem to be aetiologies rooted in situations relating to the period of the Settlement.

Several examples provide more specific test cases for how ancient recollections of the past made their way into the later biblical narrative. The Bible's description of the conquest of ʿAi details its location: "Ai, which is near Beth Aven to the east of Bethel" (Josh 7:2). Assuming the identification of ʿAi with modern et-Tell, the only prominent site east of Bethel, is correct, the story of its conquest in Josh 8 is negated by the archaeological finds. No Late Bronze Canaanite city was found at this place or in its vicinity. Thus, the conquest narrative in Josh 8 cannot be based on historical reality, despite its topographical and tactical plausibility. The story can be explained, though, in light of the archaeological evidence at the site, as an aetiological story. An Iron I village was built above the prominent ruins of the much-earlier, fortified, third-millennium (or Early Bronze III) city, and its inhabitants must have known of the older fortification, which was destroyed more than one thousand years earlier and whose ruins can partly be seen even today without excavation. It is reasonable to suppose that the story of the conquest of ʿAi was created by the Iron Age I settlers to explain the ruins upon which they had built their own village. As the site was abandoned at the end of the Iron I period, the aetiological story might have been created during the time of the Settlement (twelfth to eleventh centuries B.C.E.) and transmitted orally for centuries until it found its way into the biblical Conquest narrative.

A second example is Hazor. This seventy-hectare city was the largest in Canaan, several times larger than any other Canaanite city in the region and the capital of a sizeable city-state that is well attested in second-millennium documents from Mari on the Euphrates and from Egypt. The definition of Hazor in Josh 11:10 as "formerly the head of all those kingdoms" fits its status in the second millennium B.C.E. and could not have been invented when the book of Joshua was probably composed in the seventh century B.C.E. or later, a time when Hazor had no importance. The reference to the burning of Hazor in Josh 11:11 (an exception in this respect to all the other "conquered" cities) is supported by the archaeological evidence: a tremendous fire destroyed the Canaanite palace at Hazor and its temples sometime during the thirteenth century B.C.E. (probably during the first half of this century). Yigael Yadin did not hesitate to identify the conquerors as the Israelites led by Joshua; Amnon Ben-Tor, the current excavator of the site, finds no other candidates for the destroyers of Hazor more appropriate than the Israelites or "proto-Israelites." I would explain the biblical description as a reflection of historical memories about the traumatic event that put an end to Hazor, the largest city in Canaan. Such memories could have been retained among the Canaanite population that remained in the country during the twelfth to eleventh centuries and eventually were incorporated into Israelite tradition in the late-monarchic period, when the conquest was attributed to Joshua. The antiquity of the memory itself is significant, though the identification of the thirteenth-century B.C.E. destroyers of Hazor remains enigmatic.

Other conquest stories have no archaeological verification or explanation whatsoever. One example is the case of Arad. In the book of Numbers, the Israelites are described as crossing the Negev highlands from Kadesh-barnea and attacking "the Canaanite king of Arad who lived in the Negev" (Num 21:11 see also 21:3). Many years of archaeological research at Arad and in its vicinity have not revealed any evidence for a Canaanite settlement of the Late Bronze Age. Yohanan Aharoni, the excavator of Arad, looked in vain for an alternative site for Canaanite Arad. All that he found were two Canaanite towns of the Middle Bronze period in the region. Yet, these are too early to be related directly to the conquest story. Benjamin Mazar suggested that the phrase "king of Arad" refers to the leader of a nomadic or semi-nomadic population of which no material remains have survived. This is a very unlikely explanation. It is more feasible that the biblical stories were formulated as a much later literary creation of no historical value when the Israelites began settling this region. As we will see below, Kadesh-barnea, the Negev highlands, and Arad were settled on a wide scale during the tenth century B.C.E. and the later-monarchic periods, and so the Conquest story may have been created in relation to this later process of settlement.

The Conquest traditions concerning Transjordan can be examined against the limited available archaeological data. Numbers 21:21–32 records the wars of the Israelites against Sihon, king of the "Amorites," and of the conquest of Heshbon. At Heshbon (Tell Hesban), however, the earliest settlement has been dated to the Iron I, and even this is a sparse settlement. There is no evidence for an "Amorite" state of any kind in this region, nor is there evidence of a

Moabite kingdom at the end of the Late Bronze Age, though current research at Moab has revealed several fortified sites of the twelfth to eleventh centuries B.C.E. (see part 3).

We may conclude that in some cases there is an outright conflict between the archaeological findings and the biblical narratives, while in others, the archaeological data do not contradict the Conquest stories. Archaeology cannot confirm that Israelite tribes were responsible for the destruction of certain Canaanite cities. The devastation of Canaan did not take place in one sweeping, single military campaign. Rather, the destruction of Canaanite cities resulted from a long-drawn-out process of regional conflicts, the nature of which cannot be identified at the present time. Local destructions brought on by unknown factors such as at Hazor, or local clashes between clans or tribal groups that perhaps made up part of the later Israelite and Canaanite urban populations, may eventually have found their way into the collective memory of the Israelites. The Conquest tradition may be understood as a tele-scoped reflection of a lengthy, complex historical process in which many of the Canaanite city-states, weakened and impoverished by three hundred years of Egyptian domination, were demolished during the thirteenth and twelfth centuries B.C.E.

Two additional examples of possible historical recollections in the bibli-cal narrative should be mentioned. The first is the concept of Canaan as a country divided into many city-states. This concept is reflected in the vari-ous conquest stories that mention cities and their "kings," as well as in Josh 12, which lists thirty-one kings of Canaan. Such a geopolitical structure fits well with the reality of second-millennium Canaan, but is hardly known in the period of the monarchy or later, when the book of Joshua was written. It can hardly be conceived that a late author would invent such an idea without having some recollections of the past. At the same time, it must be noted that neither Joshua nor any other Israelite tradition makes mention of a major his-torical reality of the second millennium B.C.E., namely, that Canaan was under Egyptian domination for three hundred years.

A second example are the lists of unconquered territories in Canaan (Judg 1:27–35; Josh 13:2–6). These include mainly the Beth-shean and Jezreel Valleys and the coastal plain; cities like Beth-shean, Taanach, Dor, Jibleam, Megiddo, Gezer, and Acre are mentioned as well as cities in the valley of Ajalon and others. Archaeological exploration in many of these cities, such as at Beth-shean, Tel Reḥov, Megiddo, Dor, and Gezer, have confirmed the continuity of Canaanite urban culture throughout the Iron I period (twelfth to eleventh centuries B.C.E.), thus surprisingly supporting these biblical tra-ditions as reflecting a pre-monarchic historical reality. Another example, though less secure, is that of Shechem, which is located in the heart of the tribal allotment of Manasseh and Ephraim. In Israelite tradition, this was the place where the covenant between the tribes of Israel and their God was made (Josh 24). The story of Abimelech (Judg 9) indicates that a local Canaanite population remained at Shechem until a late stage in the period of the Judges. Indeed, in the opinion of the excavators, the Canaanite city at Shechem continued to thrive until the eleventh century B.C.E.

In sum, archaeology negates the biblical "Israelite Conquest" as an historical event, yet it may shed some light on the various ways in which memories of actual situations and events rooted in the second millennium B.C.E., early aetiologies and invented stories all found their way into the later, "melting pot" we call today the Pentateuch and the book of Joshua.

PART 3

THE HISTORICAL ORIGINS OF COLLECTIVE ISRAEL

A Summary Assessment for Part 3

Brian B. Schmidt

Having reviewed the evidence deduced by scholars that points to the compilation of Joshua and Judges as deuteronomistic works of the seventh century and therefore their secondary relevance for reconstructing the age of Israel's earliest national origins, Professor Finkelstein turns to extra-biblical texts and archaeological data for what he labels "real time" testimony to the emergence of Israel in the Cisjordanian highlands of the twelfth to eleventh centuries B.C.E. The Merneptah stele testifies to the presence of an "Israel" in Canaan in the late-thirteenth century and archaeology reveals an unprecedented wave of settlement in the highlands of Canaan that commences about the same time. These settlements continued into the Iron II period when and where they formed the heartland of the later emergent states of Israel and Judah. What remains for scholars is to ascertain the origin of these settlers in the highlands and the factors that instigated there the arrival of peoples at that time. Scholars have proposed several models or theories over the decades, for example, Albright's military conquest, Alt's peaceful infiltration, and the Mendenhall-Gottwald social revolution model. Yet, each of these presupposes the utter uniqueness of the event and each has serious shortcomings that scholars have pointed out. These include the presumed development of brand-new, heretofore-unattested technologies, like ironmaking, terrace construction, and cistern plastering, which supposedly facilitated the large-scale settlement of the highlands.

For Finkelstein, the emergence of Israel in the hill country should not be viewed as a unique or one-time event. The highlands settlements that developed at the end of the Late Bronze Age had as their precedent similar processes attested in the Early and Middle Bronze periods. Each was part of a longer-term, localized, repeated strategy of rotating sedentarization and nomadization that involved indigenous groups (that is, Canaanites) responding to changing economic, political, and environmental circumstances. Each repetition of the cycle also involved the use of technologies like hewing and plastering cisterns and terrace building. For Finkelstein, the attempt to identify the highlands settlers based on later reflections in ancient sources or modern constructs of ethnic marking is problematic. The proposals that the four-room house or the collared-rim storage jar are markers of Israelite identity are ill-fated and their development in these regions are best accounted for as features stemming from environmental and economic influences. In fact, it is impossible to distinguish the ethnic boundaries of the settlers and their material cultural traits in the Cisjordan highlands from those in the Transjordanian hill country on the bases of these two features. Yet, Finkelstein proposes as a possible alternative ethnic marker of Israelite identity the apparent taboo on pig consumption in the Iron I (1200–900 B.C.E.) highlands as indicated by the lack of corresponding faunal remains. This singular element is unique and contrasts the Iron I hill country settlers with those of earlier settlement periods in the highlands and their contemporaries in the Iron I Canaanite lowlands (and possibly those in the Transjordanian highlands). These settlers, or proto-Israelites as some would so label them, were the ancestors of the later Israelites that made up the Iron II territorial- and nation-states of Israel and Judah.

According to Professor Mazar, the biblical Settlement stories like the Conquest narratives find partial confirmation in the recent archaeological surveys that have been completed over the past few decades. These surveys document an entirely new Iron I-period settlement pattern with hundreds of new small sites in the mountainous areas of upper and lower Galilee, in the Samarian, Ephraimite, Benjaminite, and Judean hills, in the northern Negev and in parts of central and northern Transjordan. Mazar acknowledges the attendant problems in any attempt to identify individual, unambiguous "ethnic" markers from archaeology like the collared-rim jar or the four-room house, as has frequently been the case in the past, or for that matter the taboo against pig consumption proposed by Finkelstein. Instead, he concludes that it is the overall material cultural assemblage (i.e., more than just pottery forms) of the hill country population that differs from those of the contemporary lowland Canaanite and Philistine cultures and from that of the Jezreel Valley. He goes on to conclude that the socio-economic structure of the Iron I hill-country society coincides with the biblical description of Israel in the book of Judges. It is a non-urban, sedentary population living in small communities of farmers and herders without a central political authority though probably with major cultic centers like the one at Shiloh.

After surveying the various theories concerning Israel's collective origins in the hill country of Cisjordan during the Late Bronze Age to Iron 1 transition, Mazar tentatively proposes a model that views the hill-country settlers in the following manner: the Iron I settlements are a mixture of (1) previously unsettled Transjordanian peoples who entered the hill country and were known by the Egyptians in roughly contemporary sources as the Shasu; (2) local pastoralists forced by various conditions (for example, overpopulation) to return to their former hill country sedentary lifestyle of five hundred years earlier; and (3) disposed Canaanite peasants who had recently left the lowlands seeking better subsistence in the hill country. For Mazar, the Yahwists among these settlers were most likely those the Egyptians referred to as the Shasu. The proper name Yahwi appears in Egyptian sources alongside the mention of the Shasu from Seir, which in turn corresponds to the reference in Judg 5:4 that Yahweh came from Seir, that is, Edom. This society struggled for its subsistence in the harsh environmental conditions of the forested mountains and semi-arid regions of the land of Israel.

When and How Did the Israelites Emerge?

Israel Finkelstein

Setting the Stage

According to the biblical narrative, the Conquest of Canaan ended in only partial success. The book of Joshua (13:2–6) narrates that large parts of Canaan remained to be taken, and chapter 1 in the book of Judges lists Canaanite cities that remained as enclaves in the tribal territories, that is, inside the land that was conquered. This is the stage setting for what happened next, namely, the so-called period of the Judges. This was a long period between the Conquest and the establishment of the Monarchy in which Israel was ruled by charismatic leaders called judges who delivered the people from their enemies. According to the inner logic of the biblical narrative, and when placed against the history of the ancient Near East, the period of the Judges covered about two centuries, from approximately 1200 to 1000 B.C.E.

Yet, the book of Judges does not depict the realities of the Iron Age I period. Though it probably contains early materials that originated from northern Israelite sources (and that could have been put in writing before the collapse of the Northern Kingdom), in its current shape, Judges is a relatively late, deuteronomistic book, which represents the ideology of Judah in the seventh century B.C.E., hundreds of years after the alleged events took place. This can be seen in several domains:

1. Cycles of sin, retribution, and redemption clearly characterize the deuteronomistic theology.
2. Almost all the stories take place in the territories of the northern tribes. Judges 1, which also belongs, in my opinion, to the seventh-century compilation, clearly states that the northern tribes failed to cleanse the adulterous Canaanites from their midst and that the tribe of Judah was the only one successfully to do so. This explains what will come next: unlike Judah, the northern tribes fell prey, time and again, to the lure of the Canaanite deities.

3. Judges is a prelude to the rise of the Davidic dynasty in Jerusalem. It portrays the situation before the monarchy—including the relationship between the People of Israel and the God of Israel—in dark colors, and, at its end, predicts the rise of the monarchy: "In those days there was no king in Israel; every man did what was right in his own eyes" (Judg 21:25).

Therefore, though it is possible that myths and tales in Judges preserve some vague early memories of local events, most of them have little historical value for the study of the rise of early Israel. We need to turn then to extra-biblical sources and archaeology, as both provide us with "real time" testimony to the early days of ancient Israel.

The stele of Pharaoh Merneptah, which describes his campaign to Canaan in 1207 B.C.E., mentions the conquest of three cities and the subjugation—in fact, the annihilation—of a group of people named "Israel." It does not indicate the size of this group and its exact location. It only testifies that a certain group named Israel was present in Canaan in the late-thirteenth century.

Archaeology has revealed an unprecedented wave of settlement in the highlands of Canaan that commenced about that same time. In the course of the Iron Age I—the twelfth to tenth centuries B.C.E.—about 250 settlements were established in the area between the Beer-sheba and Jezreel Valleys. Since most of these sites continued to be settled uninterrupted in the Iron II when they formed the heartland of the states of Israel and Judah, their inhabitants can safely be referred to as "Israelites," or "proto-Israelites" (William G. Dever's term). This is the material background for the rise of early Israel.

Two main questions have dominated the study of the emergence of early Israel. First, what was the origin of the Iron I villagers of the highlands—the proto-Israelites? Since a similar process took place at that time in the highlands of Transjordan, one should ask the same question about the proto-Ammonites, proto-Moabites, and proto-Edomites. Second, what were the forces that stimulated the foundation of hundreds of small, isolated Iron I communities in the highlands?

Earlier scholars could not reach a consensus about the answers to these questions, and theories shifted between a complete reliance on the biblical text and the total denial of its value as an historical record. But in recent years, the spectrum of views has narrowed quite dramatically. First and foremost, most of us agree today on what we do not accept and that in itself is a remarkable achievement in historical research. Surprisingly, most scholars today will find it easy to unite behind the rejection of all three theories proposed by scholars that dominated the study of the rise of early Israel until about twenty years ago.

In part 2, I explained why William F. Albright's military conquest theory—an archaeological disguise for the biblical narrative on the Conquest of Canaan—must be dismissed. Important parts of Albrecht Alt's peaceful infiltration theory, which argued that the emergence of early Israel should be seen as a gradual sedentarization process of pastoral nomads from the steppe, cannot be accepted either because our understanding of the nature of pastoral nomadism in the ancient Near East has changed significantly. We understand today that sheep and goat pastoral nomadism is an offshoot of sedentary life, and that the sedentary-pastoral avenue was open at both ends—sedentarization and nomadization—according to changing political, economic, and social factors. In short, there was no "source" of nomads in the steppe that could have supplied the peaceful infiltrators to Canaan.

The Mendenhall-Gottwald social revolution theory—a somewhat naïve product of Marxist undercurrents in American campuses of the utopian 1960s—explained the rise of early Israel in terms of class struggle; an uprising of the exploited, rural elements in Canaanite society against their overlords. This led to their withdrawal from the lowlands to the empty highlands, where they established just, egalitarian communities. But archaeology came up short of tracing any clues to such a dramatic shift from the sedentary lowlands to the sedentary highlands in a short period of time, whether in the material culture of the highlands sites or in the settlement patterns of the lowlands. To put the latter simply, there were not enough Late Bronze settlements in the lowlands to supply a sufficient number of withdrawing people. In fact, many of these Late Bronze sites continued to be inhabited in the Iron I.

It is noteworthy that all three "classic" models described the emergence of early Israel as a unique event in the history of Palestine. In other words, consciously or unconsciously, all three followed the basic theological construct of the biblical narrative. Recent research has proven this basic premise wrong.

In what follows, I wish to present a model for understanding the emergence of early Israel that is based on two decades of intensive fieldwork in the highlands—excavations and surveys alike. Both branches of modern archaeological field research were employed in the study of the emergence of Israel. For the first time, meticulous excavations were carried out not only in the large mounds of the lowlands, but also in rural, highland sites. They shed light on the material culture and economic strategies of the Iron I people. But the "great leap forward" in the study of the emergence of early Israel was the turn, in the 1980s, to comprehensive surveys in the highlands. This made possible an almost complete reconstruction of the settlement patterns in antiquity. Most of the central hill country of Cisjordan was fully combed in the course of regional surveys. Intensive surveys have also been undertaken on the Transjordanian plateau. These surveys provide us with invaluable information on the number of sites, their size, the number of their inhabitants, and their location, including the economic factors that dictated their distribution.

I wish to start with the main conclusions, since being aware of the bottom line will make it easier to follow the complex archaeological, textual, anthropological, and ethnographic details assembled here. As far as I can judge, the rise of early Israel was not a unique event in the history of Canaan. Rather, it was another repeated phase in long-term, cyclic, socio-economic, and demographic processes that started in the fourth millennium B.C.E. The wave of settlement that took place in the highlands in the late-second millennium B.C.E. was merely another chapter in alternating shifts along the typical Near Eastern socio-economic continuum between sedentary and pastoral modes of subsistence.

THE ENVIRONMENT

Limitations on sedentary activity in the highlands stemmed from harsh topography, rock formations that were difficult to exploit and, in the distant past, dense cover of natural vegetation. These obstacles led scholars to suggest that large-scale settlement activity in the Iron Age highlands was made possible only with the introduction of one or more technological innovations—the use of iron, the construction of plastered cisterns, and the terracing of hilly slopes. These notions should be dismissed. Recent fieldwork has shown that the central hill country of Canaan was densely settled already in the third and second millennia B.C.E., and that the knowledge of hewing water cisterns and erecting terraces was mastered already in the Middle Bronze Age, probably even earlier, in the Early Bronze. The hewing and plastering of water cisterns and the construction of terraces were the result of human penetration into certain niches of the hill country, rather than the one-time event that opened the way for expansion into these areas.

The proximity to steppe areas on the east and south, the availability of green pasture in the dry summer, and the fact that the highlands were not densely populated and cultivated even in periods of settlement expansion, made these regions ideal for sheep and goat pastoral activity. They were especially convenient for "enclosed nomadism" (Michael Rowton's term), that is, a migration routine between the steppe in the winter and the highlands in the summer. In addition, the eastern flank of the highlands was especially convenient for the sedentary activity of groups that originated in a pastoral background, since they could continue to practice animal husbandry alongside dry farming.

When political and socio-economic conditions permitted, the highlands communities could benefit from specializing in a horticulture-oriented economy, which included the industrialization of the products. In early modern times, villages in certain parts of the central hill country, especially on the western slopes, specialized in olive orchards and oil production. They produced large surpluses of olive oil and exchanged it for grain, as cereal growing was an ill-fated economic strategy in these parts of the highlands.

As an introduction to the presentation of survey results, it is necessary to mention that the central hill country can be divided into two major geographical subunits, namely, the Samarian highlands between Jerusalem and the Jezreel Valley in the north and the Judean hills in the south, between Jerusalem and the Beer-sheba Valley. The Samarian highlands are the most convenient in the hill country for habitation, mainly because of the Bethel plateau and the fertile intermontane valleys further north. Indeed, they were more densely settled in the Iron I. The Judean hills region has desert fringe areas on its east and south that made pastoralism a preferable economic strategy. The central range is relatively flat and its western flank rugged and steep. Recent surveys have indicated that the Judean hills were sparsely inhabited by sedentary populations until quite late in the Iron II.

POTS, BONES, AND PEOPLE: WHO IS AN ISRAELITE IN THE IRON AGE I PERIOD?

The material culture of a given group of people mirrors the environment in which they live; their socio-economic conditions; the influence of neighboring cultures; the influence of previous cultures; in cases of migration, traditions that are brought from the country of origin; and, equally important, their cognitive world. In the case of the highlands in the Iron Age I period, a careful analysis of these factors, combined with a meticulous examination of the geographical and quantitative distribution of the finds, leads to somewhat dubious conclusions regarding the possibility of identifying "ethnic markers" of the Israelites.

Signs of continuity from Late Bronze Age traditions in pottery and other traits of material culture show no more than isolated influences from Iron I lowlands sites, which still maintained at that time traditions of the previous period. Marks of discontinuity reflect the fact that the highlands people lived in small, isolated, rural, almost autarchic communities (as opposed to the Late Bronze city-states of the lowlands). To complicate matters even more, there is no way to distinguish the material culture of the proto-Israelites from their peers in Transjordan, that is, the proto-Ammonites and others.

Still, two features have been utilized in the past as indicators of "Israelite" ethnicity, namely, pottery, especially the collared-rim jar, and architecture, mainly the four-room house.

Archaeologists tend to put ethnic labels on pottery types. Thus, we refer to "Philistine," "Edomite," and "Midianite" vessels. By doing this however, we ignore style, status, and trade factors. Therefore, with so many variables playing behind the scene, in most cases pottery cannot indicate ethnicity. This has been demonstrated in numerous examples, especially in cases in which reliable historical documents are available to supplement the archaeological data. A good example in the highlands is the medieval pottery, which does not permit any distinction between the well-documented Muslim, local (eastern) Christian, and Frankish communities.

Except for a few rare vessels, there are no special features in the pottery of the Iron I highlands sites, neither in the assemblages as a whole, nor in specific types. The distance from maritime and overland trade, the social isolation of the small communities, which were separated by topographical barriers, and the constant struggle with the ecological obstacles had a decisive influence on the pottery repertoire of the highlands people; it was limited, not to say poor, in type and quality. The collared-rim jar, once suggested as an indicator of "Israelite" sites, was subsequently found in lowland sites. Collared rim pithoi are also abundant in every Iron I site in Ammon and Moab. The dominance of this type in central hill country sites should be attributed to economic, environmental, and social factors, such as horticultural-based subsistence, and also to the great distance of some of the Iron I communities from stable water sources, rather than to the ethnic background of the population.

In certain cases, architectural forms may indicate origin and, thus, the ethnicity of past people. Ronnie Ellenblum argued that mason marks and other construction features found in medieval sites in Israel can be used to distinguish Frankish settlements, even individual houses inhabited by Franks, from Muslim communities. Unfortunately this is not the case in the Iron Age. Several scholars described the four-room house as an Israelite house type, but its full-fledged plan does not appear before the Iron IIA and it has also been found in contemporary lowland and Transjordanian sites. In this case too, its popularity in the central hill country must be linked to environmental and social factors, rather than to ethnic boundaries.

Ethnographic studies have shown that, in many cases, ethnic markers can best be identified in mortuary practices, cult, and foodways, that is, dietary patterns. Archaeology has not given us data on the first two. Not a single Iron I cemetery or sanctuary has ever been found in the highlands. We are therefore left with foodways or culinary practices, represented by the second-most-widespread find in archaeological excavations, namely, bones.

It is widely accepted that foodways tend to be conservative symbols of ethnicity. Certain groups resist change in foodways even in the face of potential assimilation. What people eat, and how they eat it, is an important aspect of their identity. Anthropologists argue that foodways often rival ideology and religion in terms of cultural conservatism, and that food is one of the primary symbols manipulated by people seeking to maintain their cultural identity and group solidarity.

A significant body of data on animal husbandry in the Bronze and Iron Ages has accumulated in recent years. Especially important for the study of ethnicity in the Iron Age are the data on the ratio of pig bones in the faunal assemblages at various sites. Brian Hesse and Paula Wapnish have shown that in Philistine sites this ratio is far larger than the average—the "normal"—for the Bronze Age. The popularity of pork consumption in the Iron I in the southern coastal plain may be related to husbandry practices brought from the Philistine homeland. In the highlands, pig husbandry was practiced in the Bronze Age and other periods. But pig bones disappear from the faunal assemblages starting in the Iron I. The most interesting fact is that contemporaneous pig bones continue to be present in significant numbers at Heshbon on the border between Ammon and Moab in Transjordan. The faunal assemblages of the Iron II reflect the same traits. Regardless of the complex factors that may influence pig distribution, this seems to mean that the taboo on pigs was already practiced in the hill country in the Iron I. Pigs were not present in proto-Israelite Iron I sites in the highlands, while they were quite popular in a proto-Ammonite site and numerous in Philistine sites.

There are two possible reasons for this phenomenon: the wide popularity of pork consumption in Philistia could have been viewed as a Philistine ethnic marker by the proto-Israelites of the highlands, who, in reaction, avoided raising pigs. No less important, avoidance of pig husbandry may have stemmed from the pastoral background of those people who settled in the highlands in the Iron I, since pigs cannot be herded over significant distances. This is the reason, many claim, why pigs became a symbol of sedentary life and why pastoral nomads in the ancient Near East avoided raising pigs.

CYCLIC PROCESSES IN THE HIGHLANDS AND THE ORIGIN OF EARLY ISRAEL

It has become conventional wisdom to view complex historical processes from a long-term perspective—*la longue durée* of the French Annales school. Indeed, the investigation of the processes that took place in the Iron Age I requires that we consider a much broader historical perspective: from the first wave of settlement in the highlands in the beginning of the Early Bronze Age (that is, the second half of the fourth millennium B.C.E.) to the outcome of the Iron I transformation—the rise of the territorial states in the early-first millennium B.C.E.

The large-scale surveys in the southern Levant that were undertaken in the 1980s indicate that, in the time frame specified above, the highlands were characterized by three waves of settlement with two intervals of social crisis between them. Settlement activity intensified from one peak period to the next. All three led to the rise of complex territorial formations, but while the first two degenerated, the third peak period resulted in the development of full-scale statehood—the kingdoms of Israel and Judah. The three peak periods (as well as the two periods of crisis) had much in common, especially in their demographic patterns, but also in the location of the sites and in certain aspects of their material culture.

The first wave peaked in the Early Bronze I, in the late-fourth millennium B.C.E. In the Early Bronze II–III, or the third millennium B.C.E., there was a decrease in both the number of sites and the total inhabited area, but large fortified centers, which characterize a more complex political system, emerged. This period was followed by a dramatic crisis in the Intermediate Bronze Age (the late-third millennium), when almost all Early Bronze sites were abandoned. There were only a few settlement sites in that period, most of them of limited size, but many cemeteries not related to nearby sedentary sites—and thus probably representing pastoral groups—have been recorded. This settlement crisis continued, even intensified, in the Middle Bronze I, that is, the early-second millennium B.C.E.

The second wave of settlement took place in the Middle Bronze II–III period (eighteenth/seventeenth to sixteenth centuries B.C.E.). About 250 sites have been recorded in the central hill country. The process started in the Middle Bronze II when scores of small sites were established in different parts of the region. In the Middle Bronze III period, several sites developed with impressive stone and earthworks serving as elaborate governmental centers for the ruling elite. This impressive settlement system collapsed at the end of the Middle Bronze. The Late Bronze Age (late-sixteenth to twelfth centuries B.C.E.) marks a second demographic crisis in the highlands; only about thirty sites were inhabited at the time. Moreover, some of the surviving sites shrank in size.

The third wave of settlement that features the rise of the "proto-Israelites," took place in the twelfth to tenth centuries B.C.E. Comprehensive surveys have recorded over 250 Iron Age I sites in the central hill country. This settlement system expanded dramatically in the Iron II when the number of sites doubled and the total built-up area (and thus, the population) almost tripled. Similar to the previous peak periods, the Iron II is characterized by the rise of large urban centers and a complex, hierarchic settlement system.

Past interpretations of such settlement oscillations as the result of the migrations of new groups from distant parts of the Levant, or alternating demographic expansion and withdrawal from the nearby lowlands, are not sufficient to explain the phenomenon. First, recent studies have shown beyond doubt that the lowland population had never come close to a "carrying capacity" point, and hence there were no land-hungry population surpluses eager to expand into new frontiers. Second, the overall character of the material culture in the highlands shows clear local features with no hint of large-scale migrations of new groups from outside. It is therefore more reasonable to explain these settlement fluctuations in terms of socio-economic change, that is, as shifts toward a more sedentary or a more pastoral society, in accordance with political, economic, and social transformations. Similar shifts in early modern times along the sedentary-pastoral continuum have been recorded in both the central hill country by David Grossman and Transjordan by Norman Lewis and Øystein LaBianca. These are more typical of the marginal areas of the Middle East, highlands and steppelands alike. Such shifts along the sedentary-pastoral continuum are well represented in the faunal assemblage from two sites in the central hill country, Shiloh and Emeq Refaim. The data correspond to shifts between plow-agriculture subsistence (that is, more cattle) in periods of settlement expansion and pastoralist societies (that is, more sheep and goats) in the crisis years.

There are additional indications for the pastoral background of the bulk of the proto-Israelite groups in the highlands. First, the few Late Bronze cult sites and cemeteries are not related to permanent sedentary communities. Second, Late Bronze texts, mainly the Amarna letters of the fourteenth century B.C.E., seem to point to a significant pastoralist component, labeled Shasu, or "plunderers," in the population. Indeed, several authorities have suggested that the early Israelites originated from these Shasu groups. Third, many of the early proto-Israelite sites are concentrated in areas of the highlands that best fit a combination of animal husbandry and dry-farming economies. Fourth, the avoidance of pig husbandry may point to the pastoralist origins of the Iron I highlands people. Fifth, certain features in the architecture of proto-Israelite sites in the highlands may point in the same direction; I refer to similarities between open-court Iron I sites and the tent encampments of pastoralist people in the Levant in early modern times. Both are characterized by a large courtyard (to protect the herds), surrounded by a belt of broad units: stone-built rooms in the distant past; tents in the more-recent past.

The factors underlying these shifts along the sedentary-pastoral continuum will not be treated here in detail. Suffice it to mention that with no historical material at hand for the third millennium, and with very limited sources for the second millennium, we have no other option but to indulge in speculative anthropological models, sometimes supported by ethnographic data from early-modern times, which take into consideration political difficulties, economic calamities, and social disturbances. It should be mentioned that pastoral nomadism is a specialization that depends on the ability of the sedentary communities to produce enough grain surpluses for exchange with the herding communities. Accordingly, the collapse of the global economic system of the Late Bronze Age must have played a major role in the widespread sedentarization of pastoralists in the Levant during the Iron I. With no surpluses of grain in the hands of the sedentary communities, pastoralists were forced to produce their own grain, that is, to shift to a more balanced, self-sufficient form of subsistence, which led to sedentarization.

I have already mentioned the significant ecological difference in the central hill country between a more amenable north and a more inhospitable south. The ecological disparities resulted in weighty demographic and settlement differences. Northern Samaria was more densely occupied with larger sites and limited evidence for non-sedentary activity. In contrast, the Judean hills were sparsely inhabited by sedentary people until the Iron II, but the number of pastoral groups was very significant. These features shaped the nature of the political entities that developed in the Middle Bronze to Late Bronze Age periods as well as in the Iron II period.

All three periods of settlement prosperity in the central hill country also point to a gradual demographic expansion from east to west. In the beginning of each settlement process, when the region was sparsely inhabited and the settlers could freely choose the location of their villages, they opted for the eastern areas, which were topographically moderate, ecologically convenient, and agriculturally promising. In addition, the eastern niches enabled their inhabitants to conduct a well-balanced, self-sufficient economic strategy. The fact that the settlers were attracted to areas suitable for a combination of dry farming and animal husbandry lends support to the proposal that many of them originated from a pastoralist background. The western slope units, typical of orchard agriculture, which bears fruit only after a relatively long period of cultivation, were occupied only in later phases of the Iron I settlement process. This was when the population was fully settled and turned to a specialized economy, including the mass production of horticultural secondary products. The westward expansion was a prominent factor in the later development of territorial entities in the highlands.

In all three periods under discussion, sedentary population growth, territorial expansion, and the demand for highland horticultural products in the lowlands led to the gradual rise of stratified, complex societies. The distinctive ecological background of the highlands brought about the formation of large territorial units, with some clear similarities between the three periods: most notably, each is characterized by two territorial polities, the northern being more sedentary and open to cultural influence from the lowlands and the southern being more pastoral and isolated in nature.

SUMMARY

The settlement processes that took place in the highlands of Canaan in the Iron I had much in common with two preceding waves of occupation in these areas. These analogies reinforce the hypothesis that much of the Iron I settlement activity was part of a long-term, cyclic mechanism of alternating processes of sedentarization and nomadization of indigenous groups in response to changing political, economic, and social circumstances. Translating these words into simple language, one can say that the early Israelites were, in fact, Canaanites.

The outcome of the Iron I settlement activity—the emergence of the Israelite and Judahite territorial states—resembles in some features the formation in the hill country of large territorial polities during the Middle and Late Bronze Ages, and possibly the Early Bronze Age. But the rise of the Northern Kingdom of Israel, which managed to expand from the highlands to the lowlands and form a true territorial state, marks a new phenomenon—a revolution—in the social history of Canaan-Israel. In other words, the genuinely exceptional event in the highlands of Palestine was not the "Israelite Settlement" of the biblical traditions, but the historical emergence of the Israelite state around 900 B.C.E. in the northern highlands.

The literary depiction of the rise of early Israel as a singular event in the annals of the region appeared only centuries after the Iron I. It was shaped by the history of the Judahite state in the late-Iron II period. The biblical description of the rise of early Israel was cast by the Deuteronomistic Historian in such a way as to serve the southern, Judahite-centered ideology and historical-national aspirations, and to convey its theological message. That narrative has prevailed until recently, when archaeology came to the center stage of historical research on Canaan-Israel.

THE ISRAELITE SETTLEMENT

Amihai Mazar

The biblical stories related to Israel's settlement period (or the biblical "period of the Judges") have been explained by the traditional approach of biblical archaeology as reflecting a genuine historical reality of the Iron Age I (ca. 1200–1000 B.C.E.), while some current scholars evaluate them as mere literary fabrications with no historical validity. Archaeology is an important research tool in this case since it may shed light on the settlement process, on the nature of society in the settlement territory, on specific sites that are mentioned in the biblical narrative, and on the nature of Israel's neighbors and their relations with the hill country settlers.

THE ISRAELITE SETTLEMENT

RESULTS OF SURVEYS

Research over the last fifty years using the modern methods of intensive surface surveys, ecological studies, and comparative ethnographic studies has facilitated a better understanding of the settlement process involving the Israelite tribes. This research has its roots in the 1930s when William F. Albright and his colleagues identified what they viewed as the basic characteristics of Israelite material culture in the hill country. The modern aspect of this research began in the 1950s with a surface survey carried out by Yohanan Aharoni in the upper Galilee. It was renewed following 1967, when Israeli scholars gained access to the territories of the central hill country of Judah and Samaria. Survey and excavations in Jordan have also added much to this growing database. The surveys revealed an entirely new settlement pattern in the Iron I as hundreds of new small sites were established in the mountainous areas of the upper and lower Galilee, in the hills of Samaria and Ephraim, in Benjamin and the Judean hills, in the northern Negev, and in parts of central and northern Transjordan.

Initial surveys in 1968 provided for the first time a general picture of this phenomenon. More intensive surveys were carried out in the following years in the central hill country, the territories of Manasseh, Ephraim, Benjamin, and Judah. In the territory of Manasseh, Adam Zertal located over one hundred Iron I sites. In this region, with Shechem at its southern end, there were several Canaanite cities near inner valleys. Only a few of these were excavated and the publications are insufficient, yet it appears that these Canaanite cities continued to survive through the Iron I, while in the hills surrounding the valleys, new settlement sites were established and in many cases in remote places, far from water resources. Zertal found a good number of such sites along the fringes of the Jordan Valley and the semi-arid eastern Samarian hills, as well as in inland Samaria, all the way to the hills overlooking the Wadi ʿAra pass.

In the land of Ephraim, about one hundred additional settlement sites were explored by Israel Finkelstein and his team. In this hilly terrain, cut through by deep valleys, the Canaanite population was sparse. Iron I settlements were identified both along the main highway as well as in remote areas on the fringe of the desert or in forested regions. Most of them were very small, measuring from a few houses to 0.5 to 0.8 hectares of built-up area. Further to the south, in the Hebron hills south of Bethlehem, the density of such sites decreases.

About forty small settlement sites were found in surveys of the Galilee, within the biblical allotment of the tribes of Asher and Naphtali. In the lower Galilee, the surveys have turned up fifteen sites, most of them in the hilly regions within the tribal territory of Zebulun. In contrast, Zvi Gal has shown that on the basalt heights of Issachar, the settlement process began only in the tenth century B.C.E., possibly in the wake of the tribe of Issachar's migration there during the period of the monarchy from its possible initial allocation in the Samarian hills. Several dozen sites were located in Gilead (the ʿAjlun region in northern Jordan) where, according to the biblical tradition, Manassaite families settled.

Results of such surveys provide a portrait of the settlement pattern and, as a result, make possible estimations of the population size, the subsistence economy, and environmental adaptation of the settlers. These subjects have been discussed in a number of studies, notably those of Israel Finkelstein and a series of articles by various researchers in the collection of essays entitled *From Nomadism to Monarchy: Archaeological and Historical Aspects of Early Israel* (Jerusalem: Yad Izhak Ben-Zvi, 1994). Population size is estimated by multiplying the known built-up area of the sites by a certain coefficient of people per built-up hectare. Using a coefficient of 250 people per built-up hectare, Finkelstein estimated the population of the central hill country alone at sixty thousand during the Iron Age I. Yet, this number is valid only on the condition that all the sites existed at the same time, that their size estimate is accurate and that the coefficient is correct. All these factors remain somewhat uncertain, and thus this population estimate must remain tentative.

THE SETTLERS' MATERIAL CULTURE

More precise details on these settlements can be obtained from excavations. However, only a few such sites have been excavated and most of these excavations were only on a small scale. The available results, nevertheless, do allow for a reconstruction of the main features of the material culture of these settlers.

The settlement process began in the late-thirteenth and early-twelfth centuries in both the central hill country of Israel and to some extent in Transjordan and the northern Negev, while most of the sites in the Galilee appear to have been established somewhat later, in the eleventh century B.C.E. The sites were mostly small, open villages with the houses arranged along their circumference, leaving large open spaces inside the settlement. At a few sites, defense walls were found, though in most cases they were poorly constructed. I had the opportunity to excavate Giloh, one of the central hill-country sites, south of Jerusalem. This 0.6-hectare site was encircled by an outer wall consisting of separately built sections, each of which can possibly be attributed to a different family or group living in the adjacent area. Large open spaces in the village probably served as livestock enclosures.

In the Galilee, in addition to small sites in the mountains, evidence for tribal settlements has been recovered at the main sites of former Canaanite cities in the Hulah Valley, namely, Hazor and Dan. Following the destruction of Canaanite Hazor during the thirteenth century B.C.E., the site was abandoned. During the Iron I period, a small temporary settlement was established, probably by a new population of semi-nomadic origin. The poor remains include dozens of storage pits and almost no other architectural remains. At Tel Dan, the Iron I settlement appears to be much larger and more substantial. Here too, many silo pits were exposed, as well as various flimsy structures and evidence for bronze production.

The typical dwellings were of the type known as "pillared houses." They contained several rectangular spaces, and, in several cases, lines of stone pillars separated those spaces. Such use of pillars is attested in several Canaanite cities and towns of southern Canaan (for example, Lachish, Tel Batash [Timnah], and Tel Harassim). In the Iron I, this architectural style became common for Israelite private and public architecture, and in the period of the monarchy, it became typical. The more elaborate form of such dwellings is the four-room house, which became common from the eleventh century onwards. The typical four-room house is rectangular or square in shape, with an entrance that usually leads to a central, rectangular space surrounded by rooms or pillared porticos on three sides.

Public buildings are practically unattested at these settlement sites. An exception is a solid square foundation (11.2 by 11.2 meters) built of large, unworked stones, which we uncovered at Giloh. It probably served as the foundation for a tall tower with inner rooms. Towers are mentioned in the book of Judges as a common feature in this period. For example, at Shechem, the tower is identified with the city temple (Judg 9:46–49), and towers are mentioned in association with Penuel (Judg 8:17), and Tebez (Judg 9:50–52). But it is surprising to find such a massive tower foundation at the small and remote site of Giloh, and its discovery raises questions about the character of the Israelite settlement sites in the hill country. Such a tower must have been designed as the settlers' stronghold in case of attack.

Settlement in the steeply sloping and forested hill country necessitated the clearing of the land, which was surely one of the more difficult tasks of the settlers. This is reflected in the words of Joshua to Ephraim: "Go up into the forest and clear land for yourself there" (Josh 17:15). Deforestation must have been followed by the construction of terraces on the steep slopes. Such agricultural terraces were essential for the Iron I settlers. They continued to be constructed in later periods, resulting in the artificially stepped landscape of the hill country that is visible even today.

Water cisterns cut in the rock, silos, and agricultural terraces demonstrate the means by which the settlers adapted to their new environmental conditions in the central hill country. Albright, followed by Aharoni, stressed the importance of plastered cisterns. These were invented, in his view, by the Israelites to facilitate settlement in the hill country. But we now know on the one hand, that cisterns were used much earlier, and, on the other, that they are in fact found at only a few of the sites that can confidently be related to the Israelite settlement. Water supply at many of these sites relied on less-significant water sources, such as springs, that were often located at a considerable distance from the settlement. Zertal has suggested that the abundance of pottery pithoi (the so-called collared-rim jars) at these sites must be related to the need for water storage.

Stone-lined silos or plastered pits were widely used in sites suitable for cereal crops. At one such site at the western base of the Ephraim hills, ʾIzbet Ṣartah, the holding capacity of the silos was calculated to be greater than the assumed quantity of grain required by the local population. This evidence for supposed grain surpluses has led to the conclusion that the economy of this and perhaps similar sites was based on trade with other inhabitants of the hill country who specialized in horticulture and herding.

The daily artifacts in these hill country settlement sites included simple pottery vessels and various grinding stones used for processing food. The pottery assemblage is generally limited to a few forms, mainly those essential for basic subsistence. There are medium-sized storage jars used for carrying and storing liquids such as oil and wine, cooking pots, and a limited selection of other shapes. The vessel forms are similar to those used by the Canaanites of the lowlands, but the Canaanite assemblage was much more varied and included painted decoration that is totally lacking in the hill country pottery repertoire. The assemblage as a whole differs widely from both that of the contemporary Canaanite-Philistine culture of the coastal plain and that of the Jezreel Valley.

The large pithos or storage jar known as the collared-rim jar was an exceptionally popular vessel in these settlements. Such vessels could typically hold as much as eighty liters of liquid, and probably were used for storing water. Due to their popularity in the settlement sites of the central hill country from the Jezreel Valley in the north to the region of Hebron in the south, they were considered for many years as a hallmark of the Israelite settlement—so much so that when such jars, otherwise unknown at sites of the Upper Galilee, were discovered at Tel Dan, the excavator Avraham Biran identified them as evidence for the northward migration of the Danites from the original settlement territory, as described in the Bible. More recent research has shown that such jars were not limited to the central hill country settlement sites. They first appear towards the end of the thirteenth century in Canaanite contexts, for example, at Tel Nami south of Haifa, Aphek, and Beth-shean. During the early Iron Age I, they were popular in the region of Amman in Transjordan (mainly at the site of Tall al-ʿUmeiri where they were found in one of the earliest-known four-room houses) and at the same time they became common in the central hill country, while they remained rare in the Shephelah and are missing from the northern Negev and Philistia. It is difficult to explain this unusual distribution in terms of ethnic identity, but it remains clear that the settlers in the hill country found these jars particularly useful for their subsistence economy.

In the Galilee, the material culture is somewhat different from that of the central hills. Pillared houses are missing, and instead of the collared-rim jars, there are other distinct types of pithoi of a Galilean type. This latter jar type had developed from a northern Canaanite form attested in the Late Bronze period at Hazor and in Syria and Cyprus.

It appears that the settlers in the hill country lacked their own pottery-making tradition and initially obtained the most necessary pottery vessels from their Canaanite neighbors. The large pithoi with their Canaanite affinities may have been produced locally by itinerant potters who brought the ceramic tradition and technical knowledge with them. When the settlers began producing pottery of their own, they manufactured a limited repertoire of forms based on various Canaanite prototypes, but did not adopt the Canaanite decoration. Though the pottery forms and a few art and craft artifacts were similar to those of the lowland Canaanites, the nature of the settlers' material culture as an overall assemblage differed to a large extent from that of the lowland Canaanites.

RELIGIOUS PRACTICES

The religious practices of the hill-country settlers are only meagerly attested. In the biblical tradition, Shiloh was the main religious center of the Israelites on the eve of the monarchy. It was the location of the tabernacle, and the biblical sources, in fact, seem to allude to a temple that stood there. Excavations at the site of Khirbet Sailun, the location of ancient Shiloh, have revealed a small town of the Iron Age I that was destroyed by a heavy conflagration, perhaps the one remembered in the biblical traditions (Jer 7:12; 26:6, 9). No remains of the cult center at Shiloh could be recovered since the central part of the site was thoroughly destroyed by erosion and by Byzantine buildings.

On Mount Ebal, north of Shechem, Adam Zertal discovered an unusual site, which he identified as the location of Joshua's altar (Josh 8:30–32; Deut 11:29; 27:4–8). The 0.4-hectare site was surrounded by a stone wall. In its earliest occupation phase, dated to the late-thirteenth century B.C.E., a circular installation was constructed on its highest point. Burnt animal bones, probably originating in this phase, were retrieved from the fill of a superseding structure. This later rectangular (eight-by-nine-meter) structure was built of massive outer walls with no opening and the inner space was filled with stones, earth, ash, and animal bones. On its southern side and attached to it were two large rooms or courtyards separated from each other by a wide wall. Zertal interpreted this rectangular structure as a large altar and identified some of the components as its parapet and ramp, yet these identifications are based on biblical and Mishnaic descriptions. This interpretation remains highly controversial since no other altar from the entire Iron Age is of such size and magnitude. An alternative interpretation is that the structure had a nonreligious function, perhaps as a podium for a watch tower like that at Giloh. While Zertal may be wrong in his interpretation of the structure, it seems possible that in the early phase of the site it indeed was utilized for cultic activity. It is not impossible that the much-later biblical account preserves an ancient memory related to this mountain and even to this particular site, the only Iron I site on the mound. In this case it would mean that the deuteronomistic literature preserved traditions that go back to the period of the settlement.

I excavated another cultic site from this period on a high ridge in the northern Samarian hills. This was an open cult place that may be identified as a biblical "high place" or *bamah*. The *bamoth* (plural) were typically built "on every high hill and under every green tree" (1 Kgs 14:23). The site was composed of a circle of large stones, some twenty meters in diameter. Inside, there was an open space and a single large, flat stone, identified as a biblical "standing stone," or *massebah*. The site has become known as the "Bull Site," after a unique, eighteen-centimeter-long bronze statuette of a bull that was found here. In Canaanite religion, the bull was related to both El, the head of the pantheon, and Baal, the storm god. The symbol of the bull in the religion of the northern tribes of Israel (compare the "golden calves" erected by Jeroboam I at Bethel and at Dan) was inherited from Canaanite religion. In northern Israel, the bull was considered either as the symbol of the god of Israel or as the deity's pedestal (recalling the function of the cherubim in the Temple of Jerusalem). Our figurine may have been produced and perhaps purchased in a Canaanite workshop. Yet the proximity of the site to several Iron I-settlement sites indicates that it probably was utilized as a cult place serving the nearby sites, which we tend to identify as settled by early Israelites.

THE PROBLEM OF ETHNIC IDENTITY: "POTS AND PEOPLE"

Who were the settlers in the Iron I hill country of the land of Israel? Can they be identified as Israelites? Most scholars indeed have accepted this identification. Yet, over the last decade some new questions have been raised. For example, were the hill-country settlers of the Iron I a self-defined ethnic entity? In recent scholarship, questions have been raised as to whether or not "national" identities existed at that time. It was formerly suspected that all that unified the settlers was their common religion, but this religion was far from being formalized during the Iron I. It is therefore questionable that the settlements in the central hill country, the Galilee, the Negev, and Transjordan should be attributed to a single "ethnic" entity. Perhaps they only represent the manifestation of similar socio-economic changes in the modes of living that resulted from the collapse of the previous Late Bronze economic and political systems.

There are two sides to the identity question: Is it possible to assume that various groups who settled the hill country during the Iron Age I identified themselves as Israelites? And, on the other hand, are we, as modern scholars, able to identify the hill-country settlers as Israelites? Both questions are debatable. The identification of the hill-country settlers as Israelites is based mainly on the biblical traditions, and these were written centuries later, as all scholars agree. The utilization of biblical sources for ethnic identification of Iron I settlers might be criticized as circular argumentation. Yet, in spite of this risk, I claim that both the socio-economic status of the settlers and the historical-geographic data fit their identity as early Israelites.

The socio-economic structure of the Iron I hill-country society coincides with the biblical description of Israel during the period of the Judges. This was a non-urban, sedentary society, living in small communities of farmers and herders, without a central political authority, though probably with central cultic centers like the one at Shiloh. The archaeological evidence appears to indicate that this was an egalitarian society that was striving for subsistence in the harsh environmental conditions of the forested mountains and semi-arid regions of the land of Israel.

Sites that, according to the biblical tradition, were major Israelite villages or towns during the period of the Judges, such as Shiloh, Mizpah (Tell en-Naṣbeh), and Dan, do appear in the archaeological record as important Iron I settlement sites. It is possible to identify them, as well as other sites with a similar material culture in the same region, as Israelite, recalling, however, the difficulties in the use of this term for this early period in Israelite history.

The problems with attempting ethnic identifications become more pronounced, however, when one considers certain biblical references. For example, Jerusalem and the four Gibeonite cities to its northwest are portrayed in the Bible as non-Israelite, Jebusite, and Gibeonite enclaves during the pre-monarchic period. Excavations in Jerusalem by three different expeditions (led by Kathleen Kenyon, Yigal Shiloh, and Eilat Mazar) revealed Iron I material culture (in particulary pottery assemblages dated to late-thirteenth to early-eleventh centuries B.C.E.) identical to that found in other Iron I settlement sites in the hill country, which we usually identify as populated by "Israelites" or "proto-Israelites." This case demonstrates the contradiction between the biblical text and archaeology: nothing in the archaeological record hints at the existence of Jebusites or Gibeonites as separate ethnic entities. The site of Giloh, just three miles southwest of Jerusalem, on a ridge overlooking Jerusalem, yielded material culture identical to that found in Jerusalem and in other hill country sites of the twelfth century B.C.E. Was Giloh an Israelite village situated opposite Jebusite Jerusalem, or was it a settlement in the territory of Jerusalem? Or perhaps we have to admit the limitations of archaeology in refining ethnic identities in this period of change and restructured group identities in the hill country of the land of Israel. Similar questions can be asked concerning the identity of settlers in other parts of the country, such as in Upper Galilee or at the important site of Tall al-ʿUmeiri near Amman in Transjordan.

Lack of pig bones at the hill country sites, in contrast to their presence at contemporary Philistine sites, has been considered evidence for the observance of a prohibition against pork consumption that is also found in biblical traditions. Yet, as very few pig bones have been found in any of the major Canaanite sites of the lowlands, it does not seem that the hill country differed much in this respect from Canaanite dietary customs. The taboo on swine consumption among the Israelites should be explained as rooted in local dietary manners of the second millennium B.C.E., which were perhaps related to ecological conditions, as well as to the pastoralist background of many of the hill-country settlers (since pastoralists in general avoid pigs).

To conclude, when I use the term "Israelite" in relation to the Iron I, I refer to several groups of people or tribal units who lived in a specific socioeconomic mode of life in the central hill country, in the Galilee, the northern Negev, and the Transjordanian plateau. The central hill country constituted the heartland of the land of Israel. Since the various population groups there eventually became part of Israel during the time of the monarchy, it is legitimate in my view to use this term to refer to the Iron I settlers as well.

MERNEPTAH STELE

A cornerstone in the study of the emergence of Israel is the victory stele known as the "Israel Stele" erected by Pharaoh Merneptah (1213–1203 B.C.E.), the successor to Ramesses II. This poetic text describes an Egyptian military raid against Canaan. The conquest of such cities as Ashkelon, Gezer, and Yenʿoam is mentioned, as well as the victory over Israel, which appears here for the first and only time in Egyptian sources. The name Israel appears in this inscription with a determinative sign referring to "people" and Merneptah specifically emphasizes that "Israel is laid waste. His seed is not" (translation by John A. Wilson, in Ancient Near Eastern Texts Relating to the Old Testament [ed. James Pritchard; Princeton: Princeton University Press], 378). As such, Israel is the only "people" mentioned in this royal inscription, and its mention in this context is puzzling. Was Israel at the end of the thirteenth century B.C.E. a sizeable confederation of tribes posing a threat to an Egyptian empire that had ruled Canaan for almost three hundred years? And if so, where did this Israel live? The answers to these questions continue to be disputed. Revisionist scholars who do not accept the traditional reconstruction of the early history of Israel attempt to dismiss the reference to Israel in this text. Others, like Michael Hasel in a recent study, have convincingly suggested that Israel in this text must be the name of an important population group in Canaan. As he and others have proposed, it is tempting to identify this Israel with the population that participated in the wide-scale settlement in the hill country west of the Jordan as well as in Transjordan from the late-thirteenth century B.C.E. onwards, as reflected in the archaeological record.

THE ORIGIN OF ISRAEL

Can archaeology shed new light on the question of the origin of Israel? Various theories have been suggested. Following Albrecht Alt's 1925 suggestion, Aharoni, Zertal and others claim that the settlers in the hill-country sites were semi-nomadic pastoralists who arrived from Transjordan and settled in a slow process that started in the Jordan Valley and gradually moved towards the west. Manfred Weippert suggested in 1979 that the settlers were local pastoralists living in the hill country both west and east of the Jordan, and that they were referred to in the Egyptian sources as the Shasu. The Egyptians depicted them as wearing a specific headdress (or perhaps a hairdo) and a leader of such Shasu tribes appears on a large carved stele found in the territory of Moab standing in front of the Egyptian deity. The reasons for settlement were explained by Weippert as resulting from overpopulation of the nomadic tribes. Donald Redford also identified the early Israelites as Shasu nomads. Israel Finkelstein has pointed out the resemblance between the settlement process in the central hill country in Iron I and a parallel phenomenon in this region that took place in the Middle Bronze period, about five hundred years earlier. He has proposed that the Middle Bronze sedentary population, after having been forced to adopt a pastoralist and semi-nomadic existence in the Late Bronze Age, returned to sedentary life when conditions changed at the end of the Late Bronze Age. All these explanations are rooted in the recognition that the Israelites emerged from unsettled, Late Bronze population groups known from written sources, such as the Shasu attested in Egyptian sources.

A different interpretation has been suggested by archaeologists like Joseph Callaway and William G. Dever, who follow the social-historical theories of George Mendenhall and Norman Gottwald. They claim that the settlers were none other than dispossessed Canaanite peasants, who abandoned the deteriorating Canaanite society of the lowlands and looked for better subsistence opportunities in the hill country.

Nothing in the archaeological findings from this period points to the foreign origin of the hill-country settlers. There are no objects or traditions that might have been brought by the settlers from outside the country, and the poor artifacts that are attested were inspired from local Canaanite ones. This situation could support all three theories. If the settlers were semi-nomadic peoples, it makes sense that during the settlement process they adapted local fashions and traditions, and perhaps purchased goods from Canaanite cities or itinerant merchants and craftsmen. In my view, a combination of components from all three theories may explain the hill-country settlement wave and the origins of Israel. We may imagine the settlement as a complex process in which various clans and groups of people found it necessary to look for new modes of subsistence in the harsh mountainous terrain. As claimed by Benjamin Mazar, Ann Killebrew, and others, the origin of such groups could have been quite diverse; some could have been local pastoralists, others perhaps were pastoralists arriving from Transjordan or other parts of the country. Aspects of the archaeological evidence appear to depict a settlement process involving tribal groups who once conducted a tribal, pastoral mode of life. No actual material evidence of this previous lifestyle can be located, but its heritage is felt in the distribution of the settlement sites, their planning and their economy. In addition, some of this population could include displaced Canaanites or immigrants from Syria or even further north, where the Late Bronze political system collapsed around 1200 B.C.E., causing refugees to scatter through the Levant.

One must still ask several questions. What is the origin of the nuclear group that initiated Yahwism? Who was responsible for the traditions concerning the sojourn in Egypt, the Exodus, Mount Sinai, and the figure of Moses? Finally, were all these late fabrications? A clue might be at our disposal in the phrase "Shasu of Seʿir" mentioned in an Egyptian inscription from the days of Ramesses II, alongside a proper name, Shasu Yahwi. The equation of Seir with Edom as the place from which Yahweh comes is known in the Song of Deborah (Judg 5:4) and hinted at in the blessing of Moses (Deut 33:2), both considered by many scholars to be among the earliest biblical texts. The Shasu are related to Edom in a number of Egyptian sources. Several scholars, in particular Frank M. Cross, propose that the "Moses group" migrated during the thirteenth and twelfth centuries along the route from Egypt to Midian and Edom, bringing the new religion, Yahwism, with them. At present, archaeology can contribute little to this question.

Israel's Neighbors

Within the framework of this essay, I can mention only briefly the immense amount of data pertaining to Israel's early neighbors that has accumulated in the archaeological record. I treat here only a few details that are directly related to the evaluation of the historical aspects of the biblical text and to the mutual relations between Israel and these peoples, namely, the Canaanites and their descendents, the Phoenicians, Philistines, Arameans, the people of Transjordan (Moabites, Ammonites, and Edomites), as well as desert people like the Midianites.

THE CANAANITES AND PHOENICIANS

Throughout the twelfth and eleventh centuries B.C.E. (Iron Age I), Canaanite cities continued to survive in certain parts of the country, in particular in the valleys of Jezreel and Beth-shean and the coastal plain from the Carmel ridge northward. Megiddo in the eleventh century B.C.E. (Stratum VIA) is an excellent example of a densely built, flourishing city that was destroyed by conflagration in ca. 1000 B.C.E., perhaps by an earthquake. It yielded many metal objects, jewelry, various small artifacts, and abundant painted pottery of Canaanite tradition as well as some features related to the world of the Sea Peoples. Limited trade with Cyprus is also evident. This is a very different material culture from that of the settlement sites in the hill country, and it corroborates the biblical account in Judg 1:27–29, as mentioned in part 2. Such continuity of Canaanite life has also been identified at Beth-shean, Tel Reḥov, Dor, and additional sites in the region.

In ancient coastal cities, such as Tyre and Sidon, in what is today modern Lebanon, a new aspect of Canaanite culture was developing in the first millennium. It is commonly referred to as the "Phoenician culture," a term based on the Greek word for the descendants of the Canaanites who developed their own civilization and established colonies throughout the eastern and, later, western Mediterranean. Phoenician sites of the eleventh century B.C.E. onwards have been excavated farther south along the Carmel coast (at Dor) and in the valley of Acre. The finds from these sites include specific pottery groups and burial customs. By means of trade, Phoenician pottery found its way to Philistia, the northern Negev, Egypt, and Cyprus, and provides solid evidence for the spread of Phoenician commerce. In the settlement sites in the upper Galilee, some indicators of connections with the Phoenician cities (in particular to Tyre) were found in the form of peculiar large pottery pithoi of "Tyrian" type.

THE PHILISTINES

The Philistine culture is known to us due to intensive excavations at Ashkelon, Ashdod, Ekron, and Gath, four of the five major cities of the Philistines mentioned in the Bible. In accordance with the biblical tradition, the Philistine culture that has emerged from recent archaeological work was an urban culture of immigrants who arrived from the west—either Greece itself or the eastern Aegean islands, Asia Minor, or Cyprus. They brought with them Aegean traditions, which were preserved in many aspects of daily life such as architecture, pottery production, artistic styles, weaving, and dietary customs (for example, they raised pigs, unlike the Canaanites and the hill-country settlers). One cannot imagine a greater difference in the mode of life between that of the Philistines and that of the Israelite settlement sites.

The Bible identifies the homeland of the Philistines as "Kaphtor," probably referring to Crete, or it was used as a more general designation for the Aegean world (Amos 9:7; Jer 47:4; compare also Zeph 2:5 and Ezek 25:16). These biblical references, along with others that mention the five main cities of the Philistines as well as other minor towns like Timnah (Tel Batash) finds confirmation in the current archaeological picture in a rather surprising manner. In other words, the stories referring to the Philistines in Judges and Samuel as well as other biblical traditions related to the Philistines must have been based on historical realia of the twelfth to eleventh centuries B.C.E.

THE NORTHERN NEGEV

In the semi-arid Arad and Beer-sheba Valleys, where Canaanite cities of the Late Bronze Age did not exist, a few sites were established in Iron I. The most prominent is Tel Masos, one of the largest settlements from this period in the entire country. Dwelling structures comprising what typically have been described as four-room houses were located at the northern part of the site, while in its southern part, different buildings were erected, namely, a courtyard building of a Canaanite type and a fortified structure that looks like an administrative building. The concentration of population in this one central site was perhaps due to a combination of ecological factors (particularly available water sources), security considerations, and the economic role of this site in the trading system that connected the Arabah and Transjordan with the coastal plain. The material culture at Tel Masos closely approximates that of the coastal plain and the finds point to connections with Philistia, Phoenicia, and the Arabah Valley. Canaanites, and perhaps Philistines, probably settled there alongside the local tribal population, which may have comprised part of the Israelite tribal complex. The finds are indicative of wealth and it seems that the southern part of the site served merchants who perhaps traded with those controlling the copper-producing industry in the Arabah Valley.

THE PEOPLES OF TRANSJORDAN

According to the biblical narrative, the tribes of Reuben and Gad and the half tribe of Manasseh settled in Transjordan alongside the Edomites, Moabites, Ammonites, and Amorites. To what extent is this ethnic diversity reflected in the archaeological finds? Several ancient texts hint at the antiquity of the biblical traditions, yet they do not go beyond the ninth century B.C.E. The ninth-century B.C.E. stele of the Moabite king Mesha mentions Gad as the ancient population of northern Moab, the land north of the Arnon River, thus confirming some of the biblical account. Literary texts citing the writings of Balaʿam son of Beʿor were found written on an eighth-century wall of a house or chapel at Tell Deir ʿAlla in the eastern Jordan Valley, confirming that the traditions associated with this diviner who so prominently appears in the book of Numbers (chapters 22–24) were well known in the Transjordan during the Iron Age.

All additional information on the antiquity of the Transjordanian peoples and states depends on the silent archaeological testimony. However, the material culture of Transjordan in the Iron I is only partially known. In the ancient territory of Ammon, excavations at the sites of Sahab and Tall al-ʿUmeiri have revealed towns with material culture that share many traits with the settlements in the western hill country. For example, the pillared houses and collared-rim jars discussed earlier are found in abundance. Again, these findings raise the question of the ethnic affiliations of these population groups. Larry Herr has suggested that Tall al-ʿUmeiri was related to the settlement of the tribe of Reuben in the early-twelfth century B.C.E., though this identification may be challenged, and others would claim that no ethnic or political entity can be identified in this region during the period in question.

In the ancient land of Moab, excavations of major towns mentioned in the Bible, such as Dibon and Heshbon, have yielded only meager remains from the Iron I. Yet several sites along the Arnon River, notably Lahun and Khirbet al-Mudayna al-ʿAlyiah, were surprisingly well-developed towns in the late-eleventh century B.C.E. and both were surrounded by casemate walls. These sites hint at the emergence of a new entity in the region, perhaps a forerunner of Moab.

Edom of the Iron I is barely attested, but recent explorations in the copper mines of Feinan indicate that during the Iron I period, mining and smelting were performed on a large scale, replacing the earlier copper mines of Timnaʿ, further to the south. Thomas Levy, who conducts explorations at the impressive site of Khirbet en-Naḥas in the Feinan region, claims that this new discovery may indicate the emergence of Edom as a state much earlier than previously assumed.

These rather recent discoveries may change our understanding of the emergence of the Transjordanian states. The archaeological picture there is complex and heterogeneous, as is the ethnic composition of the region. In the final analysis, it seems that the biblical traditions concerning Transjordan including the emergence of Edom and Moab and the Israelite settlement in Gilead and the valley of Succoth were not completely fictitious, and were partially rooted in actual memories of the past.

Part 4

The Tenth Century: The New Litmus Test for the Bible's Historical Relevance

A Summary Assessment for Part 4

Brian B. Schmidt

As the historian moves into the early-Iron II period, which is tradition-ally held to correspond with the literary construction of that period in the Bible, namely, the age of David and Solomon, both Professors Mazar and Finkelstein embrace positions somewhere between those who assume the his-toricity of all, or the vast majority, of the biblical account pertaining to David and Solomon and those who reject it in its entirety. Both authors acknowledge that much, but not all, of the narrative materials regarding David and Solo-mon can be read as fiction and embellishment written by later writers. While Finkelstein upholds the historicity of David and Solomon, he rejects the his-torical likelihood of a tenth-century United Monarchy altogether. Instead, Finkelstein relocates swhat might constitute just such a united monarchy a century later, in the ninth century, and in the north; a monarchy ruled by the Omrides from Samaria.

Finkelstein avers that much of the David and Solomon narrative in Samuel and Kings cannot be read as a straightforward historical testimony of the tenth century B.C.E. and that their monarchy was not a grand, united empire in nature but a marginal chiefdom of the southernmost portion of the Levant, which was never united in the tenth century by either of these two figures. Yet, he does recognize David and Solomon as historical figures and founders of what eventuates into the later Davidic dynasty in Judah. This he bases largely on the reference to the Davidic dynasty or "House of David" (*bytdwd*) in the Tel Dan inscription. As such, he disagrees with both the maxi-malists and the minimalists as to the facts of history, and then also as to their reliability when it comes to both these two key personages and the polity to be attributed to them.

He outlines the arguments against the traditional view on the historic-ity of the United Monarchy or what Finkelstein refers to as the "conventional theory" based on earlier archaeological data. First, he concludes that this theory had been constructed ultimately in the light of a single biblical text, 1 Kgs 9:15. In other words, for those who advocate a tenth-century United

Monarchy, the sizeable construction projects attested in the archaeological record that date from the general time period in question at sites like Megiddo, Hazor, and Gezer were, as 1 Kgs 9 might suggest, Solomonic-sponsored and therefore constitute a major part of Solomon's efforts to fortify and consolidate his budding empire.

At one point or another, three previous expeditions to Megiddo identified various archaeological and architectural structures as Solomonic; horse stables, (see 1 Kgs 9:19), a six-chambered city gate, and two elaborate palaces. As Finkelstein notes, however, successive excavation teams at Megiddo have further clarified the dates that should be attributed to these structures. Based on the emerging archaeological evidence, it has become clear that these various structures were not built during the same period. The stratigraphic contexts of these structures differ. They represent successive levels and time periods at Megiddo. For example, the so-called stables were subsequently interpreted by Yadin as the undertaking of King Ahab in the ninth century B.C.E., who was apparently renowned for his chariotry according to the Assyrian king Shalmaneser III's description of Ahab in one of his royal inscriptions. The two palaces and gate were deemed Solomonic by Yadin. Yet, Finkelstein argues that the city gate at Megiddo dates to a later period than those of Hazor and Gezer. First, the city gate at Megiddo connects to a wall that runs over the two palaces; in other words, it comes from a later stratigraphic level. Moreover, Finkelstein points out that similar city gates are attested in much later periods and in areas beyond the borders of what has been proposed—on the basis of biblical descriptions—as the boundaries of the United Monarchy. Add to this the following factors and for Finkelstein the conventional theory should be abandoned altogether: territorial states in the Levant did not arise prior to the expansion of the Assyrian Empire in the early-ninth century B.C.E.; the destruction levels associated with the two palaces at Megiddo are more likely the work of Hazael, king of Damascus, who invaded the north during the ninth century (see for example, the Tel Dan inscription) than that of the Egyptian pharaoh Sheshonq; Jerusalem has failed to reveal any meaningful building activity for the tenth century and the old argument that such evidence had been eradicated by subsequent activity hardly holds up in the light of the fact that Middle Bronze and Iron II monumental fortifications there survived later occupations.

Finkelstein then outlines the positive evidence in support of his view. One of the two palaces at Megiddo conventionally assumed to be from the tenth century B.C.E. preserves what he describes as highly distinct masons' marks on the surfaces of the ashlar blocks used to build the palace. Such marks appear otherwise only on the palace of Omri and Ahab at Samaria, which is clearly to be dated to the ninth century B.C.E. on the basis of the fact that both Ahab and his predecessor, Omri are attested in Assyrian texts with Omri clearly viewed as the founder of the dynasty in Israel (that is, the north). Here, Finkelstein invokes the references to the Northern Kingdom as the "house of Omri" or *bit omri*. Furthermore, at the site of Jezreel, the material cultural assemblage there has been dated to the ninth century B.C.E. and parallels the assemblage that others have dated to the tenth century at Megiddo. Since at Jezreel, the major building structure associated with the above assemblage is identical to that identified at ninth-century Samaria, both it and the corresponding assemblage at Megiddo must date to the ninth century.

These factors, along with some recent dating results derived from ^{14}C radiocarbon analysis of several sites, including, among others, Megiddo and Rehov, compels Finkelstein to date what were formerly considered Solomonic monuments and levels later, to the ninth century (900 to 835 B.C.E.). That so much of the archaeological record is to be moved down to the ninth century is for Finkelstein justified by what we know from the broader ancient Near Eastern testimony. Only the Northern Kingdom of the ninth century B.C.E. ruled by Omri and later Ahab, was recognized in the contemporary international climate as an important regional power. Shalmaneser III of Assyria, Mesha of Moab, and Hazael of Aram-Damascus all clearly indicate this in their respective royal inscriptions. This for Finkelstein was the first great Israelite state and as such, if there ever was an Israelite kingdom that united north and south then it was that of the Omride dynasty and it ruled from Samaria, not from Jerusalem, in the ninth century.

In sum, the biblical story of a great United Monarchy is the product of a later Josianic ideal to unite the two states under a southern or Judahite capital in Jerusalem. Megiddo, Hazor, and Gezer are included in the later biblical writer's text since they were the most important cities in the north during the eighth century B.C.E., thereby justifying what Finkelstein views as the later author's pan-Israelite aspiration to bring the entire region under Jerusalem's rule when Josiah reigned as king. If Solomon once ruled these cities—and the region—then Judah should rule them again, only this time (theologically speaking . . .) the way it should have been.

In support of what he tags as "the historicity of the United Monarchy," Mazar reviews several lines of supporting evidence. First, he articulates what he calls his "Modified Conventional Chronology" (or MCC), in which both the tenth and ninth centuries must be viewed together as a single, longer archaeological period. For example, at Tel Rehov, Mazar identified three distinct archaeological layers spanning the tenth to ninth centuries B.C.E. all with the same pottery assemblage. In other words, what is conventionally referred to by historians as the United Monarchy (tenth century) and the subsequent Omride dynasty (ninth century) are both to be included in a more lengthy,

single archaeological period. Therefore it would be very difficult to date with
any greater precision a specific structure or artifact found in this period to
either of these centuries.

Mazar then highlights the importance of the campaign list of the Egyptian
pharaoh Sheshonq I (or Shishak). This list establishes the historicity of some
sites known also from the biblical account of that same event. For Mazar, the
only plausible explanation for the mention of sites in the central hill country
in Sheshonq's list must be the existence of a political power there that was
significant enough to warrant Egypt's attention and intervention. The only
sensible candidate would have been Solomon's kingdom. As to whether or not
specific sites in the region can confidently be identified from the archaeological record as having been actually destroyed by Sheshonq, Mazar remains, in
the final analysis, non-committal since the evidence is ambiguous. Nevertheless, he is of the conviction that archaeologists and historians should make
every effort to identify any and all of the sites mentioned in the list. This is so
since in Mazar's view the place-names are not fictional nor based entirely on
scribal copying from topographical lists known to be available back in Egypt,
as has been suggested in the past. After all, some of the names in Sheshonq I's
campaign list appear exclusively in his inscription originally displayed on the
Temple of Amun at Karnak.

Mazar next surveys the archaeological indicators that point to Jerusalem's
status as a power base in the tenth century (though admittedly not a capital
of a large state). The size of the Stepped Stone Structure on the narrow ridge
of the Eastern Hill and the monumental building to its west currently being
excavated by Eilat Mazar have no parallels anywhere in the land of Israel
between the twelfth and ninth centuries B.C.E. For Mazar, this indicates Jerusalem's unique status during this period, as does the biblical tradition's details
of construction with regard to Solomon's temple and his palace. The use of
large hewn stones (and combined with cedar wood) also fits temple and other
building techniques known in the second millennium and the Iron Age, as
does the palace architecture. Many of these are unknown, however, after the
eighth century in the Levant. In other words, the biblical description of the
Jerusalem Temple and palace cannot be an invention of the seventh century
or later. We are left then to infer that such traditions are early and historically
reliable.

Mazar then notes the evidence for growing urbanization and increased
population density at other known sites and in the wider region during the
tenth century. He concludes that a population estimate of twenty thousand
in Judah during the tenth century, complimented by the populations in the
north and in the Transjordan, for a grand total of fifty to seventy thousand,
would comprise a sufficient demographic base for an Israelite state in the

tenth century. The dearth of Hebrew inscriptions from the tenth century and, for that matter, from the ninth century in the north—where all would agree that we can assume the existence of a central administration—is likely due to the widespread use of perishable writing materials and is not evidence for the lack of literacy. The few that we do have written on stone and pottery point to the reality of literacy at this time and so it is safe to conclude that there were Israelite and Judahite scribes and officials who could write in the tenth century. Mazar also reviews the tenth century archaeological evidence for the beginnings of urbanization among Israel's neighbors who are mentioned in the biblical stories; the Philistines, Edomites, Moabites, Ammonites, Phoenicians, and Arameans. Based on specific cases supported by the archaeological record, Mazar raises the likelihood that tenth-century Israel was in trade relations with more than one of these groups.

Lastly, Mazar highlights the fact that history cannot satisfactorily be written on the basis of deterministic modes of study that do not allow for the role or impact of individual personalities in history even if their influences may elude the archaeological record. Leaders with exceptional charisma and personal abilities could have created short-lived political states with significant military power. When one compares David with the achievements of an earlier hill-country leader like Labayu, the Amarna Age Apiru ruler over Shechem who dominated a sizeable territory and threatened cities like Megiddo and Gezer, this becomes all the more self-evident. Keeping in mind that Labayu achieved all this in spite of the domination of Canaan by Egypt in the New Kingdom period, David might be similarly envisioned, and he operated in a day when Egyptian, or any other foreign, intervention was lacking and when the Canaanite cities were in decline. In fact, the only power that stood in the way of David's rule was that of the Philistine city-states. In the end, many of the achievements of David may well be beyond the tools of archaeology to detect. Yet, the great changes that archaeology can identify as having taken place during the tenth century may be the result of his influence.

The United Monarchy for Mazar was a state in the early stage of development, though far from the imperial state portrayed in the Bible. Its capital was more like a medieval European burg surrounded by a medium-sized town. Sheshonq's invasion was probably in reaction to the growing influence of this state. In agreement with his Modified Conventional Chronology for resolving issues of tenth-century dating, Mazar upholds much of what had been identified as Solomonic monumental building projects by Yadin and others. In any case, the Tel Dan inscription clearly eliminates for Mazar the notion that David and Solomon were the mere invention of later biblical authors since David was still recognized by a foreign power a century or more later as the founder of the dynasty that ruled over Judah.

King Solomon's Golden Age: History or Myth?

Israel Finkelstein

The story of the United Monarchy of David and Solomon is one of the greatest epics of western civilization. A young shepherd boy kills the giant Goliath with a single stone slung from his sling, at once saving Israel from the Philistines and becoming western culture's heroic example of the weak overcoming the mighty. But he then must flee from the rage of King Saul, the first tragic monarch of Israel, who later commits suicide on the battlefield. Conquering Jerusalem, David embarks on an unprecedented campaign of territorial expansion and establishes a great empire. At the height of his fast-rising career, he receives an exceptional, unconditional promise from God: his dynasty will rule in Jerusalem forever.

David's son and successor, Solomon, has likewise captivated the western literary and religious imagination. His wisdom is the standard by which all rulers are rated. His wealth and opulence were reportedly so great that he became the ideal that countless later kings attempted to emulate.

No wonder that David and Solomon have always been revered in western tradition. From Constantine to Charlemagne, from the "David Throne" of the kings of England through the coronation of the Franks at Reims to the "Crown of Solomon" of the Ottonian kings of Germany, David and Solomon have supplied the greatest monarchs of the world with a model of kingship: pious, wise, courageous, but at the same time capable of moral weakness.

Yet, the question remains, is this great epic historically reliable? What if David and Solomon were, as some scholars now contend, purely legendary characters with no more historical substance than King Arthur or Helen of Troy?

Let me begin at the end. This essay presents "the view from the center." Against the conservative or maximalist camps, I argue that much of the David and Solomon narrative in the Bible cannot be read as a straightforward historical testimony and that their kingdom was far more modest than traditionally perceived. At the same time, against the so-called minimalists,

I contend that David and Solomon are historical figures—the founders of a dynasty based in the Judahite city of Jerusalem.

THE CONVENTIONAL THEORY

The quest for the historical United Monarchy—the glamorous empire of David and Solomon—has been the most spectacular venture of biblical archaeology's legacy. The obvious place for early scholars to start the search was, evidently, Jerusalem. Yet, Jerusalem proved to be a hard nut to crack. The nature of the site made it difficult to peel away the layers of later centuries and the Temple Mount has always been out of reach for archaeologists.

Therefore, the search for the great United Monarchy of David and Solomon was redirected to other sites; first and foremost among them, Megiddo in the Jezreel Valley. Megiddo is specifically mentioned in 1 Kgs 9:15 as having been built by Solomon. For more than a century now, Megiddo has become the focus of the endeavor to put flesh and bones on the Bible's literary portrayal of the great Solomonic kingdom. Strategically located on the international highway that connected Egypt and Mesopotamia, Megiddo has been excavated by no fewer than four separate expeditions and, as such, it has yielded more "biblical" monuments than any other site in the Holy Land, including walls, gates, palaces, and water systems, to name but a few.

The University of Chicago's Oriental Institute excavation at Megiddo was the most comprehensive dig in the history of biblical archaeology. Close to the surface of the mound, the excavators unearthed two sets of large public buildings, each divided into three aisles, separated by two sets of stone pillars and troughs. Based on the Megiddo-Solomon linkage in 1 Kgs 9:15 and on the mention in 1 Kgs 9:19 of Solomon's cities of chariots and horses, P. L. O. Guy, one of the directors of the dig, identified these buildings, now being reinvestigated by a Tel Aviv University-led team, as horse stables, and attributed them to King Solomon (fig. 2).

The stables paradigm became the final word and the mirror for the great achievements of Solomon over the next thirty years. The change came with the 1950s excavations of Yigael Yadin farther north at Hazor. Yadin noticed the similarity between the six-chambered city gate that he uncovered at Hazor and the one that the University of Chicago team had unearthed at Megiddo. Yadin turned to 1 Kgs 9:15, which states, "this is the account of the forced labor that King Solomon conscripted to build the house of the Lord and his own house, the Millo and the wall of Jerusalem, and Hazor, and Megiddo, and Gezer," and decided also to dig Gezer. But he did not excavate the field. Rather, he searched in the old Gezer reports of the British excavations from the beginning of the twentieth century. Indeed, he discovered there a similar

Fig. 2. The stable in the northeastern sector of Megiddo. Photo courtesy of the
Tel Aviv University Megiddo Expedition.

city gate hiding in the drawn city plan of what had been formerly described
as a "Maccabean castle." For Yadin this was a perfect match between text and
archaeology. Yadin no longer hesitated and so he described all three gates as
the "blueprint architecture" of the Solomonic era (fig. 8).

Yadin proceeded to carry out soundings at Megiddo and revised the previous stratigraphy and historical interpretation of the Oriental Institute team.
According to him, Solomonic Megiddo was represented not only by the city
gate, but also by two beautiful palaces built of ashlar blocks—one discovered
by the University of Chicago team in the 1920s (Palace 1723) and the other
partially traced by him in the 1960s (and almost fully excavated of recent by
the Tel Aviv University-led team; Palace 6000; fig. 3). Both buildings were
found under the city of the "stables."

Two more finds at Megiddo seemed to support Yadin's interpretation:
the major city under the city of the palaces—one that still features Canaanite
material culture—was destroyed by a terrible fire, and the next city, built on
top of the palaces, featured the famous "stables." Yadin's interpretation seemed
to fit perfectly the biblical testimony:

1. Canaanite Megiddo was devastated by David.
2. The palaces represent the Golden Age of King Solomon; their
   destruction by fire should be attributed to the campaign of Pharaoh
   Sheshonq I in the land of Israel, which is mentioned on the walls of
   the Temple of Amun at Karnak, Upper Egypt, and in 1 Kgs 14:25.

Fig. 3. Palace 6000 at Megiddo. Photo courtesy of the Tel Aviv University
Megiddo Expedition.

3. The stables (which are later than the palaces) date to the early-ninth
   century B.C.E., to the days of King Ahab who, in an Assyrian inscription, is reported to have faced the great Assyrian king Shalmaneser III
   in Syria with a huge force of two-thousand chariots.

It is no wonder Yadin's interpretation became the standard theory on the
United Monarchy.

WHY THE CONVENTIONAL THEORY IS WRONG

Yet, Yadin's theory was haunted by severe problems from the outset. First,
the city gate at Megiddo seems to have been built later than the gates at Hazor
and Gezer; simply put, it connects to a wall that runs over the two palaces.
Second, similar city gates have been discovered at other places in the region,
among them sites that date to late-monarchic times, centuries after Solomon
(for example, Tel 'Ira in the Beer-sheba Valley and Ashdod on the coast), and
sites built outside the borders of the great United Monarchy even as defined
by the maximalist view (Ashdod in Philistia and Khirbet Medeineh eth-
Themed in Moab). No less important is the fact that all three pillars of Yadin's

theory—stratigraphy, chronology, and the biblical passage—cannot withstand thorough scrutiny. Following is the most pivotal citation from Yadin:

> Our decision to attribute that layer to Solomon was based primarily on the 1 Kings passage, the stratigraphy and the pottery. But when in addition we found in that stratum a six-chambered, two-towered gate connected to a casemate wall identical in plan and measurement with the gate at Megiddo, we felt sure we had successfully identified Solomon's city. (Y. Yadin, "Megiddo of the Kings of Israel," *Biblical Archaeologist* 33 [1970]: 67)

Obviously, stratigraphy provides us only with relative chronology—that is, what is earlier and what is later. Unfortunately, the same holds true for old pots. In the case of pottery, archaeologists have committed the ultimate mistake. Some scholars argue that the Solomonic strata at Megiddo, Hazor, and Gezer were dated according to a well-defined family of vessels—red-slipped and burnished ware—which dates to the tenth century. Following is a citation from William G. Dever:

> The pottery from this destruction layer included distinctive forms of red-slipped . . . and hand burnished pottery, which have always been dated to the late tenth century. . . . Thus, on commonly accepted ceramic grounds— not on naive acceptance of the Bible's stories—we dated the Gezer walls and gates to the mid-to-late tenth century. (W. G. Dever, *What Did the Biblical Writers Know and When Did They Know It?* [Grand Rapids, Mich.: Eerdmans, 2001], 132)

The opposite is true. Dever dated this pottery to the tenth century because it had been found in the so-called "Solomonic strata." In other words, how does Dever know that these strata were constructed by Solomon? From the Bible—another classic case of circular reasoning.

So, we are back to square one. Yadin's stratigraphy and chronology tell us nothing when it comes to absolute dating. In order to reach a date, we need an archaeological find that would anchor the archaeology of Israel to the securely dated monarchs of Egypt and Assyria. The problem is that no such anchor for the tenth century B.C.E. exists. In fact, there is no such anchor for the entirety of the more-than-four-centuries of the Iron Age that span the mid-twelfth to the late-eighth centuries B.C.E.! The fragment of the Sheshonq I stele found in the 1920s at Megiddo could have given us such an anchor, but unfortunately, it was recovered out of context. The same holds true for the Mesha stele from Dibon in Moab (in modern Jordan) and the Hazael inscription from Tel Dan in northern Israel. This means that the connection between the remains in the ground and the historical sequence is based on one's interpretation of the biblical material. Hence, Yadin's theory relied on the biblical verse, 1 Kgs 9:15, and nothing but the biblical verse. This must be made clear: the entire reconstruction of the great Solomonic state—by Yadin as well as by others—has been based on a single biblical verse.

So we should take a close look at this verse. There is no question that the material in the books of Kings was put in writing not earlier than the late-seventh century B.C.E., three centuries after Solomon, and that its description of the United Monarchy paints a picture of an idyllic golden age, one that is wrapped in the theological and ideological goals of the time of the authors. Is it possible that despite all this, the author did know about Solomon's building activities in the north? The commonsensical answer would be that he could have consulted with a Solomonic archive in Jerusalem. But over a century of archaeological investigations in Judah has failed to reveal any meaningful scribal activity before the late-eighth century. The idea of a Solomonic archive is therefore no more than wishful thinking. If this is the case, how should we understand 1 Kgs 9:15? I would argue that the author referred to the three most important lowland cities of the Northern Kingdom in the eighth century B.C.E., namely, Megiddo, Hazor, and Gezer, in order to justify his own pan-Israelite ideology that the great Solomon ruled from Jerusalem over the entire country including the lands of the Northern Kingdom (though in the writer's time, the North had already been destroyed).

To sum up this point, Yadin's stratigraphy and pottery tell us nothing at all as regards a United Monarchy and the biblical verse can tell us nothing about the days of Solomon. As far as I can judge, the conventional theory rests on a somewhat simplistic reading of the biblical text, the importance of which has been magnified by wishful thinking.

Now, there are many more reasons to reject the conventional theory. It raises severe historical and archaeological problems. Following are three examples:

1. The rise of territorial states in the Levant was an outcome of the westward expansion of the Assyrian Empire in the early-ninth century B.C.E. Indeed, extra-biblical sources leave little doubt that all major states in the region, namely, Aram-Damascus, Moab, Ammon, and northern Israel, emerged in the ninth century B.C.E. It is extremely difficult to envision a great empire ruled from the marginal region of the southern highlands a century before this process.

2. Affiliating the destruction of the Megiddo palaces with the campaign of Pharaoh Sheshonq I leaves us with no destruction layers in the north for the well-documented later assault of Hazael, king of Aram-Damascus, on the Northern Kingdom in the mid-ninth century.

3. Most problematic of all is the fact that over a century of archaeological explorations in Jerusalem—the capital of the glamorous biblical

United Monarchy—has failed to reveal evidence for any meaningful tenth century building activity. The famous Stepped Stone Structure— usually presented as the most important archaeological remnant of the United Monarchy—was probably built later (fig. 6). Pottery that dates to the ninth century, if not later, was found between its courses. The excavator has interpreted the foundations of a building recently unearthed on the ridge of the City of David above this structure as the remains of the palace of King David. But a careful examination of the architecture and the finds indicates that this building should be dated to the later phase of the Iron II, if not later. The common pretext for the absence of tenth-century remains in Jerusalem—that they were eradicated by later activity—should be brushed aside. Monumental fortifications from both the Middle Bronze Age and late-monarchic times (that is, the sixteenth and eighth centuries B.C.E. respectively) did in fact, survive later occupations. To make a long story short, tenth-century Jerusalem—the city of the time of David and Solomon—was no more than a small, remote highlands village, and not the exquisitely decorated capital of a great empire.

An Alternative Theory

So much for the negative evidence; more straightforward clues as to the appropriate dating of finds come from two sites related to the great Omride dynasty, which ruled over the Northern Kingdom in the ninth century—Samaria in the highlands, its capital, and Jezreel in the valley, generally considered to be its winter palace.

Ashlar blocks uncovered in the foundations of one of the so-called Solomonic palaces at Megiddo preserve distinctive masons' marks on their surfaces. Such marks have been found only in one other building in Israel, namely, the ninth-century palace of Omri and Ahab at Samaria. I should stress that we are not speaking about two sites, or two strata, but about two buildings! These masons' marks are so distinctive that they must have been executed by the same group of masons. Yet, one palace was dated to the tenth century and the other to the ninth century B.C.E. There are only two alternatives here: either we push the Megiddo building ahead to the ninth century, or we pull the Samaria palace back to the tenth century. The answer to the riddle lies in the biblical source on the building of Samaria by King Omri of Israel. This source must be a reliable one since it is supported by Assyrian texts that refer to the Northern Kingdom as *bit omri*, that is, the "House of Omri," the typical phraseology employed when referring to a state that had been named after the founder of its capital. Therefore, there is hardly any doubt that down-dating the Megiddo palaces to the ninth century is the only option.

The recent Anglo-Israeli excavations at Jezreel, located less than ten miles to the east of Megiddo, revealed equally surprising results. The destruction layer of the royal compound there, dated to the mid-ninth century B.C.E., yielded a rich collection of vessels identical to a Megiddo assemblage that has conventionally been dated to the late-tenth century B.C.E. Again, we need either to push the Megiddo assemblage ahead or to pull the Jezreel one back. Since the Jezreel compound is architectonically identical to that of Samaria, it must date to the ninth century. In this case too, then, there is only one option: one must down-date the Megiddo palaces to the ninth century B.C.E.

So far I have dealt with traditional archaeology and biblical exegesis. Can we add to these circumstantial considerations a more accurate method? The answer is positive and it comes from the exact sciences. In recent years, samples from Iron Age strata of several sites in Israel have been subjected to ^{14}C dating procedures. The resultant dating of a large number of readings from Dor on the Mediterranean coast, Tel Hadar on the eastern shore of the Sea of Galilee, Megiddo, and Yoqne'am in the Jezreel Valley, Tel Reḥov south of Beth-shean, Hazor in the north, and Rosh Zayit near Acco were found to be lower than expected by almost a century according to the conventional chronology. A comprehensive study by the Weizmann Institute and the University of Arizona laboratories has placed the transition from the Iron I to the Iron II, which is traditionally dated from around 1000–980 B.C.E. to 920–900 B.C.E. Destruction layers, which have conventionally been dated to the late-tenth century, provide dates in the mid- to late-ninth century B.C.E.

A set of readings from Tel Reḥov has been interpreted by Amihai Mazar as supporting the conventional dating. Yet, a more thorough reading of the Tel Reḥov radiocarbon data (that is, taking into consideration all readings rather than a selection of results) can be interpreted as supporting the down-dating of the Iron Age strata (that is, the Low Chronology). In addition, comparison of the pottery assemblages of Tel Reḥov and Megiddo indicates that the Megiddo palaces should be placed in the later phase of the period labeled "Iron IIA," that is, in the first half of the ninth century B.C.E.

In sum, the radiocarbon results confirm my earlier conclusions: the date of the "Solomonic" monuments should be lowered by seventy-five to one-hundred years.

BACK TO HISTORY

What is the meaning of all this for biblical and historical studies? The mention of the "House of David" in the Tel Dan inscription from the ninth

century B.C.E. leaves no doubt that David and Solomon were historical figures. And there is good reason to accept that many of the David stories in the
books of Samuel—mainly the heroic tales and the description of his life as a
bandit on the fringe of the Judean highlands—contain genuine, early historical memories. These in turn were transmitted orally and put in writing not
before the late-eighth century B.C.E. But the great biblical story of the United
Monarchy is left with no material evidence. In the tenth century B.C.E., places
such as Megiddo in the north still featured Canaanite material culture. The
kingdom of David and Solomon was no more than a poor, demographically
depleted chiefdom centered in Jerusalem, a humble village.

The beautiful Megiddo palaces—until recently the symbol of Solomonic
splendor—date to the time of the Omride dynasty of the Northern Kingdom,
almost a century later than Solomon. They were probably constructed by King
Ahab. This should come as no surprise. Contemporary monarchs—Shalmaneser III of Assyria, Mesha of Moab, and Hazael of Damascus—all attest to
the great power of ninth-century Israel. The biblical story about the reign of
the Omride princess Athaliah in Jerusalem, which is widely considered to
be a reliable historical testimony, indicates that the Omrides dominated the
marginal, powerless Judah to their south. The great, powerful, and glamorous Israelite state was the Northern Kingdom—the wicked kingdom in the
eyes of the biblical historians—not the small and poor territory dominated
by tenth-century Jerusalem. If there was a United Monarchy that ruled from
Dan to Beer-sheba it was that of the Omride dynasty and it was ruled from
ninth-century Samaria.

If these are the facts on the ground, what is the origin of the biblical tale
of an illustrious United Monarchy? In order to answer this question, we need
to remember that the biblical narrative of the ancient history of Israel—the
Deuteronomistic History—was put in writing in the late-seventh century
B.C.E., in the days of King Josiah, who is described in the book of Kings as
the most righteous monarch of the lineage of David. The Deuteronomistic
History was intended to serve Josiah's agenda of centralization of the cult in
Jerusalem and territorial expansion into the northern lands of vanquished
Israel after the withdrawal of Assyria. It is not difficult to identify the landscapes and costumes of late-monarchic times—the time of the compilation of
the text as well as the immediate past—as the stage setting behind the biblical
tale of the United Monarchy. The stories of Solomon's cities of chariots and
horsemen must reflect a memory of the great horse-breeding and training
facilities of the Northern Kingdom in eighth-century B.C.E. Megiddo. King
Hiram of Tyre must be identified with the only Hiram known from reliable
extra-biblical texts—the contemporary of Tiglath-pileser III in the eighth
century; the story of the trade relations with him was designed to equate the

grandeur of Solomon with that of the great monarchs of the Northern King-dom. The lavish visit to Jerusalem of Solomon's trading partner, the Queen of Sheba, undoubtedly reflects the participation of late-eighth and seventh-century Judah in the lucrative Arabian trade under Assyrian domination. The same holds true for the description of the trade expeditions to lands afar that set off from Ezion-geber on the Gulf of Aqaba—a site that was not inhabited before late-monarchic times.

As I have mentioned, some of the David stories in the books of Samuel may contain earlier, even tenth-century B.C.E. traditions. But they too had been put in writing much later, possibly in the late-eighth century, and were then inserted into the larger history of Israel in the seventh century. At that stage, they absorbed the realities and ideology of the later time. The armor of Goliath, for instance, which resembles that of a Greek hoplite of the seventh or sixth century B.C.E. (and not an early Aegean warrior), should probably be understood against the background of the service of Greek mercenaries in the army of seventh-century Egypt. That was a time when tiny Judah faced mighty Egypt of the Twenty-sixth Dynasty, which inherited the Assyrian territories in the Levant. So, the victory of David over the giant Goliath—described as a Greek hoplite and thus symbolizing the power of Egypt—could have depicted the hopes of Judah in Josiah's time.

But why was it so important to project these late-monarchic images back into the early history of Israel? The tale of a glamorous United Monarchy had an obvious meaning for the people of Judah in the days of the compila-tion of the text. In a time when the Northern Kingdom was no more than a memory and the mighty Assyrian army had faded away, a new David—the pious Josiah—came to the throne in Jerusalem, intent on "restoring" the glory of his distant ancestors. He was about to "replay" the history of Israel. By cleansing Judah of the abominations of the nations and undoing the sins of the past, he could stop the cycle of idolatry and calamity that character-ized the history of ancient Israel. He could "recreate" the United Monarchy the way it should have been, before it went astray. So Josiah embarked on reestablishing a United Monarchy. He was about to "regain" the territories of the now-destroyed Northern Kingdom, and rule from Jerusalem over all Israelite territories and all Israelite people. The description of the glamorous United Monarchy served these goals.

While all this may seem somewhat to belittle the stature of the historical David and Solomon, in the same breath we gain a glimpse into the grandeur of the Northern Kingdom—the first true, great Israelite state. No less impor-tant, we are given a glimpse into the fascinating world of late-monarchic Judah whose authors created the image of the great United Monarchy.

THE SEARCH FOR DAVID AND SOLOMON: AN ARCHAEOLOGICAL PERSPECTIVE

Amihai Mazar

As one reads the Hebrew Bible, one imagines David and Solomon as rulers of a powerful, mature state (sometimes denoted as an "empire") and Jerusalem as a large and prosperous capital, at least large enough to contain Solomon's one thousand wives. One would also expect dense urban settlements throughout the country, official inscriptions and various art forms. It has been the professional opinion of many historians and archaeologists that indeed this was the case, and the depiction of Solomon's kingdom that for so long had been developing in archaeology seemed to fit the traditional image portrayed in the Bible.

Yet, during the last two decades, a good number of scholars have grown increasingly skeptical concerning both the historical validity of the biblical descriptions, as well as the archaeological conclusions regarding the tenth century B.C.E., the supposed time of David and Solomon. While others retained the older, conservative approach, accepting much of the biblical narrative at face value, there have been several arguments cited against the historicity of the United Monarchy: the kingdom is not mentioned in any written sources outside of the Bible; Jerusalem, its supposed capital, was either entirely unsettled or comprised only a small village during the tenth century; literacy is hardly attested during this period; the population density was sparse; there is no evidence for international trade, and so forth. Scholars have also claimed that the biblical texts relating to David and Solomon should be read as fictional literature, theologically and ideologically motivated national sagas intended to glorify a supposed past golden era in the history of Israel.

As I will attempt to show, this deconstruction of the United Monarchy has gone too far. Though indeed many of the biblical narrative stories related to this period should not be taken at face value, it is a long way to go from there to the total negation of the United Monarchy as an historical reality.

Let us start with the fact that many of the same scholars who deny the historicity of the United Monarchy do accept the historicity of the Northern Kingdom of Israel ruled by Omri and Ahab in the ninth century. They do so to a large extent since the latter is mentioned in Assyrian, Moabite, and Aramean documents external to the Bible. Yet, the time lapse between the United Monarchy and the Omride dynasty is less than a century, while several centuries separate the ninth century from the supposed time when the biblical texts were composed, namely the seventh century B.C.E. If in fact the early version of the Deuteronomistic History is to be dated to the seventh century B.C.E. or later, as generally accepted, and if the Bible preserves accurate information regarding the Omride dynasty of the ninth century, then why should one accept the view that all of the information concerning David and Solomon is imaginative? Furthermore, the ninth-century Assyrian inscriptions mentioning Israel result from the fact that the Assyrian Empire was established during that century and left us historical inscriptions, while for the tenth century such documents are lacking, since there was no external power to write them. The one exception is Sheshonq I's inscription from the Temple of Amun at Karnak, to which we will return later. There is no logic in acknowledging the historicity of the biblical account regarding ninth-century northern Israel but discrediting the historicity of the United Monarchy of the tenth century or for that matter, that of Judah in the ninth century—that is, unless the claim is based on clear archaeological indications. This is why archaeology has become so important for evaluating the historicity of the United Monarchy. In the light of this argumentation, let us examine how archaeology may or may not support one of the two positions outlined above, or perhaps how it might guide us in a third direction.

IRON AGE CHRONOLOGY AND HISTORICAL INTERPRETATION

A condition for archaeological interpretation of any period is an accurate chronology that will enable one to comprehend the nature of the material remains from a certain time period, in our case the tenth century B.C.E. The archaeological period under discussion is termed by most archaeologists "Iron IIA." It is characterized by a significant change in material culture, as particularly expressed in pottery production. The earlier Canaanite painted-pottery traditions that survived in the plains until the early-tenth century gave way to a new style, characterized by both new forms and the appearance of red slip and irregular hand-burnished wares. This new pottery tradition and the cities and settlements where it was found were traditionally dated to the tenth century B.C.E., the time of the United Monarchy. Israel Finkelstein has suggested lowering the chronology of archaeological assemblages in Israel that were traditionally attributed to the twelfth to tenth centuries by seventy-five to one hundred years. This wholesale lowering of dates results in the removal of archaeological assemblages from the tenth century that have served for about half a century of scholarship as the bases for the archaeological portrait or paradigm of Solomon's kingdom. This suggested "Low Chronology" supposedly supports the replacement of this paradigm by a new one (in fact, similar to one presented earlier by David Jamieson Drake and others), according to which the kingdom of David and Solomon either did not exist or comprised at best a small local entity. According to this suggestion, the first Israelite state documented in the archaeological record was northern Israel under the Omrides of the ninth century B.C.E.

This reconstruction has generated an extensive debate that is still ongoing. A major issue is the perennial chicken-or-the-egg question: Was the Low Chronology born out of an independent archaeological endeavor or as an archaeological response to a certain historical paradigm? In each of Finkelstein's papers on this issue, the archaeological discussion is intermingled with an evaluation of state formation in Israel and Judah in a manner that does not allow for any differentiation between cause and effect. So, one gains the impression that the archaeological conclusions have been influenced or even biased by the desire to deconstruct the traditional view and replace it by an alternative one. Let us examine this particular issue in greater detail.

The time frame under discussion is secured by two chronological anchors: the earlier is the end of the Egyptian presence in Canaan during the twelfth century B.C.E. and the later is related to the Assyrian conquests of Israel, Philistia, and Judah between 732 and 701 B.C.E. Between these two anchors, which are four-hundred years apart, we have very few reference points. One such point is the site of Jezreel, where excavations carried out during the 1990s revealed the royal enclosure of Ahab and Jezebel well known from 1 Kings. This immense enclosure was destroyed during the late-ninth century B.C.E., probably by Hazael, king of Damascus, soon after the end of the Omride dynasty in ca. 840/830 B.C.E. The pottery from this destruction layer must thus be dated to that time. It soon became clear that this pottery resembled the pottery found at nearby Megiddo in buildings traditionally attributed to Solomon. This is one of Finkelstein's major arguments in favor of his lowering the date of the Megiddo buildings to the ninth century (see above p. 114). However, similar pottery was found at Jezreel also in construction fills below the foundations of the royal enclosure, probably associated with an earlier town or village. Such a pre-Omride occupation could date to the tenth or early-ninth century B.C.E. This suggests that throughout much of the tenth and ninth centuries, the same pottery repertoire was in use. Reflecting back on the buildings at Megiddo, we can conclude that they were constructed

Fig. 4. Tel Reḥov. Photo courtesy of the Tel Reḥov excavations.

during, and remained in use throughout, the time frame represented by this particular pottery (designated as Iron IIA in the most common current division of the Iron Age), that is, either the tenth or the ninth centuries, or both (see further below). These buildings thus could have been built either by Solomon or by Omri or Ahab.

A second important chronological reference point is Arad in the northern Negev. This site appears in the list of place-names in the land of Israel that was inscribed on a wall of the Temple of Amun at Karnak in Upper Egypt during the reign of Sheshonq I, the pharaoh who conducted a military raid against Israel. Sheshonq I can safely be identified with the Shishak mentioned in 1 Kgs 14:25 as threatening Jerusalem in the time of Rehoboam five years after the death of Solomon. Since Arad is mentioned in Sheshonq's list, there must have been a settlement there prior to Sheshonq's invasion. Thus, at least the earliest settlement at Arad should be dated to the tenth century B.C.E. (or the time of Solomon). Excavations conducted in the earliest settlement (Stratum XII) by Yohanan Aharoni at Arad revealed pottery similar to that found in other occupation strata in Judah that traditionally has been attributed to the tenth century, such as that recovered from Beer-sheba or Lachish. Such a comparative relative chronology is a fundamental research tool in archaeology, and, as in the case at hand, it negates Finkelstein's Low Chronology, according to which all these other sites should postdate the tenth century, and thus are later than the Solomonic era. Yet, somewhat surprisingly, Finkelstein himself accepts the dating of Arad Stratum XII to the time period prior to Sheshonq, and by doing so he pulls the rug out from underneath his own theory.

Meticulous research substantiates a series of correlations between many sites throughout the country, thus enabling us to use Arad as a key reference point and to create horizons of contemporary occupation strata elsewhere. Such an approach indicates in my view that Finkelstein's Low Chronology cannot be accepted as is, since it creates unresolved problems in the study of the Iron Age. The archaeological research at Hazor, Jezreel, and at my own Tel Reḥov excavations in the Beth-shean Valley (fig. 4) convinces me that indeed we have to modify somewhat our conventional chronology. But, unlike Finkelstein, who simply moves all the tenth-century assemblages to the ninth century, I propose that the pottery assemblage under consideration had a long life span and that it overlapped both the tenth and ninth centuries B.C.E. According to what I term the Modified Conventional Chronology (MCC), the Iron IIA lasted approximately from 980 to 840/830 B.C.E. (fig. 5).

During the last decade, a good number of archaeologists who excavate or study Iron Age IIA sites have adopted this "long duration" perspective for the pottery assemblage in question as the most acceptable one, including the excavators and researchers of Hazor, Jezreel, Beth-shean, Tel Reḥov, Gezer, Beth-shemesh, Timnah (Tel Batash), Jerusalem, Gath (Tell eṣ-Ṣâfi), Arad, and Beer-sheba. Currently, there are attempts to divide the Iron IIA period into two subphases, an earlier one in the tenth century and a later one starting at the end of the tenth century and continuing into the ninth century B.C.E. Some confirmation of this proposal has been tested at both Tel Reḥov in the north and the Beer-sheba–Arad region in the south (the latter by Zeev Herzog and Lili Singer-Avitz).

Attempts to use ^{14}C dates to resolve the debate over Iron Age chronology have been made in the last decade in several research frameworks. More than sixty samples from Tel Reḥov dated at the Groningen University laboratories by J. Van der Plicht and H. Bruins provide a sequence of dates for a series of

THE CONVENTIONAL CHRONOLOGY (after *The New Encyclopedia of Archaeological Excavations in the Holy Land* [E. Stern, ed.; Jerusalem: Carta, 1993])

Iron IA: 1200–1150 B.C.E.
Iron IB: 1150–1000 B.C.E.
Iron IIA: 1000–925 B.C.E.
Iron IIB: 925–720 B.C.E.
Iron IIC: 720–586 B.C.E.

THE MODIFIED CONVENTIONAL CHRONOLOGY

Iron IA: 1200–1150/1140 B.C.E.
Iron IB: 1150/1140–ca. 980 B.C.E.
Iron IIa: ca. 980–ca. 840/830 B.C.E.
Iron IIb: ca. 840/830–732/701 B.C.E.
Iron IIc: 732/701 B.C.E.–605/586 B.C.E.

Fig. 5. Divisions of the Iron Age in Israel.

strata from the twelfth to the ninth centuries B.C.E. The Early Iron Age Dating Project directed by E. Boaretto, A. Gilboa, I. Sharon, and T. Jull, utilizing the laboratories of the Weizmann Institute in Israel and the University of Arizona, intends to sample as many sites as possible; more than fifty dates stemming from this project have been published so far. Additional dates from various sites have been measured in recent years. The emphasis in these current projects is on high-quality dating of as many short-life samples (for example, seeds and olive stones) as possible from secure contexts, calibration with updated software, and statistical processing of the results. The major question is, what is the material culture related to the time frame attributed to David and Solomon in traditional historical reconstructions, namely, the bulk of the tenth century B.C.E.? Traditionally, this period would be included in the Iron Age IIA. The Low Chronology as suggested by Finkelstein would move the Iron Age IIA to the ninth century, and include the tenth century in the Iron Age I. Analysis of sixty-four ^{14}C dates from Tel Reḥov point to a date between 992 and 962 B.C.E. for the transition from Iron I to Iron II; thus, the Iron IIA would cover much of the tenth as well as much of the ninth centuries B.C.E. The early results of the Early Iron Age Dating Project (published by E. Boaretto *et al.* in the journal *Radiocarbon* in 2005), which pointed to ca. 900 B.C.E. as the date of the end of the Iron Age I period and thus supporting the Low Chronology, have been checked more recently in an as-yet-unpublished study by myself together with Ch. Bronk Ramsey in light of several additional dates. The results point to a transition date from Iron I to Iron II between 964 and 944 B.C.E. We also calculated the destruction of three major sites related to the end of Iron Age I (Megiddo, Yoqneʿam, and Tell Qasile) as occurring around the end of the eleventh or beginning of the tenth century B.C.E. Thus, the transition from Iron I to Iron IIA occurred most probably somewhere during the first half of the tenth century B.C.E., allowing sufficient time in the tenth century B.C.E. for the Iron Age IIA to be correlated with the Davidic/Solomonic era. Yet, the study has also shown how sensitive statistical models of ^{14}C dates are. New published dates or elimination of published dates for certain reasons (such as outliers, wood samples that are much too old, and questionable contexts or dates), may change the results substantially.

The outcome of the Modified Conventional Chronology is that both the United Monarchy and the Omride dynasty are included in a single, more lengthy archaeological period, denoted Iron IIA. This revised periodization in turn creates a greater flexibility in the interpretation of the archaeological data, and makes life more difficult for those who wish to utilize archaeology for secure historical interpretations in the southern Levant during the tenth and ninth centuries B.C.E. Since in many cases it would be difficult to conclude with any certainty whether a specific building was constructed either during the tenth or the ninth century, unless the subtle ceramic divisions between Early Iron IIA and Late Iron IIA will one day prove to be valid and utilized in a more controlled manner. This cannot be done at the present time for many of the older excavations, and in particular at Megiddo, since, out of the two palaces attributed by Yadin to the time of Solomon, the southern one was preserved to the level of the foundation courses only, while, from the northern one, the published pottery does not allow such a subtle dating inside the boundaries of the Iron IIA period. The modified chronology would mean that any comprehensive archaeological synthesis of the Solomonic period is tentative and may be interpreted in more than one way. And finally, it rejects the strict and one-sided Low Chronology as suggested by Finkelstein. In what follows, I will examine a few of the more crucial issues relating to our subject in the light of this Modified Conventional Chronology (MCC).

THE IMPORTANCE OF THE SHESHONQ I (SHISHAK) RAID

The lack of external sources relating to a kingdom like that of David and Solomon should not surprise us, since there were no empires or major political powers during the tenth century B.C.E. that could leave behind substantial written documents. The only external source relating to this period is the Sheshonq I inscription mentioned above, which refers to a military raid against the land of Israel that took place in about 920 B.C.E. First, we must realize that the mention of Sheshonq's campaign in 1 Kgs 14:25–28 cannot be explained away as an invention of an author of the seventh-century B.C.E. or later since the writer must have had records of some sort. This by itself is important evidence regarding the historical dimension of the biblical narrative and the way it emerged.

Unlike any of the earlier Egyptian New Kingdom military campaigns in Canaan, Sheshonq's list mentions sites north of Jerusalem, like Beth Horon and Gibeon. The only plausible explanation for this must be the existence of a political power in the central hill country that was significant enough in the eyes of the Egyptians to justify such an exceptional route for the campaign. The only sensible candidate for such a power is the Solomonic kingdom. Finkelstein's proposal that it was Saul's kingdom that was Sheshonq's target seems to be farfetched (see below, p. 148) and in contrast to any biblical inner chronology, which dates Sheshonq's raid to the reign of Rehoboam. If indeed the raid followed Solomon's death, perhaps Sheshonq was trying to take advantage of a time of weakness and strike a blow against the emerging Israelite state. The fact that Jerusalem is not mentioned in the inscription does not mean much—if the city surrendered, perhaps there would have been no reason to mention it; or alternatively, its mention could have appeared on one of the broken parts of the inscription.

As to the remaining stages of the route, most scholars (except Nadav Na'aman) reconstruct a route that crossed the central mountain ridge towards the Jordan Valley. The references in the inscription to Reḥov, Beth-shean, and "The Valley" (probably referring to the Beth-shean or Jezreel Valleys or both) in a continuous line fits this reconstruction.

There are various views concerning the question of whether or not Sheshonq actually destroyed the cities along his route, and if so, which archaeological levels can be identified as those he destroyed. The commonly held view is that such destructions indeed occurred, and that it is possible to identify destruction layers that resulted directly from this military campaign. Violent destructions that can be dated to this time, and which may have been the result of this raid, were tentatively identified at a number of sites, in particular in the Beth-shean and Jezreel Valleys, such as Tell el Hama, Tel Reḥov, Megiddo, and Taanach. In my view, however, the question of whether cities were indeed destroyed is less important than the very mention of certain names in the list. It is not conceivable, as some scholars have suggested, that Sheshonq's scribes merely copied names from earlier Egyptian topographic lists at Karnak, since there are many place-names known only from Sheshonq's inscription. For archaeologists, it is important to recognize that any place-name that appears in this list must have been in existence before the raid and that where possible, it should therefore be identified in the archaeological record; Arad, the Negev highland sites, Taanach, and Reḥov are all good examples of sites that are mentioned in the Sheshonq inscription and that yielded Iron IIA occupation layers. In some of these (for example, Arad and the Negev highlands, for which see below) there is no alternative but to attribute the Iron IIA occupation layers to the tenth century B.C.E., preceding Sheshonq's raid. This is an important chronological anchor, one that negates the Low Chronology.

JERUSALEM OF THE IRON I–II PERIOD

The evaluation of Jerusalem as a city in the tenth to ninth centuries is crucial for defining state formation in Judah—if there was no capital, there likely was no kingdom. In several papers published in recent years, David Ussishkin has proposed that Jerusalem was not settled in the tenth century, while Finkelstein has defined Jerusalem of the tenth century as a small village. These assessments should be examined in some detail since they are crucial for our subject.

Prior to its expansion in the eighth century B.C.E. towards the Western Hill, Jerusalem was limited to the narrow ridge of the Eastern Hill, crowned by the Temple Mount. The area of this entire ridge is about twelve hectares (ca. thirty acres), a large area for any Iron Age city in Israel or Judah. The entire upper part of this hill is located below the huge artificial platform from the Second Temple period. South of the Temple Mount, the ridge becomes narrower, surrounded by the deep ravines of the Kidron and Tyropoeon Valleys. This was the location of early Jerusalem, the original Canaanite city. The area of this part of the ridge is about four hectares. A main structure uncovered near the summit of this part of the hill known as the Stepped Stone Structure is enormous and was most probably intended to support an exceptionally large monumental building (fig. 6). The earliest possible date of its construction can be deduced from pottery found within its foundations, which dates no later than the twelfth to eleventh centuries B.C.E. Pottery found on the floors of structures above the lower part of this stepped structure indicate that it started to go out of use during the Iron IIA, that is, some time in the tenth or ninth century. Therefore, the Stepped Stone Structure must have been constructed between the twelfth and tenth centuries B.C.E. It is thus legitimate to conclude that the building was either constructed or continued to be in use during the tenth century, the alleged time of David and Solomon (cf. below, p. 151).

Excavations carried out recently by Eilat Mazar on the summit of the hill to the west and very close to Stepped Stone Structure have revealed a monumental building with walls over two meters wide, which extends beyond the limits of the excavation area in all directions. A continuation of the same

Fig. 6. The Stepped Stone Structure in Jerusalem. Photo courtesy
of Zev Radovan.

building was excavated by Kathleen Kenyon (in her Area H) and identified by
her as a "casemate" structure dating to the tenth century B.C.E. The data relating to the date of this building are very similar to that of the Stepped Stone

Structure. Its foundation rests upon, and is abutted by, an earth layer containing twelfth to eleventh century pottery, and tenth to ninth century pottery was found in an earth layer relating to some of its walls, where evidence for repairs and changes to the building have been detected. This building appears to be the anticipated monumental building or citadel that was supported by the Stepped Stone Structure. In terms of their magnitude, neither the Stepped Stone Structure nor the building recently discovered to its west has a parallel anywhere in the land of Israel between the twelfth and early-ninth centuries B.C.E., and this is, in my view, a clear indication that Jerusalem was much more than a small village; in fact it contained the largest-known structure of the time in the region and thus could easily serve as a power base for a central authority. Eilat Mazar suggested identifying this building with the palace attributed to David in 2 Sam 5:11. A more plausible identification in my view would be with Metsudat Zion—"the fortress of Zion"—mentioned in the biblical description of David's conquest of Jerusalem. David is said to have changed the name of this citadel to ʿir dawid, or "the City of David" (2 Sam 5:7, 9). Such identification remains, of course, hypothetical, yet it might appeal to those who believe that the biblical narrative did preserve many ancient traditions and some knowledge of the past.

In addition to this huge building, only a few remains were found in the City of David that can be attributed to the tenth century. These are mainly pottery sherds found in all the excavation areas, and only a few architectural remains. The latter situation is probably the result of the bad state of preservation of structures on the steep slope at this peculiar site, and of the continuous reuse of buildings over the centuries. Massive fortifications discovered by Ronni Reich and Eli Shukron around the Gihon spring at the foot of the City of David have been dated to the Middle Bronze period (eighteenth to sixteenth centuries B.C.E.), and were among the mightiest fortifications from this period in the entire country. Such immense fortifications could have continued to be used for centuries, including into the time of David and Solomon, though there is no direct proof to support this proposal, and it remains a circumstantial argument only. But compare, for example, the situation at other major cities of the ancient Near East where Middle Bronze monumental structures continued to be in use for many centuries, sometime well into the Iron Age (such as the palace in the city of Assur, the temple of the storm god at Aleppo, the temples at Shechem and Pella, and more).

The temple and palace that Solomon supposedly built should be found, if anywhere, below the present Temple Mount, where no excavations are possible (fig. 7). If the biblical account is taken as reliable, Solomon's Jerusalem would be a city of twelve hectares with monumental buildings and a temple. Should Solomon be removed from history, who then would have been responsible

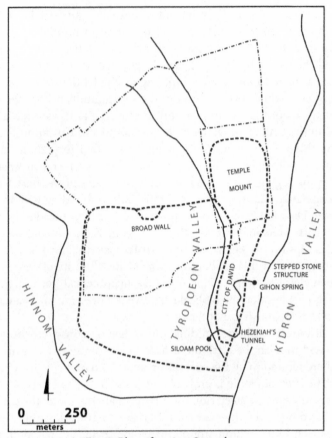

Fig. 7. Plan of ancient Jerusalem.

for the construction of the Jerusalem Temple? There is no doubt that such a temple stood on the Temple Mount prior to the Babylonian conquest of the city, but we lack any textual hint for an alternative to Solomon as its builder.

Solomon's temple, as described in the Bible, was built according to a tripartite plan well known in the region from the second millennium B.C.E. to the eighth century B.C.E. Close parallels are known from the Iron Age temples at Tell Tayinat and ʿAin Dara in northern Syria. They provide examples of architectural details that appear in the description of Solomon's temple, such as the two pillars at the front of the main entrance (biblical Yachin and Boas), the corridors surrounding the building, and the special type of windows. The details of construction in the biblical tradition, such as the use of large hewn stones combined with cedar wood, also fit building techniques known in the second millennium and the Iron Age. Such temple plans are unknown after the eighth century B.C.E. in the Levant and, thus, the biblical description of the Jerusalem's temple could not have been an invention of the seventh century or later.

The decoration of the temple and its furnishings, like the molten sea, the gourds, the wheeled stands of bronze, the cherubim, the shovels, and the basins, all have parallels in archaeological finds. The decorations fit artistic motifs that are known in Phoenician art. Most of the parallels come from objects dated to the ninth to eighth centuries, but many of them are rooted in second-millennium traditions, and are evidence for the continuity in cultural traditions between the second and first millennia. Solomon's temple could signify this same continuity. The main detail that seems exaggerated is the huge amount of gold in the structure—it seems unlikely that such a large quantity of gold was available in Jerusalem, though Allan Millard has argued for the feasibility of this detail as well.

The description of Solomon's palace compound and its various components can be compared to palace architecture in the Levant and northern Syria. Such a comparison indicates close similarities to well-known palace compounds such as those at Zinjirli, the capital of Sam'al (in southeastern Turkey) and other Syrian cities. It thus appears that the biblical descriptions of both the temple and the palace fit the architecture and decorative arts of the Iron Age as known to us from archaeology.

Yet, is it feasible that such splendid structures stood in tenth-century Jerusalem? One may doubt that Solomon's kingdom was strong and rich enough to afford such buildings and furnishings. It may well be that the biblical description is based on the shape of the Temple at the time of writing—the eighth to seventh centuries, when Jerusalem was at its peak—and even then it seems to be much exaggerated. Such an explanation, however, does not exclude the possibility that the temple and palace were indeed established during the tenth century, and later renovated.

In summary, Jerusalem during the time of David was most likely a city of about four hectares, which could have reached an area of twelve hectares during the reign of Solomon. At the summit of the core city (the "City of David") stood a large citadel, the nature and dimensions of which are exceptional for this period. Such a city cannot be imagined as a capital of a large state like the one described in the Bible, but it could well serve as a power base for local rulers like David and Solomon, providing that we correctly define the nature of their kingship and state.

YADIN'S PARADIGM: MEGIDDO, HAZOR, AND GEZER

In the early 1930s, the excavators at Megiddo from The Oriental Institute of the University of Chicago uncovered in their Stratum IV, huge compounds or structures that were interpreted by them as royal stables. They identified these as Solomonic projects following the references in the Bible to chariot cities constructed by Solomon (1 Kgs 9:19). In an earlier level, Stratum V, the Chicago excavators, as well as Yigael Yadin of the Hebrew University, revealed an unfortified city with two palaces constructed of ashlar stones (today, this city is usually denoted as Stratum IVB–VA). The history and dates of these two cities became the subject of a longstanding debate among archaeologists and it remains an unresolved issue, although crucial for our subject. One major question relating to Megiddo is the date of the so-called six-chambered gate; a city gate constructed of ashlar stones that definitely was in use during the time of the "chariot city," but according to several scholars was already established in the earlier "palaces city" (or Stratum IVB–VA). William F. Albright, Yadin, and others dated the "palaces city" to the time of Solomon and the "stables city" (Stratum IVA) to the time of Ahab in the ninth century.

Following his excavations at Hazor and Megiddo in the 1960s, Yadin developed his renowned thesis concerning Solomonic architecture. At Hazor he discovered a six-chambered gate similar to that of Megiddo, and at Gezer he identified a similar gate that was partly excavated by Stuart Macalister many years earlier. Based on the mention of Hazor, Megiddo, and Gezer among Solomon's building activities in 1 Kgs 9:15, Yadin suggested that all three gates were constructed by Solomon's architects according to a similar "blue print" (fig. 8). Thus, these gates and the cities to which they belonged were considered by him to be markers of Solomon's kingdom. Later excavators at both Hazor and Gezer appeared to confirm the tenth-century dates of these gates. At Hazor, the gate was found in the earliest of at least six Iron Age

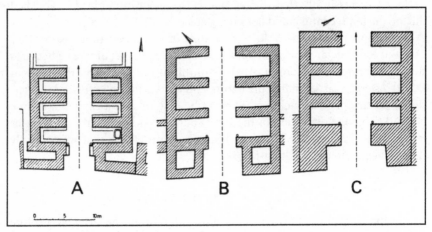

Fig. 8. Plans of the six-chambered gates at Gezer (A), Hazor (B), and Megiddo (C).

strata preceding the Assyrian conquest of 732 B.C.E.; three of these strata (X, IX, and VIII; the two early ones have subphases) are from the tenth to ninth centuries B.C.E., with Stratum VIII probably ending no later that ca. 830 B.C.E. The six-chambered gate and the casemate wall belong to the earliest of these strata, and thus it makes sense that this fortification system was constructed during the tenth century B.C.E.

Yadin's view concerning Megiddo was criticized in light of indicators that the six-chambered gate could not have been constructed earlier than the "stables city" and the latter must be later than Solomon according to Yadin himself. In my view, the gate could have been part of the palaces city (Stratum IB–VA) and continued in use into the ninth century. A more radical view is that of Israel Finkelstein, who has suggested that the entire "palaces city" (Stratum IVB–VA) was constructed by Ahab, and the "stables city" (including the six-chambered gate) was built by Manasseh in the eighth century B.C.E. This continues to be a debated issue, and there are diverse views even among the three directors of the current excavations at Megiddo (Israel Finkelstein, David Ussishkin, and Baruch Halpern). As mentioned above, the Modified Conventional Chronology enables one to date the pottery found in the "palaces city" to either the time of Solomon or to the time of Ahab. This situation demonstrates the variety of possibilities in the interpretation of archaeological data for historical reconstruction. I still hold to the notion that the tenth-century date of the "palaces city" is the correct one, though it would be difficult to provide final proof for that. The "palaces city," though it might have had a monumental gate, lacked a city wall and it would be hard to accept the notion, as suggested by Finkelstein's Low Chronology, that Ahab's Megiddo was an unfortified city, since this warrior king had huge fortifications at his nearby royal enclosure in Jezreel, as well as at other cities of his kingdom. The stables of Megiddo would fit the time of Ahab who is mentioned in the Assyrian sources as the owner of a huge number of war chariots. To sum up, Yadin's thesis concerning Solomonic architecture at Megiddo, Hazor, and Gezer might be correct.

THE JUDEAN SHEPHELAH

Several other excavated sites throughout the Israelite territories point to a process of urbanization during the tenth century B.C.E. This would be the first stage in an urban development that continued in most of these cities without interruption until the Assyrian conquests in the late-eighth century B.C.E. It should be mentioned though that many of the sites remained unfortified and were not sufficiently developed to qualify as urban centers during the tenth century. The new style would continue to survive through most of the tenth and ninth centuries, thus making it difficult to differentiate between these two centuries, and this complicates matters in regard to historical interpretation.

The case of Lachish, Judah's second-most-important city, is a good example of the chronological dilemma. After a long occupation gap beginning in the twelfth century B.C.E., a new unfortified town (Stratum V) was established during the tenth century (according to the conventional chronology) or the ninth century (according to the Low Chronology adopted by Ussishkin, the excavator). The first phase of a monumental palace located at the center of the mound was perhaps established at this time (as suggested by the British excavators and by Ussishkin during his excavations) or only in the later city (Stratum IV; as maintained by Ussishkin in the final publication). An accurate date for this building is important for historical reconstruction. If the palace were to be dated to the tenth century, it would accord well with the archaeological situation in Jerusalem as described above, and could serve as evidence for the emergence of Judah as a state in the tenth century. Yet, the answer is not definitive and we find ourselves in the same quandary of being subjected to preconceived historical paradigms when making a choice between the two alternative interpretations of the archaeological data.

Lachish is included in the list of Rehoboam's fortified cities (2 Chr 11:8). His fortification of Lachish may be identified with that of Stratum IV, which included a massive city wall and a six-chambered gate similar to the ones mentioned above. The problem is that the date of this biblical list is debated: several scholars claim that it was created in a much later period and should not be considered historical. Yet, this remains an unresolved question. Although the list is included in the less historically reliable book of Chronicles, this book may retain authentic traditions and citations from ancient documents.

In the northern Shephelah, along the Sorek Valley, the cities of Beth-shemesh and Timnah (Tel Batash) were built in the tenth century, perhaps within the framework of the emerging Israelite United Monarchy. Two short Hebrew inscriptions, one found at each of these sites in tenth-century contexts, preserve the name Ḥanan, which can be related to Elon Beth Ḥanan, a place-name mentioned in Solomon's second administrative district, right in this region (1 Kgs 4:9). This seems to be more than mere coincidence. Perhaps the family of Ḥanan settled this region, and the name was preserved in both inscriptions and in the biblical name. In this case, the tenth-century date of the inscriptions may support the authenticity of the biblical list of Solomon's districts.

THE NEGEV

The Negev highlands are a hilly region bounded by the oasis of Kadesh-barnea on the southwest. The region was not settled during the second millennium B.C.E., but, rather abruptly, about fifty massive, well-planned buildings (so-called fortresses) and about five-hundred scattered houses were constructed in this region during the tenth century B.C.E. They survived for only a short time and then were destroyed and abandoned. The well-planned fortified structures and four-room houses built according to a typical architectural plan and building technique, as well as about half of the pottery found in these sites, could not be of local nomadic origin, as suggested by a number of scholars. They must indicate influence from, and connections with, settled regions further north, be it the northern Negev, Judah, or the coastal plain. The more simple, scattered structures, as well as the other half of the pottery (rough and handmade "Negebite" pottery) can indeed be attributed to local pastoral, semi-nomadic populations. All this is probably evidence for a symbiosis between settlers who came from Judah or the southern coastal plain and local desert nomads. Various explanations have been offered for this phenomenon. In my view, it is the outgrowth of external influences, perhaps that of the emerging Israelite United Monarchy. The motivation was probably economic, perhaps related to the vast copper smelting industry that was established at the same time at Feinan east of the Arabah Valley (see below). In the middle of the Arabah Valley, opposite Feinan, the site of 'Ein Hazevah might have been a trading post situated along one of the routes of such a trade network.

The Sheshonq list (see above) includes dozens of place-names in the Negev. Some of these appear to be common Hebrew names such as *hgr abrm* (Hagar Abraham) and *hgr ard rbt* (Hagar Arad Rabat). Hagar could have been the Hebrew term for the large structures surrounded by belts of rooms, which are common in the Negev highlands. It is thus probable that Sheshonq destroyed this short and intensive settlement wave in the Negev highlands. This southern branch of his campaign was probably intended to put an end to the exceptional network of settlements and trade in the region, which perhaps was considered by the Egyptians as competing with or threatening their own economic interests. I reject Finkelstein's suggestion that these Negev highland sites were part of a "chiefdom" centered at Tel Masos in the Arad–Beer-sheba Valley. The main occupation phase at Tel Masos appears to precede those Negev highlands sites and Tel Masos lacks Negebite handmade pottery, which is a major hallmark of these sites.

An excellent example of misinterpretation of an archaeological discovery is the case of the identification of Ezion-geber with Tell el-Kheleifeh (between

Aqaba and Eilat). The Bible relates that Solomon carried out an active trade with Sheba and Ophir, apparently to be identified with southern Arabia and Somalia respectively (1 Kgs 9:26–28; 10:1–13). Ezion-geber, the port of call for this trade, was identified by Nelson Glueck in 1937 with Tell el-Kheleifeh, at the head of the Red Sea. He described a large building that he uncovered there as a smelting center for copper ores brought from the Timnaꜥ mines, about thirty kilometers to the north. Nelson Glueck's proposals became widely publicized due to his popular books and reputation. However, more intense research at Timnaꜥ and a reassessment of the finds many years later proved that the entire theory had no foundation. The Timnaꜥ mines were earlier than Solomon by some three-hundred years, and the Iron Age fortified settlement at Tell el-Kheleifeh was probably established long after Solomon's time (though this is not secure, since pottery recovered by Glueck in the earliest level there was neither published nor preserved).

DEMOGRAPHY

One of the arguments against the historical reality of the United Monarchy is the supposed low settlement density and lack of urbanization in the tenth century. Yet, studies of settlement density and ancient demography are strewn with methodological problems, as they rely on the interpretation of surface surveys. It is difficult to assess the results of such surveys at sites that were settled continuously for most of the Iron Age. The pottery collected would come from the last occupational phases of these sites, and only meticulous excavation could detail their full occupational history. Thus, the history and extent of such sites remain enigmatic, and calculations of population based on such studies are to be used with caution. A comparison of the settlement pattern in the Iron I to that of the eighth century B.C.E. points to a gradual increase in settlement over this time span of about five hundred years. An average estimation of approximately twenty thousand people in Judah during the tenth century appears to be realistic. If we add to this the unknown population numbers in the Israelite territories of northern Israel and parts of Transjordan, we may estimate the population in the Israelite territories at somewhere between fifty and seventy thousand people. Such a population may be considered sufficient as a demographic base for an Israelite state in the tenth century.

LITERACY

Another argument against the existence of the United Monarchy is the dearth of inscriptions dating to the tenth century B.C.E. This may mean a lack of literacy and thus the improbable existence of a central administration and, consequently, a state. However, the Northern Kingdom of Israel, the existence of which is undisputed in the ninth century B.C.E., certainly has not yielded a large number of ninth-century inscriptions either! It might be assumed that the dearth of inscriptions from both these centuries is due to the wide use of perishable materials like parchment or papyrus for writing. The few inscriptions incised on stones or pottery vessels for daily use from a tenth century context hint at the spread of literacy already in this time, and thus it can be assumed that some officials and professional scribes did exist in the tenth century.

ISRAEL'S NEIGHBORS IN THE TENTH CENTURY

In the biblical narrative relating to David and Solomon, Israel's neighbors play an important part. We read about the Philistines, the Ammonites, the Edomites, the Arameans and the city of Tyre. To what extent does archaeology throw light on these various geo-political units? The last three decades of archaeological research were revolutionary concerning some of them, while others remain largely unknown. The following is a short summary of the evidence and of several debated questions.

THE PHILISTINES

The Bible excludes Philistia from the territory of David's conquests, and this fits the archaeological situation in Philistia, where the independent cities continued to thrive. However, current research has indicated an interesting shift in the balance between the main Philistine cities. During the preceding Iron Age I, Ekron (Tel Miqne), located inland and close to the border of the Shephelah, was one of the largest Philistine cities, with an area of about twenty hectares. Gath (Tell eṣ-Ṣâfi) to the south of Ekron, was possibly also a very large city of about twenty to thirty hectares. Yet, during the tenth century, Ekron diminished to an area of only four hectares, while coastal Ashdod increased its settled area from about eight hectares to about forty hectares. Gath maintained its size. One possible explanation for the shifts is pressure from the east by the emerging kingdom of David and Solomon. This may have affected Ekron, which perhaps lost much of its hinterland south of the Sorek Valley, and many of its people had to move to Gath or Ashdod, perhaps contributing to the expansion of the latter.

EDOMITES, MOABITES, AMMONITES

Our information on the tenth-century states of Transjordan is limited. Recent research has brought new data and raised new questions concerning the emergence of Edom. Excavations conducted by Thomas Levy at Khirbet en-Naḥas, the main Iron Age site in the vast copper mines of Feinan, east of the Arabah Valley at the foot of the Edom mountains, have revealed intensive copper-ore mining and smelting industry. A large fortress, several massive structures, and huge piles of copper-production slags belong to several activity phases, dated by radiometric dates and various finds to a time span between the eleventh and the ninth centuries B.C.E. This well-organized and vast copper industry was certainly of immense economic importance and must have been maintained by a central authority. It also must have been related to an extensive trade system, in which the sites in the Negev highlands, the regions of Arad, Beer-sheba, and perhaps the coastal cities of Philistia and Phoenicia took part. Who were the operators of this large-scale production center? The early Edomites are the natural candidates. Yet, the traditional view, based on the finds in the Edomite highland sites, was that Edom did not emerge as a state before the eighth–seventh centuries. Excavations at Bosrah (Buseirah), the capital of Edom, located to the east of Feinan, revealed monumental architecture that is no earlier than the eighth to seventh centuries B.C.E. The new finds at Feinan call for a reassessment of the history of Edom. It might be, as Levy argues, that the Edomite state at least emerged during the tenth century B.C.E. The Feinan mines were perhaps operated by a central authority that must have been in nearby Edom; perhaps future excavations at Bosrah will reveal earlier occupation periods there. The subject is currently under debate, and specialists in Edomite archaeology like Piotr Bienkowski have rejected Levy's hypothesis. Yet, the new evidence appears to be strong and convincing. The Feinan copper mines must have been well known during the tenth century B.C.E., and this might be the background for the mentioning of Edom in the biblical narrative in relation to the United Monarchy.

We have already mentioned the possible emergence of Moab in the twelfth to eleventh centuries, yet no direct finds related to the tenth century are known in either Moab or Ammon. David's wars against the Ammonites thus cannot be corroborated. This may change in the future, if and when systematic excavations can be carried out on the mound of Rabbath Ammon (at the center of modern Amman) and related sites.

TYRE AND THE PHOENICIANS

The Bible often mentions relations between Hiram, king of Tyre, and Solomon. Tyre belongs to what was at the time an emerging new entity, which we call today (following the Greek term) "Phoenicia." Not much is known about the major Phoenician cities Tyre and Sidon as they have not sufficiently been undertaken, yet specific pottery styles can be related to the Phoenician cities of the tenth century B.C.E. Greek Euboean pottery found in probes conducted at Tyre indicates international trade relations in which Tyre was involved already during the tenth century B.C.E.

The sarcophagus of Ahiram, king of Byblos, preserves both a royal burial inscription, as well as a finely executed bas relief. It has been considered a hallmark of Phoenician art and evidence for the flourishing of Phoenicia during the tenth century B.C.E. A recent attempt by Benjamin Sass to lower the date of this monument to the ninth century is inspired by the Low Chronology and is highly questionable in my view.

Coastal sites in northern Israel, such as Dor and Achziv, have revealed several stages in the emergence of the Phoenician culture, from the end of the eleventh century B.C.E. onwards. Horvat Rosh Zayit in the western Galilee is of special interest. It seems to have been a trading post between Tyre and northern Israel during the late-tenth and early-ninth centuries B.C.E. Its location close to the modern village of Cabul led the excavator Zvi Gal to suggest its identification with biblical Cabul mentioned in the story about the land of Cabul that Solomon delivered to Tyre (1 Kgs 9:10–13). This story perhaps stems from the political and economic relations between Tyre and the Israelites at that time.

Phoenician pottery and other artifacts found at Israelite sites of the tenth century are evidence for trade relations between Tyre and Israel. Though most of these finds come from northern Israel, some evidence from Jerusalem and other southern sites indicates relations between Phoenicia and Judah already in the tenth century B.C.E., although admittedly these are indeed few and of small scale.

Arameans and Neo-Hittites

Due to the paucity of archaeological data from southern Syria, we lack direct archaeological evidence for the emergence of the Aramean states of Damascus and Aram-Zobah mentioned in the biblical narratives concerned with David's wars in Syria. It is highly questionable whether David indeed ever conducted wars in Syria and whether Toi, king of Hamath, was actually an historical figure and ally of David, as described in the biblical narrative. Yet, it is interesting to recall a rather recent archaeological discovery: the main temple of the storm god at Aleppo in northern Syria was recently excavated and found to contain monumental reliefs in Neo-Hittite style, dated tentatively to the eleventh century B.C.E., while the temple itself continued to be in use until the ninth century B.C.E. An inscription found in the temple identifies a king named Tauta whose kingdom encompassed a vast territory in northern Syria, including Hamath, where another inscription mentioning the same king was found. The name Tauta is of non-Semitic origin and might be echoed in the biblical name Toi, and thus this new discovery could shed light on the origin of the biblical traditions relating to Toi, king of Hamath. We cannot judge whether David's relations with Hamath actually occurred or not, but we can claim that the biblical story may have been based on the actual existence of a large tenth-century kingdom in northern Syria.

Archaeology has managed to shed some light on the small Aramean kingdom of Geshur mentioned several times in the biography of David. This kingdom existed to the northeast and east of the lake of Galilee, where two sites have been excavated, namely, Tel Hadar and Bethsaida. Tel Hadar was an administrative center with a large granary and a storehouse and has been dated by both conventional research as well as recently published radiometric dates to the eleventh or early-tenth century, the supposed time of David. Bethsaida, an eight-hectare city, was fortified during the tenth century B.C.E. by massive fortifications. Though Geshur was the smallest Aramean state, its fortifications and public structures are evidence for a strong central authority and economic power from the eleventh century B.C.E. down to the Assyrian conquest of the mid-eighth century. Here again, the archaeological evidence provides an early backdrop to the biblical narrative.

Conclusions

To be sure, much of the biblical narrative concerning David and Solomon can be read as mere fiction and embellishment written by later authors. The stories of David's conquests in Transjordan and Syria, Solomon's wisdom, the visit of the Queen of Sheba, the magnitude and opulence of Solomon's buildings, and so on, should not be read as historical accounts. Nonetheless, the total deconstruction of the United Monarchy as suggested by some current authors is, in my view, unacceptable

In evaluating the historicity of the United Monarchy, one should bear in mind that historical development is not linear, and history cannot be written on the basis of socio-economic or environmental-ecological determinism alone, as was common during the processual phase that dominated historical studies and archaeology in the 1970s and 1980s. The role of the individual personality in history should be taken into account, particularly when dealing with figures like David and Solomon. Such an approach has received renewed legitimacy in post-modernist thinking. It enables one to assume that leaders with exceptional charisma and personal ability could have created short-lived political entities or states with significant military power and territorial expansion. I would compare the potential achievements of David to those of an earlier hill country leader, namely, Labayu, the Amarna Age

Apiru leader from Shechem who managed during the fourteenth century to rule a vast territory of the central hill country, and threatened cities like Megiddo in the north and Gezer in the south. All this he achieved in spite of Egyptian domination of Canaan. David can be envisioned as a ruler similar to Labayu, except that he operated in a time free of intervention by the Egyptians or any other foreign power, and when the Canaanite cities were in decline. A talented, charismatic, and politically astute leader in control of a small yet effective military power could, in my view, have taken hold of a large part of a small country like the land of Israel and united diverse population groups under his leadership. These groups may have been descendants of the local Canaanite populations and/or tribal groups in the hill country and the Negev. The only powers that stood in David's way were the Philistine city-states, which, as both the Bible and archaeology inform us, were large, fortified, and independent urban centers during this time, and which indeed engaged David both militarily and politically.

While short-lived political and territorial achievements like those of David may be beyond the capability of the tools of archaeology to detect, the great changes that took place in the material culture during the tenth century may have been the result of these new ethnic, social, and political alliances and configurations. This new material culture is emblematic of the beginning of a new era that reached its zenith in the ninth and eighth centuries.

The United Monarchy can be described as a state in an early stage of development, far from the rich and widely expanding state portrayed in the biblical narrative. Its capital during the time of David can be compared to a medieval burg surrounded by a medium-sized town, yet it might well have been the center of a significant regional polity that included most of Cisjordan. Sheshonq's invasion of the Jerusalem area probably came as a reaction to the growing significance of this state, and his list of conquered towns and territories at Karnak may reflect the major territories ruled by David and Solomon. The identification of Solomon's buildings remains a debated issue, though the archaeological chronology that I utilize allows for the dating of the monumental structures to the tenth century. Therefore such buildings might have been Solomonic in origin.

The mention of *bytdwd*, or the "House of David," as the name of the Judean kingdom in the Aramaic stele from Tel Dan, possibly erected by King Hazael of Damascus, indicates that approximately a century and a half after his reign, David was still recognized throughout the region as the founder of the dynasty that ruled Judah. His role in Israelite ideology and historiography is evidenced by his impact on later Judean collective memory, and cannot be explained as merely an invention of later authors.

PART 5

ON MORE SECURE GROUND? THE KINGDOMS OF
ISRAEL AND JUDAH IN THE IRON II PERIOD

A Summary Assessment for Part 5

Brian B. Schmidt

Professor Finkelstein summarizes the lengthy time span that covers the late-tenth century to the late-eighth century B.C.E. in the Cisjordanian region in four episodes: the emergence of a settlement hierarchy first in the northern highlands; the eventual establishment of the Omride state there; the subsequent development of the southern highlands; and, finally, the sudden growth of Judah following the demise of the north. This is the period that has been viewed traditionally as the last remaining period of political viability for both the northern and southern hill country populations until their respective, and successive, devastations at the hands of the Assyrians (in the north) and then the Babylonians (in the south).

In the northern hill country, the majority of the 250 or so Iron I sites thus far identified continued to be populated throughout the Iron II period. The one exception is the area immediately north of Jerusalem. Finkelstein identified this area as the one that the Egyptian pharaoh Sheshonq also campaigned against in the mid- to late-tenth century B.C.E. The sites in his campaign list from Karnak coincide with the archaeological data pointing to the abandonment of sites in this area. For Finkelstein, this means that this area, which also coincides with the biblical traditions that describe the region surrounding Gibeon, must have posed a threat to Egypt. When these data are viewed together, Finkelstein argues that this can best be understood as the historical background for the biblical traditions' portrayal of the emerging polity of Saul—a chiefdom of sorts—centered at Gibeon. For Finkelstein, archaeology, an extrabiblical written source (Sheshonq's list), and the biblical traditions (for example, 2 Sam 2:9) all converge in support of this proposal. He then employs it as a means of explaining or providing background to several other biblical texts relating to Saul and his times. In the end, he concludes that the Egyptian campaign resulted in the sudden demise of this political entity, namely, the Saulide chiefdom, but that it was soon replaced by another emergent power based farther north in Samaria, that of the Omrides.

For Finkelstein, the northern hill country reached full statehood in the days of the Omride dynasty of the early-ninth century. This finds confirmation in the archaeological data (Samaria, Jezreel, Megiddo, Hazor), extra-biblical written sources (the inscriptions of Shalmaneser III, Mesha, and Hazael) and the biblical traditions. It was not an entirely unique development however, as many aspects of this developing polity had their parallels or aspirations anticipated in the fourteenth century B.C.E. Amarna-period flourishing of Shechem and its ruler, Labayu. Finkelstein also notes that pressures from the east—Assyria—and from the local region—Aram—were important factors in the burgeoning of the north and the emergence of the Omride state, but also that these factors also led to its eventual demise.

As the pressures from Aram increased in the latter part of the ninth century, the Omride dynasty lost power over the wider area, as did the Philistines farther south. As Omride and Philistine control of regions farther south eased, those regions were able to grow and develop. Finkelstein proposes that this background best explains the emergence of Judah as a state in the late-ninth century and continuing into the early-eighth century. By the late-eighth century, Jerusalem had grown to be the largest city in Judah and with the eventual destruction of the northern state by the Assyrians, Judah experienced a surge in growth, first as a result of being incorporated into the global Assyrian economy, and then as the outgrowth of the sudden appearance of at least two waves of refugees from Israel. Archaeological surveys suggest that the majority of those refugees apparently came from the southern portions of the Northern Kingdom, near where the memories and traditions of the older Saulide chiefdom that had concerned Pharaoh Sheshonq originated and, perhaps, still persisted. This would explain for Finkelstein two subsequent developments— the need for Judahite kings like Hezekiah to consolidate and centralize the Southern Kingdom against the backdrop of the sudden and sizeable appearance of a northern population in the south, and the preservation of northern traditions (for example, in the Deuteronomistic History), but also ultimately, the subversion of those traditions via what Finkelstein labels an *apologia* for the Davidides by its pro-southern writers. For Finkelstein, this *apologia* served to bolster what he referred to as earlier as the pan-Israelite ideology of the Southern Kingdom and the attempt to reconcile and unify north and south within Judah, with primacy, of course, given to the latter (rather than within, and to, the former northern territories).

Professor Mazar reviews the archaeological evidence that has been recovered over the past few decades and its increasing contribution to our understanding of the later stages of the Iron II period (930–586 B.C.E.), or what scholars often refer to as the period of the Divided Monarchy in the biblical narration based on the narration in the Bible of a split between the northern half of the country, Israel, and the south, Judah. He then turns his focus to three areas where major advances have been made in recent years; the emergence of Judah as a polity over against Israel, the impact of warfare on everyday life, and some rather new developments within Israelite religion. Mazar argues that Judah, like Israel, emerged as a state in the ninth century and not later, in the eighth, although Judah was undoubtedly poorer and smaller than its contemporary counterpart. By the eighth to seventh centuries, literacy was sufficiently developed to have resulted in the writing of various biblical and other literary texts. The technology of warfare led to the development of massive fortifications and sophisticated water supply systems, the latter being unique to the immediate area. Warfare also fortuitously preserved many artifacts, lifeways, and writings in its destruction layers, many of which we would otherwise be without. Mazar concludes his survey of Iron II society by noting the contribution of archaeology to modern understandings of Israel's religion, specifically its strong Canaanite or indigenous orientation (more so in the north than in the south), the prominence of the goddess Asherah, and the apparently late rise of monotheism. He also surveys some fragmented archaeological details of temple plans and various pieces of evidence for local cult practice such as figurines and standing stones.

THE TWO KINGDOMS: ISRAEL AND JUDAH

Israel Finkelstein

In this chapter, I wish to deal briefly with four episodes in the history of Israel. Though they cover different periods of time—from the tenth to the late-eighth centuries B.C.E.—and though they took place in different parts of the territories of Israel and Judah, they are all connected in a chain of events and are crucial for understanding the history of the kingdoms of Israel and Judah.

THE RISE OF THE FIRST ISRAELITE ENTITY IN THE NORTHERN HIGHLANDS

If there was no great United Monarchy in the days of David and Solomon, what was the first Israelite territorial entity? In contrast to previous periods, the settlement patterns in the highlands in the late-Iron I period (the late-eleventh and much of the tenth centuries B.C.E.) show a more-advanced settlement hierarchy and hint at a more-sophisticated economic production, which can be identified in the growing number of sites in the horticultural niches of the highlands. But even so, there is no direct proof in the archaeological record for the existence of an elaborate polity in the highlands.

Yet, one phenomenon stands out. One of the most obvious characteristics of the Iron I sites in the hill country is that most of them—over ninety percent of the approximately 250 that have been recorded—continued to be inhabited without interruption in the Iron II. An exception to this rule—a clear cluster of sites abandoned in the late-Iron I or very early-Iron II periods, that is, in the mid- to late-tenth century, is found in the area immediately north of Jerusalem and near Gibeon and Bethel.

The exact same niche to the north of Jerusalem is the only area in the highlands that is specifically mentioned in the list of settlements taken by Pharaoh Sheshonq I in his campaign to Palestine in the second half of the tenth century B.C.E.. In contrast to the concentration of sites in this area, other parts of the highlands are missing from this list. I refer to Jerusalem and the hill country to its south and, with one possible exception, northern Samaria—the most densely settled area in the hill country in the Iron I.

In the time of the New Kingdom in Egypt, pharaohs refrained from penetrating into the sparsely settled, wooded, rugged and hostile hill country of Canaan. The march of Sheshonq I in the second half of the tenth century B.C.E. against the peoples of this area is therefore an exception. Elsewhere, I have removed the possibility that the target of the campaign was Jerusalem. One needs to ask, therefore, what it was that attracted the attention of the Egyptian pharaoh to this relatively remote part of the highlands, an area that had no real geopolitical importance. The only reasonable answer is that the area around Gibeon was the hub of an emerging territorial-political entity strong enough to threaten Egyptian interests in the region.

The next question should be, do we have any clue in the literary sources for a late-Iron I territorial formation centered in the vicinity of Gibeon? The only possible clue is in the biblical account of the reign of King Saul and his dynasty. The Sheshonq I list and the biblical description of the Saulide chiefdom refer to the very same niche in the hill country and, no less important, both refer also—of all places—to the Jabbok River area in Transjordan. Sheshonq's list mentions a group of four towns located along the Jabbok River, an area that was never of great interest to other Egyptian pharaohs. The biblical description of the days of the Saulide dynasty specifically connects the Gibeon area with this same region. This can hardly be a coincidence. What we have here is a unique case in which archaeology, a highly important extrabiblical historical source, and the Bible both, "speak the same language." I should note that the conventional dating of Sheshonq I and the early-Israelite monarchs do not stand in the way of this proposal. Both are proximate enough to allow for some flexibility in the second half of the tenth century B.C.E. The biblical author might have placed the Shoshenq (his Shishak) campaign in the fifth year of Rehoboam for theological reasons, namely in order to demonstrate his cycles of sin and retribution: sinful monarchs are humiliated by military campaigns of foreign adversaries. As I will try to show later, the (oral) traditions of the Saulide state preserved in the book of Samuel could have been brought to Judah in the late-eighth century, after the fall of the Northern Kingdom, by refugees who originated from the highlands north of Jerusalem—the ancient hub of the Saulide chiefdom.

A memory about the extent of the Saulide polity in the highlands may have been preserved in 2 Sam 2:9, which states that Saul's son Ishbosheth was made king "over Gilead and the Ashurites and Jezreel and Ephraim and Benjamin and all Israel." This description has usually been taken as a genuine historical memory of the territory ruled by the Saulides, among other reasons because it does not use late-monarchic terminology and does not correspond to any later reality in the history of Israel. A Saulide rule over the entire northern highlands with an extension into the margins of the Jezreel Valley, may provide the reason for Sheshonq I's penetration into the hill country. It clarifies the otherwise difficult-to-explain memory in 1 Samuel, namely that Saul died in battle on Mt. Gilboa and that his corpse was displayed on the wall of Beth-shean, the ancient Egyptian stronghold in the valley. It also sheds light on the otherwise strange mention of the Philistines in the battle of Gilboa. No united Philistine army could march on Beth-shean in the late-Iron I. The Bible may retain an ancient memory of an Egyptian military presence with assistance from the forces of the Philistine city-states. Yet, by the time this material was put in writing, Egypt was long gone, leaving the Philistines as the only threatening reality.

The rise of a northern Israelite entity in the highlands and Shoshenq I's campaign should be seen as indicators of a significant social development in the history of ancient Israel. Yet, the early-Israelite entity immediately north of Jerusalem soon collapsed and the Egyptian presence did not last long. This opened the way for the rise of another Israelite entity, much more powerful and diverse. But this process took place in the hill country farther north of the Saulide region.

The Omride State of Northern Israel

The Northern Kingdom reached full-blown statehood in the days of the Omride dynasty in the early-ninth century. This is attested by both text and archaeology. Shalmaneser III, king of Assyria mentions "Ahab the Israelite" as his most powerful opponent in the battle of Qarqar in western Syria in 853 B.C.E. The ninth-century Mesha stele recounts how the Omrides had conquered territories in Moab, and the Tel Dan inscription, most probably written by Hazael, king of Damascus, states that before his time Israel took territories from Aram. Archaeologically, the skills and power of the Omrides are reflected in their great building operations. At Megiddo, the Omrides constructed two or three elaborate ashlar palaces. Samaria, Jezreel, and Hazor evince similar characteristics of monumental architecture with large-scale filling and leveling operations. The palace at Samaria is the largest and most elaborate Iron Age edifice known in the Levant.

Still, the rise of Israel in the north was not a total novelty. Indicators of continuity with second-millennium Canaan can be traced in almost every cultural trait of the Northern Kingdom. Most significantly, ninth-century Samaria fulfilled the fourteenth-century vision of Shechem, namely, of establishing a territorial state comprised of both highland and lowland areas. Nadav Na'aman and I have recently demonstrated the close geographical and historical similarities between the expansion attempts of Labayu, the ruler of Shechem in the Amarna period and those of the Omrides of the Northern Kingdom.

Northern Israel was a multi-faceted state and so it differed from a tribal or "nation"-state such as we find later in Judah. It was comprised of several different ecosystems and a heterogeneous population. Ample evidence—archaeological and historical—indicates that the hills of Samaria—the core territory of the state and the seat of the capital—was inhabited by the descendants of its second-millennium sedentary and pastoralist population. In the northern lowlands—the Jezreel and the Jordan Valleys—the rural population consisted of mainly local, indigenous elements, that is, rural Canaanites. Surveys and excavations alike attest to impressive settlement continuity in the northern valleys from the second millennium down to the eighth century B.C.E. Culturally, this continuity is exquisitely manifested in the famous cult stands from Taanach, in the architecture of the rural sites, and in the nature of central sites such as Megiddo, which continued to feature some older second-millennium Canaanite traits, at least in their layout.

The ethnic and cultural diversity of the Northern Kingdom, which also included Phoenician and Aramean elements in the northwest and northeast, may explain the monumentality of the Omride architecture, since state-establishing dynasties that engaged in territorial expansion into neighboring territories must seek legitimacy. In the case of the Omrides, this was especially important since, at the same time, a strong competing state was emerging in neighboring Damascus. Controlling the population of the "Canaanite" valley and the border areas in the north must have been the most important task on the agenda of the Israelite monarchs of the north. Indeed, the northern valleys became the backbone of the economy of northern Israel. Whoever controlled them could profit from their agricultural output, utilize their manpower for further military exploits, and control some of the most important trade routes in the Levant.

The construction of fortified compounds in the Jezreel Valley at Megiddo and Jezreel, on the border with Aram-Damascus at Hazor, on the border of Philistia at Gezer and, according to the Mesha stele (and seemingly also archaeology) in Moab (at Jahaz, probably Khirbet Medeineh eth-Themed), should therefore be seen in the light of two objectives. They were built as administrative or defense centers to control the "non-Israelite" population areas of the newly established state, and they served the propagandistic and legitimacy needs of a dynasty ruling from the highlands.

Yet, this was a relatively short episode in the history of the country. In the mid-ninth century, the political circumstances in the region changed dramatically. A short break in Assyrian pressure in the west and the growing prominence of Aram brought about the collapse of the Omride state. This, in turn opened the way for the rise of the first genuine "national states" farther to the south, first and foremost in Judah.

HAZAEL OF DAMASCUS AND THE RISE OF JUDAH

Judah was different than Israel, mainly in the sense that it was a true, demographically cohesive, nation-state. In the tenth and early-ninth centuries B.C.E., the southern hill country in general and Jerusalem in particular still featured what I would describe as an "Amarna-like" demographic and territorial-political reality: a relatively poor village, Jerusalem ruled over a very sparsely inhabited southern highland. The first signs of statehood in Judah—certainly relative to what we know about the Late Bronze–Iron I–early-Iron II continuum—appeared during the ninth century. Most of the evidence for this early stage—fragmentary as it may be—comes from the periphery of Judah, namely, the Shephelah in the west and the Beer-sheba Valley in the south.

In the Shephelah, two sites are of special importance, namely, Lachish and Beth-shemesh. Lachish was the "second city" of Judah, the most important administrative center in the lowlands. Excavations have shown that its fortifications and palace were first built in the ninth century. Recent excavations at Beth-shemesh have uncovered a system of massive fortifications and an elaborate water system. Their construction seems to be contemporary to the first phase of fortifications at Lachish. Two Judahite sites in the Beer-sheba Valley—Arad and Beer-sheba—were also fortified for the first time in the ninth century.

In Jerusalem too, the first signs of significant building activity seem to date to the ninth century B.C.E. Two sets of elaborate structures, known as the "Terraces" and the Stepped Stone Structure (fig. 6), were built on the eastern slope of the City of David, near the Gihon spring, in order to stabilize the slope and facilitate the construction of large buildings on the ridge. The latest sherds from the original phase of the Stepped Stone Structure—a sort of a mantle that wrapped around some of the old terraces—included early-Iron II red-slipped and burnished wares. This means that the structure was built during the ninth- or very early-eighth century B.C.E. It is the earliest elaborate Iron II building found so far in Jerusalem. The remains of monumental walls recently discovered by Eilat Mazar above the Stepped Stone Structure may also date to this period of time, though a later date is also possible.

What brought about the sudden rise of Judah in the ninth century? The process could have started in the early-ninth century, when Judah was under northern Israelite domination. The Omrides, who engaged in military expansion in the east and northeast, must also have dominated the marginal

Judahite polity to their south. In fact, 2 Kings, in what seems to be a reliable historical witness, and indirectly supported by the Tel Dan stele, reveals that the Omrides may have tried to take over Judah, perhaps even annexing it, by a royal, "diplomatic" marriage of the Israelite princess Athaliah and the Davidide king Jehoram. For a few decades in the first half of the ninth century, Israel managed to establish a great United Monarchy—an actual United Monarchy—which stretched from Dan in the north to Beer-sheba in the south. Yet, this United Monarchy was ruled from Samaria, not from Jerusalem.

All this changed with the fall of the Omrides under the pressure of Aram-Damascus in the 840s. Hazael, king of Aram, invaded the Northern Kingdom, took back territories in the northeast and the Gilead, destroyed many of the Israelite centers in the valley, and forced the northern kings into a limited territory in the highlands around Samaria. As a result, the Northern Kingdom's grip over Judah eased, and a coup in Jerusalem brought a supposed Davidide, Jehoash, back to power. No less important, other events took place at that time in the Shephelah. Hazael campaigned in the coastal plain, besieged Gath and conquered it. Recent excavations by Aren Maeir at Tell eṣ-Ṣâfi in the western Shephelah—the location of ancient Gath—revealed dramatic evidence for these events. In the ninth century, Gath was a huge city that stretched over an area of about forty hectares. A sophisticated siege system, which included a deep trench, was laid around it, probably by Hazael. Inside the city, excavations revealed that Gath was put to the torch and was completely destroyed. It never fully recovered from these events.

For a short time in the second half of the ninth century, a window of opportunity opened for Judah. In the north, Israel was severely weakened by the Aramean assaults, while in the west, Gath, the most powerful Philistine city, was destroyed by Hazael. Judah, taking advantage of this situation, expanded to the west and built the administrative centers of Lachish and Beth-shemesh. In the south then, the most significant change from the Amarna-like situation to a territorial state, took place in the second half of the ninth century B.C.E. in the wake of the temporary decline of the Northern Kingdom and the destruction of powerful Philistine Gath.

Judah's Great Leap Forward

The situation that I have just described, that is, the first signs of statehood in Judah, continued into the beginning of the eighth century B.C.E. Several decades later, the Southern Kingdom was utterly revolutionized.

In the late-eighth century, Jerusalem grew to be the largest city in the entire country. It was surrounded by a system of massive fortifications consisting of two walls on the eastern slope of the City of David and a seven-meter-thick wall on the Western Hill. Water was supplied by the Siloam tunnel, which led from the Gihon spring to a pool at the southern tip of the Tyropoeon Valley, which separated the ridge of the City of David from the Western Hill, a location that was more accessible for the many inhabitants of the new city quarters in the west (fig. 7). Elaborate, rock-cut tombs began to be hewn around the city, testifying to the existence of an affluent elite.

In the southern hill country, as well as in the plateau to the north of Jerusalem, the number of settlements and the total built-up area increased dramatically. Both grew considerably also in the Shephelah and the Beer-sheba Valley. In the late-eighth century, Judah reached its peak territorial expansion and its largest population ever. Well-planned countryside towns, such as Beer-sheba (Stratum II) and Tell Beit Mirsim (A), represent this emerging, highly-organized state.

The high level of organization of late-eighth century Judah is indicated by several other lines of data. Monumental inscriptions—in the Siloam tunnel and on the facades of the Siloam tombs—appear at this time, and the number of seals, seal impressions, and ostraca increase dramatically. Standardized weights also appear for the first time. The *lmlk* storage jars and seal impressions of officials found on some of the jars also attest to an advanced bureaucratic apparatus. Finally, this is the time when the economy of Judah grew considerably. For the first time, pottery was mass produced and Judah engaged in large-scale, state-controlled olive-oil production in the Shephelah.

In a very short period of time then, in the second half of the eighth century B.C.E., Judah developed into a highly bureaucratic state. Two momentous events seem to have stimulated these developments. The first is the incorporation of the kingdom into the Assyrian global economy, which must have started in the 730s, in the days of Tiglath-pileser III of Assyria and King Ahaz of Judah, and continued through the fall of the Northern Kingdom in 722–720 B.C.E. Starting in 732 B.C.E., Judah participated in the Assyrian-dominated Arabian trade. This was the main reason for the prosperity in the Beer-sheba Valley along the routes that led from Arabia via Edom to Mediterranean ports, which were turned into Assyrian emporia. Somewhat later, apparently after the destruction of Ashdod and the rise of Ekron in the days of Sargon II, Judahite olive oil must have been sold to Assyria and other clients possibly via the olive-oil production center at Ekron. Other equally important events took place alongside these developments after the fall of the Northern Kingdom.

The key phenomenon—which cannot be explained solely against the background of economic prosperity—was the sudden growth of the population of Jerusalem in particular, and of Judah in general. In only a few decades in the late-eighth century, Jerusalem grew in size from about five hectares to about sixty and in population from around one thousand inhabitants to over ten thousand. The population of the Judahite countryside also grew dramatically. The number of settlements in the hill country to the south of Jerusalem swelled from about thirty-five in the Iron IIA to 120 in the Iron IIB or the late-eighth century. In the Shephelah, the number increased from about twenty to 275. To estimate that the population of Judah doubled in a matter of only a few decades in the eighth century would be a modest—probably understated—evaluation.

This sudden increase in the population of Judah cannot be explained as a natural growth or as a result of a peaceful migration from neighboring areas. The only reasonable way to explain this unprecedented demographic development is to view it as the direct result of a flow of refugees from the north following the conquest of Israel by Assyria in 722. In Jerusalem and the southern hill country, such growth probably continued with a second wave of refugees who arrived after the devastation of the Judahite Shephelah and the Beer-sheba Valley by Sennacherib in 701 B.C.E.

All this means that "the great leap forward" in the demography of Judah took place in a very short period of time, between 732 (but mainly 722) and 700 B.C.E. (or a few years later). In two to three decades, Judah was totally revolutionized. It was transformed from an isolated, formative tribal state into a developed nation-state, fully incorporated into the Assyrian global economy. And no less important, the population dramatically changed from "purely" Judahite to a mix of Judahites and ex-Israelites. The proposal that as much as half of the Judahite population in the late-eighth to early-seventh centuries B.C.E. was of northern Israelite origin cannot be too far from reality.

A close look at the results of archaeological surveys in the highlands seems to indicate that many of the Israelites who moved to Judah came from the area between Shechem and Jerusalem. This is the region where one can detect a dramatic decline in the number of settlements and their overall built-up area in the transition from the eighth century to the Persian period or the fifth century B.C.E. Even if the long period between these two data lines saw several oscillations, it is clear that southern Samaria suffered a major demographic blow in the wake of the conquest of the Northern Kingdom by Assyria. Indeed, this is also indicated by the fragmentary clues to the locations in the territory of vanquished Israel where the Assyrians settled Mesopotamian deportees.

These clues seem to point specifically to the southern part of the Northern Kingdom and the vicinity of Bethel as the region from which the majority of northern refugees came to Judah. Many Israelites seem to have fled this area in fear of deportation, and foreign groups were settled in their stead. These people must have come to Judah with their own local traditions. Most significantly, the Bethel sanctuary must have played an important role in their cult practices. The memories and myths of the Saulide dynasty, which originated from this area, could have played an essential role in the northern refugees' understanding of their own history and identity.

In Judah, the new demographic situation must have presented a challenge to the leadership as the need became ever more urgent to unite the two segments of the society, Judahites and Israelites, into one entity. The main problems that needed to be addressed were probably the different—not to say alien and hostile—cults and royal traditions of the northerners who settled in Judah. Indeed, in the late-eighth century B.C.E., King Hezekiah and his Jerusalem elite focused the new nation exclusively on Jerusalem's Temple and the Davidic dynasty.

Hezekiah is remembered in the Bible as one of the most righteous kings, who carried out a sweeping religious reform in Judah. Scholars have debated the historicity of this reform, some accepting it as reliable and others raising doubts or rejecting it altogether on purely textual grounds. We have no direct information about the possible changes made to the Jerusalem Temple in this period, as it lies inaccessible to archaeologists beneath the Muslim shrines on the Temple Mount. Yet, there is evidence in some of the outlying centers of the kingdom that dramatic changes in the nature of public worship were underway by the end of the eighth century B.C.E. Excavations at three sites, Arad, Beer-sheba, and Lachish, seem to have unearthed evidence for eighth-century shrines, or cult places, that were abolished before the end of the century. It is no less important to note that none of the many seventh and early-sixth century B.C.E. sites excavated in Judah produced evidence for the existence of a sanctuary.

It seems plausible that in the late-eighth century, Judahite countryside sanctuaries were abolished probably as part of an effort to centralize the state cult in Jerusalem. Yet, this process should be seen as the outgrowth of socioeconomic and political, rather than strictly religious, motivations. Such were probably aimed at strengthening the unifying elements of the state—the central authority of the king and the elite in the capital—and at weakening the old, regional, clan-based leadership of the countryside. No less important, it was essential to deal with the northern cult traditions that the Israelite refugees brought to Judah. The most important of these traditions were those of the Bethel temple, situated as it was in the midst of their ancestral villages. It seems that Hezekiah's solution was a ban on all sanctuaries—both countryside shrines in Judah and the Bethel temple—the lone exception being the royal temple in Jerusalem.

Setting down the early history of the Davidic dynasty in writing was another tool in the "remaking" of Judah. Scholars have divided the story

(1 Sam 16 through 1 Kgs 2) into two main narratives: the History of David's Rise to Power and the Court or Succession History. Both contain information about the Saulides, the first northern dynasty, and neither is entirely complimentary of King David. They include subtle allegations against the founder of the Jerusalem dynasty for cooperating with the Philistines; for betraying his fellow Israelites; for being responsible for the death of the first king of Israel; for being liable in the death of other key figures related to Saul; and for being guilty of other murders and wrongdoing. Most of these accusations deal with themes related to the Saulides and the north.

Most scholars have dated these narratives to the tenth century B.C.E. or immediately thereafter and argued that they were put in writing in order to legitimize David and Solomon. These traditions were aimed at explaining how David came to power and why Solomon, who was not the first in line to the throne, succeeded him in Jerusalem. But why would the authors and later redactors leave the negative stories and accusations against King David in the text? Scholars suggested that much of the material was written as an *apologia*—to counter these allegations, to vindicate King David of any wrongdoing and to explain "what really happened" according to the point of view of his dynasty.

The idea of a tenth-century compilation derives from a broader perception that the reign of Solomon was a period of exceptional enlightenment during which great historical works had been written in Jerusalem. And this theory was based, in turn, on the biblical description of a great Solomonic empire—another case of circular reasoning. As I have already stressed more than once, archaeology has shown that full-blown statehood in Judah did not develop until the late-eighth century B.C.E. This included the appearance of elitist literacy and scribal activity. Over a century of archaeological excavations in Jerusalem and in almost every important mound in the countryside of Judah has failed to find any significant inscription before this time.

The *apologia* theory is also somewhat problematic as it fails to deal with a key question: Why should the author deal with these accusations at all? In a great Davidic-Solomonic empire, the author could simply have ignored these stories. The fundamental question in dating and understanding the story of the early Davidides should therefore be, what is the period that best fits the compilation of a saga that takes into account negative northern traditions about the founder of the Jerusalem dynasty? To state this differently, what is the most likely period in which an author, undoubtedly a Judahite, needed to counter these traditions with an *apologia* since he could not simply ignore or eliminate them?

On the one hand, the answer to this question must fit what we know about literacy in Judah, that is, it can hardly be anytime before the second half of the eighth century B.C.E. On the other hand, these biblical texts cannot be dated too late, because it is quite obvious that they went through a late-seventh century B.C.E. redaction by what scholars have identified as a deuteronomistic writer or school.

When we situate all these factors against the background of the broader historical situation, the most reasonable period is the late-eighth century B.C.E., after the fall of the Northern Kingdom. This is when the population of Judah swelled dramatically, including among its members a large number of Israelite refugees. Parallel to the centralization of the Judahite cult in Jerusalem, the Judahite royal family and its entourage must have engaged in a program of strengthening the power of the dynasty by uniting southerners and northerners around the Davidic king. To that end, they needed to bridge the two narratives regarding the early days of the dynasty: the supportive southern traditions about David, its founder, and Solomon, the builder of their temple, as well as the disapproving northern traditions.

As I have already indicated, many of the northerners who lived in Judah must have come from southern Samaria. This was the area where the first northern chiefdom emerged and where the Saulide traditions were probably still influential. So, as Judah tried to accommodate its various social and political constituencies, an attempt was made to reconcile the two traditions. Instead of ignoring the northern accusations, the author(s) included them in the official history, but ultimately precedence was given to the southern traditions that vindicated David from almost all wrongdoings.

The great *apologia* served to reconcile southerners and northerners within Judah. As such, it served a new, powerful platform for the rise of the pan-Israelite ideology. This was the moment when the pan-Israelite concept first appeared, and behind it was the drive to unite "all Israel" within the borders of Judah (the ideology of "all Israel," including the territory of the former Northern Kingdom, appeared somewhat later in the deuteronomistic writings of the seventh century B.C.E.). This was also the point of departure for over three centuries of scribal activity resulting in the biblical history of Israel as we know it.

The Divided Monarchy: Comments on Some Archaeological Issues

Amihai Mazar

The divided monarchy, which parallels most of the Iron II period (see fig. 5), is known thanks to extensive archaeological research in Israel and Jordan. Surface surveys have facilitated the analysis of settlement patterns and located various kinds of sites like towns, farmsteads, citadels, watchtowers, and agricultural installations. Archaeological research in the arid zones of the Negev and Judean desert has facilitated the study of the precise settlement history of these marginal zones. A large number of excavations in various types of sites have yielded abundant data on many aspects of the material culture in Israel, Judah, and in the territories of their neighbors and opened new research subjects on many aspects of the material culture of the region. Settlement patterns, demography, town planning, fortification systems, architecture of public buildings and dwellings, water systems, building techniques, various aspects of the ancient economy involving both internal and international trade, agriculture and land use, terracing and irrigation systems, animal herding, and industries like weaving, oil production, pottery making and distribution, household equipment, and metallurgy comprise only a partial list of possible research subjects. Religious beliefs, official and popular religion, and cult practices can partially be reconstructed on the basis of temples, local cult places, and various works of art that preserve the symbolism and iconography of these ancient societies. Burial customs can inform us about supernatural beliefs and social structure. For the first time, significant numbers of inscriptions, including inscribed seals and seal impressions, ostraca, and inscriptions on stone, wall plaster, and pottery vessels have become available, and are a gold mine of information on the language, private names, administration, economy, and religion of Israel and, in particular, of Judah during the eighth to seventh centuries B.C.E. In many cases, the finds can be related to biblical texts of all kinds—a large portion of which were probably written during this period.

These rich archaeological data provide a panoramic view of Israelite and Judean society and culture, as well as of their neighbors. In fact, the reconstruction of this society, its economic background, and geopolitical development currently present the major challenge to modern archaeological research relating to this period. Yet, in spite of the growing amount of data and general agreement among scholars concerning many issues, disagreement still remains concerning some major topics. While the last decades of research have solved some of the major debates of the past, several new questions have surfaced over the years. One example is the controversy between so-called maximalists and minimalists concerning the size of Jerusalem, which had been a hotly debated topic during the 1950s and 1960s. The excavations on the Western Hill of Jerusalem since 1968 have made it clear that Jerusalem indeed was a large city of some seventy hectares (175 acres), but this expansion did not occur before the eighth century B.C.E. Thus, both sides in this debate were partially correct. During the last fifteen years a new debate has emerged, this time concerning the status of Jerusalem in the tenth century B.C.E.

A second example is the old debate concerning the chronology of Judean sites in the eighth to seventh centuries B.C.E.: a central point in this debate was the destruction date of Lachish Stratum III. While Olga Tufnell, in the fiinal publication of the Lachish excavations, attributed this destruction to Sennacherib's invasion in 701 B.C.E., William F. Albright and his followers dated this destruction and other sites with similar pottery to an assumed first-wave Babylonian invasion in 597 B.C.E. This latter view was for many years influential for many archaeological studies of Judah. Yet the renewed excavations at Lachish by David Ussishkin, as well as by myself at Tel Batash (biblical Timnah), have convincingly confirmed Tufnell's view and thus corrected Albright and his followers' error in understanding the development of material culture in Judah. Nevertheless, new questions and debates have emerged, mainly concerning the status of Judah in the ninth and early-eighth centuries B.C.E. Thus, while much of our knowledge on the period has become a constant and is accepted by all, other important questions remain contentious.

It would be impossible to cover even a small part of these newly debated issues here. I thus confine myself to the emergence of Israel and Judah as independent states in the ninth century B.C.E., the status of Judah in the eighth and seventh centuries B.C.E., and examples of short-term events versus long-term processes in Israelite archaeology.

ISRAEL AND JUDAH IN THE NINTH CENTURY B.C.E.

More than three centuries separate the establishment of the kingdoms of Israel and Judah as separate political entities (traditionally dated to ca. 930

B.C.E. or somewhat later) and the destruction of Jerusalem by Nebuchadnez-zar in 586 B.C.E. As I pointed out in part 4, the very existence of the United Monarchy has been called into question recently; of course, if there was no United Monarchy, there was also no split of such a kingdom into two separate states. Rather, as Israel Finkelstein has proposed, both Israel and Judah could have emerged later and at different times. As explained in part 4, I still adhere to the concept of an Israelite United Monarchy in the tenth century and I retain the accuracy of the biblical narrative concerning the establishment of two Israelite kingdoms following the short period of the United Monarchy. To be sure, these two kingdoms had very different fates: the northern one passed through several dynastic changes and only survived about two hundred years until it was destroyed by the Assyrians in two blows—in the years 732 B.C.E. (i.e., the conquest of Galilee) and 722 B.C.E. (the destruction of the capital city, Samaria). Judah, on the other hand, lasted more than three-hundred years and was ruled during this entire period by a single dynasty, the House of David.

The geographical and environmental conditions of the two kingdoms dif-fered to a large extent. The kingdom of Israel included vast territories: the Samarian hills, parts of the coastal plain, the Jezreel Valley, the Jordan Valley, the Galilee, and, occasionally, some parts of Transjordan. Judah, on the other hand, was much smaller and limited to the harsh terrain of the Judean hills, the Shephelah, the northern Negev and the Judean desert. Thus, the economic resources of the two kingdoms were dissimilar; the northern kingdom had an abundance of fertile land and water sources, extensive control over the main roads of the country, including the international highway that connected Egypt with Syria and Mesopotamia, and direct access to the coast and to trade routes with Phoenicia, Syria, and Transjordan. Judah was more isolated. Its economic resources were limited and the capital city of Jerusalem was located on a hilly terrain far from the main roads, fertile lands, and resources of the region. The deserts on its east and south forced Judah either to protect itself from nomadic raiders or to maintain economic relations with them. On the west, the strong Philistine city-states, in particular Gath (until its destruction in the late-ninth century) and Ekron (mainly during in the seventh century B.C.E.), blocked access to the international trade route that ran along the coastal plain, as well as access to the Mediterranean Sea. In the east, the Trans-jordanian states of Ammon, Moab, and Edom, separated from Judah by the Judean desert, the Jordan Valley, the Dead Sea, and the Arabah, tended to be hostile and competitive.

THE NORTHERN KINGDOM OF ISRAEL

The status of the Northern Kingdom in the ninth to eighth centuries as a strong regional state is generally recognized by all scholars, since it is documented as such in various ninth-century B.C.E. written sources from the ancient Near East. The most telling of these is the description of King Ahab in Shalmaneser III's monolithic inscription from Kurkh as an important member of allied force that participated in the battle of Qarqar in central Syria in the year 853 B.C.E. At Qarqar, the allies tried to stop the Assyrian army in an early phase of Assyrian expansion to the west. Ahab is mentioned in this inscription as leading two thousand chariots and ten thousand infantry in the battle against Assyria. Though this number may be a propagandistic exaggeration, it still should be noted that Ahab is listed as having the largest number of chariots among the allies mentioned in this inscription. The conquests of Ahab in northern Moab, east of the Dead Sea, are recorded in the ninth-century commemorative stele of Mesha, king of Moab, discovered at Dibon. The inscription describes in detail the area north of the Arnon river, which had been under Israelite domination in earlier years, and commemorates the liberation of this region from Israelite control. Jehoram, the last king of the Omride dynasty, is most probably the king of Israel that is mentioned on the Tel Dan inscription. Jehu, the founder of the next dynasty in the north, is depicted and mentioned on the Black Obelisk of Shalmaneser III as having surrendered to the Assyrian king (ironically, he is mentioned as "Jehu, son of Omri"). Israel continued to flourish during the eighth century B.C.E., mainly during the time of Jeroboam II, until its abrupt and final conquest by the Assyrians.

The excavations at Samaria and Jezreel open a window to the realia behind the often colorful stories in the books of Kings related to both these places. They confirm that during the ninth century B.C.E., Ahab and perhaps other members of the Omride dynasty initiated large-scale, monumental architectural building projects that required significant amounts of material, a centralized administration and planning, and numerous skilled laborers and artisans. At both Samaria and Jezreel, large rectangular enclosures were constructed and surrounded by a double wall system with a spacious courtyard at its center. The royal enclosure at Jezreel was fortified also by an imposing rock-cut moat that isolated the enclosure from its surroundings. At Samaria, the remains of an elaborate royal palace were uncovered inside the well-planned and fortified royal enclosure. The use of ashlar masonry, carved stone capitals of the so-called Proto-Ionic style, and thick lime-covered floors in the courtyards are features of royal architecture that may have been inspired by Phoenician prototypes (though they are as yet hardly attested in Phoenicia proper due to the lack of excavations).

In addition to architecture, Phoenician (Tyrian) influence is manifested in the Northern Kingdom by various artifacts such as high-quality pottery, clay figurines and especially by the elaborately carved ivory furniture inlays that were recovered from Samaria. These were carved in typical Phoenician style and included Phoenician-Egyptian religious and mythological scenes, such as the figure of "a woman in the window," stylized plant motifs, and so on. Such examples of the close connections between northern Israel and Tyre, the most important Phoenician city of the time, can be linked to the biblical account of Ahab's marriage to Jezebel, the daughter of the king of Tyre. Thus, the archaeological evidence from Samaria and Jezreel clearly supports the status of northern Israel as a territorial state with royal palaces, an elite social class, a centralized administration, and significant economic and military power.

Excavations at a number of other major cities in the Northern Kingdom like Dan, Hazor, Kinneret, Megiddo, Yoqneʿam, Taanach, Beth-shean, Reḥov, Dothan, Tell el-Farʿah (Tirzah), Shechem, Dor, and Gezer as well as surface surveys in the Galilee and Samaria hills and excavations in village sites, farms and citadels, reveal a flourishing kingdom with a complex and dense hierarchical settlement system, immense population growth, expanding international trade relations, a flourishing artistic tradition and the increasing use of writing during the ninth and eighth centuries. My own work at Tel Reḥov, for example, has revealed a well-planned, densely built ten-hectare city, which, during the tenth and ninth centuries, was at the peak of its development as it conducted economic relations with Phoenicia, Cyprus, and Greece.

Judah

Unlike northern Israel, the time frame of, as well as the processes that led to, the emergence of Judah as a state remain controversial among scholars. According to the traditional view, and in line with the biblical narrative, Judah continued to develop during the tenth and ninth centuries from being part of the United Monarchy to an independent state alongside Israel, its northern partner. This reconstruction, however, has been criticized by some current scholars, in particular by Professor Finkelstein, who claims that Judah was of no importance until the eighth century B.C.E., and in fact, not until the fall of Samaria in 722 B.C.E., when many refugees from the north found their way to Jerusalem and the rest of Judah. According to this view, kings like Rehoboam, Asa, Jehoshaphat, and Uzziah were either mere literary figures or insignificant local rulers. The argumentation is based on an evaluation of the supposed minimal number of settlements and populations, the lack of significant architecture for the ninth century occupation strata in Judah, the supposed weakness of Jerusalem during that time, and the lack of inscriptions and elite objects.

In my opinion, this viewpoint is unjustified. First, it contradicts the reference to Judah as a state under dynastic rule in the Tel Dan inscription—the "House of David" (or *bytdwd*)—which was an ally of the Northern Kingdom in the war against Hazael, king of Damascus, around 830 B.C.E. This inscription alone is sufficient to conclude that Judah was an important power in the region already by the mid-ninth century. While one may claim that at this time, following the rule of Athaliah at Jerusalem, Judah was a vassal state of Israel, it still cannot be denied that it was a state. Perhaps the Omrides had good reason to seek control of this state. Second, the archaeology of Judah, based on extensive evidence from a good number of excavated sites in the Judean hills, the Shephelah, and the northern Negev, confirms, in my judgment, the existence of a Judean state in the ninth century. The evidence tells a story of gradual growth and development from the late-tenth century onwards.

At this point, the reader might ask, how does it happen that archaeologists arrive at such contradicting conclusions? The answer lies in part in the different archaeological chronologies used, as well as in the vastly different interpretations of the same archaeological data. In order to understand accurately the archaeology of Judah, one should use my Modified Conventional Chronology (see part 4), according to which the Iron IIA period lasted from about 980 to about 830 B.C.E. and to understand the peculiar conditions of cultural continuity in Judah for that time period. Unlike its northern sister, Judah did not suffer from any severe military attacks until Sennacherib's invasion in 701 B.C.E., and Jerusalem was not noticeably affected even by that invasion. The lack of destruction layers and the durability of massive stone buildings in the Judean hills and the Shephelah indicate that the same stone buildings were in use for a long period of time. There is also considerable longevity in the pottery production in Judah: the changes were gradual, covering a long period of time. This longevity of the material culture in Judah has blinded the eyes of archaeologists who wish to define in detail the development of Judean material culture in the ninth century as opposed to that of the previous or later centuries. It appears that cities and towns that were founded in the late-tenth or ninth centuries continued to survive in Judah with little change until the late-eighth century when Sennacherib destroyed many of them. This can be demonstrated in Jerusalem, Beth-shemesh, Lachish, Tell Beit Mirsim, and other sites where only few occupation strata are attributed to these centuries.

In Jerusalem, massive stone buildings were in continual use for a long time. The monumental building, perhaps a royal citadel, that was recently exposed in the City of David by Eilat Mazar and that was retained by a massive Stepped Stone Structure, continued to be in use throughout the period and passed through changes and additions of new walls, with fine dwellings constructed above the lower part of the stepped stone revetment. Occupation strata from the Iron IIA (tenth to ninth centuries B.C.E.) were found all over the City of David and they can be attributed to both (or either) the tenth and ninth centuries B.C.E. The most recent discoveries in the City of David (by Reich and Shukron) have revealed a fill of debris in an earlier rock-cut pool south of the Gihon spring. The fill contained, in addition to ninth-century B.C.E. pottery, thousands of fish bones, as well as over 130 seal impressions on clay bullae (sealings of containers and papyri). The seal impressions do not preserve any inscriptions as they probably preceded the invention of inscribed seals carrying the name of the owner, which would become common in Judah and Israel only from the eighth century B.C.E. onwards. Many of the decorative motifs on the Jerusalem seal impressions are Phoenician in style, indicating Phoenician influence on Judah during the ninth century B.C.E. Similar seals and seal impressions have been found in other sites in Israel, such as at Tel Reḥov, in tenth- and ninth-century levels. They indicate the existence of a central administration and organized commerce, as should be expected in an established state.

Beyond Jerusalem, various sites in Judah indicate the existence of a state in the ninth century B.C.E. The citadel of Arad in the northern Negev was established in Stratum XI on top of the ruins of the village of Stratum XII, which, as we saw in part 4, is anchored in the Solomonic era of the tenth century B.C.E. This early citadel can thus be dated to the ninth century B.C.E. and is followed by three additional strata of rebuilding and changes, culminating in a violent destruction of Stratum VIII, which, as agreed by all, should be dated to ca. 700 B.C.E. Arad thus provides a convenient starting point for the study of Judean pottery chronology. The pottery from the strata X–VIII at Arad is almost identical, illustrating the longevity in the pottery production in Judah. Based on the dating of Arad, and comparing its pottery assemblages to those from other sites, one can conclude (in contrast to Ussishkin's conclusions in the final report but in line with his previous view on this matter) that Lachish Stratum V was founded during the tenth century and continued to develop during the ninth century (Stratum IV). At this time, Lachish became second in importance to Jerusalem, with a royal citadel or palace at its center, and fortifications consisting of two city walls, which were entered through a well-fortified six-chambered gate.

Other sites in Judah were either excavated in the early years of archaeological research and are not sufficiently known, or have been excavated recently only on a small scale and the evidence is far from sufficient for full analysis. Yet, the existing evidence indicates that urbanism (including public architecture), fortifications, and water supply systems were well-known features in ninth-century Judahite towns like Beth-shemesh, Tell Beit Mirsim, and Beer-sheba, and this supports the existence of a state in Judah in the ninth century B.C.E.

One of the claims against the existence of a Judahite state in the ninth century has been the minimalistic calculation of the number of settlements and population in Judah during the tenth to ninth centuries. This calculation is based, however, on interpretations of surface surveys in areas that were settled continuously for most of the Iron Age. Such interpretations are strewn with methodological problems. During surface surveys of sites that were continuously settled during several centuries, it is often impossible to find sufficient evidence for the earlier occupation phases without systematic excavation. Indeed, there are various alternative evaluations of the number of sites and the population estimates for ninth-century Judah. A major study of the Judean hills by Avi Ofer indicates a slow and gradual growth of population from the eleventh to the eighth centuries B.C.E. Occasional excavations at other Judean sites, for example, the large site of Moza west of Jerusalem, have revealed a continuous occupation from the tenth or ninth century until the Babylonian destruction in the early-sixth century, and this is probably the case at other still-unexcavated sites as well.

In sum, an overall analysis of the finds negates the claim that Judah did not emerge as a state until the late-eighth century B.C.E. While Judah was not a wealthy state like its northern counterpart and its population density and urbanization were much less developed, the evidence does justify the existence of a state, one significant enough to be mentioned in Hazael's Tel Dan inscription. Thus, biblical references that portray Judah as a state in the ninth century should *not* be dismissed as unreliable.

THE STATUS OF JUDAH DURING THE
EIGHTH AND SEVENTH CENTURIES B.C.E.

Following the Assyrian conquest of northern Israel in 722 B.C.E. and the surrender of the Philistine city-states in approximately 714–712 B.C.E., Judah stood alone as the only independent state in the region. The adventurous rebellion initiated by Hezekiah against Sennacherib almost resulted in the destruction of the entire state. The Assyrian invasion of 701 B.C.E. desolated large parts of Judah, although Jerusalem itself remained unconquered. Soon after, during the later years of Hezekiah and his son Manasseh in the seventh century, Judah recovered, entered a golden age, and enjoyed growing prosperity during the first half of the seventh century, when Assyria ruled most of the ancient Near East. Although Judah remained an independent state, it held the status of vassal state under Assyria. Judah's prosperity continued long after the retreat of Assyria in about 630 B.C.E. under the kingship of Josiah. Only the expansion of the Babylonian Empire led by Nebuchadnezzar brought an end to this prosperity, culminating with the destruction of Jerusalem and Judah in 586 B.C.E.

During the eighth century B.C.E., Judah and Jerusalem developed considerably. Jerusalem grew in area and population, and towards the end of the eighth century it became a fortified city of seventy hectares. Add to this an area of neighborhoods outside the city walls of some ten to twenty hectares, and Jerusalem became at this time one of the largest cities in the entire Levant. It was the only major city in the region that was not conquered by the Assyrians, and its population, estimated at about ten to twelve thousand people, was almost equal to the entire population of the rest of Judah. Most of the other cities and towns in Judah were not more than three hectares in area, with the exception of Lachish, which encompassed eight hectares. This disparity in size and population between Jerusalem and the rest of Judah meant that Jerusalem was a virtual city-state where the majority of the state's population was concentrated (as in some modern urban societies). The biblical idiom "Jerusalem and Judah" (2 Kgs 21:12; Jer 52:3) illustrates this special status of Jerusalem over the rest of Judah.

The expansion of Jerusalem was directed towards the Western Hill, the ridge to the west of the Tyropoeon Valley where today the Jewish, Armenian, and Christian quarters of the Old City are located. When did this expansion occur? In 1972, Magen Broshi, followed by others (in particular Israel Finkelstein), suggested that the growth of Jerusalem resulted from the arrival in the city of many refugees from the Northern Kingdom following its fall in 722 B.C.E., namely during the time of Hezekiah. However, it is questionable that this is the only or even the main explanation for the expansion. The Western Hill must already have been in the process of being settled prior to the eighth century B.C.E., since the massive city wall that was built there and which is commonly attributed to Hezekiah, obliterated earlier buildings. These could have been constructed earlier than Hezekiah and 722 B.C.E., but the fact is that we lack the ability to date these earlier structures more precisely. It is reasonable to assume that a certain number of Israelite refugees settled in Jerusalem following 722 B.C.E., yet we have no way to evaluate their number and the assumption that they were a major power in the development of Jerusalem in the late-eighth century remains no more than an educated guess.

At Ramat Rahel (biblical Beth-hakerem?), on a ridge overlooking Jerusalem to its south, stood a military stronghold during the time of Hezekiah, as evidenced by a large number of royal seal impressions found there. During the seventh century, an elaborate palace was constructed at this site, overlooking Jerusalem and Bethlehem. Its plan and architectural decorations resembled (though on a smaller scale) those of the palace of Samaria that was destroyed several decades earlier. It appears that one of the kings of Judah (perhaps Manasseh?) tried to reconstruct the glamour of Samaria by building this palace.

Outside Jerusalem, new towns and farmsteads were established in the Judean hills around Jerusalem, in the northern Negev, and in the Judean desert, which was not settled before the seventh century. However, in the west, Judah lost important territory in the Shephelah as a result of punitive operations by the Assyrians following the 701 B.C.E. war. These lands were probably planted with olive groves, which supplied olives for the important Judean oil industry during the eighth century. Control of these Judean olive groves appears to have been transferred by the Assyrians to the Philistine city of Ekron, which flourished during the seventh century and inherited Judah's role as a major olive-oil producer. Judah perhaps found some economic compensation by developing trade with the south and east.

Fortresses and stations along the Negev roads leading to the Red Sea and Edom and along the Dead Sea are evidence for this activity, which perhaps related to the emerging incense trade that originated in Yemen and south Arabia. The fortresses of Hazevah (in the mid-Arabah Valley) and Kadesh-barnea (on the border between the Negev and the Sinai peninsula) probably played important roles in this trade, as they controlled the two main roads leading to the Red Sea. It appears that the use of camels for crossing desert routes became common during this period and facilitated such a long-distance trade. Two unique cult places, one near the entrance to the Hazevah fortress and the other at Horvat Qitmit (in the northern Negev southwest of Arad) were located along the eastern road, and both yielded rich assemblages of unusual clay cult objects, including molded human faces on pottery stands, various other stands that could be used for burning incense, and other artistic depictions in clay with various motifs. These outstanding cult places and works of art are foreign to Judah and may have been built and used by Edomites, thus marking the initial penetration of Edomites into the Arabah Valley and the northern Negev and their involvement in trade. Alternatively, these cult places may have been built by other local people, perhaps of nomadic origin, who were involved in the long-range trade.

The knowledge of writing spread during the eighth to seventh centuries, as evidenced by various inscriptions. The Siloam inscription in Jerusalem, the burial epitaphs in the village of Siloam, and a few fragments of other inscriptions found in Jerusalem are evidence for the existence of formal lapidary writing in the capital of Judah. Other inscriptions include literary texts and prayers written on plastered walls (at Kuntillet 'Ajrud and Tell Deir 'Alla, both outside Judah), blessings incised on silver amulets, short inscriptions incised on pottery vessels and rock-cut caves, collections of letters written in ink on potsherds (ostraca) from Lachish, Arad, and several additional sites, stone-inscribed seals and seal impressions on clay bullae, which sealed unpreserved papyrus documents, and even small fragments of inscribed papyri preserved in the dry Judean desert. All of these, however, are just the tip of the iceberg, as most writing was done on perishable materials, such as parchment and papyrus. This rich epigraphic material provides us with an incredible amount of information on many aspects of Judean life. It is but one facet of unusually vigorous intellectual activity in Judah, and in particular in Jerusalem, during the late-eighth century and lasting until the end of the Judean monarchy. It is in this period that large parts of the biblical texts were written, Judean monotheistic theology articulated, and religious laws consolidated among elite groups of priests and spiritual leaders concentrated around the temple of Jerusalem, as evidenced by much of the prophetic and historiographic texts in the Hebrew Bible.

Short-Term Events and Long-Term Processes in Israel and Judah

Two major types of evidence for investigation of the past are revealed by archaeological research, namely, those that relate to short-term events, and those that throw light on long-term developments within human societies. In biblical archaeology, the former type of evidence can often be related directly to biblical and extra-biblical narrative history, for example, royal building operations known from the scriptures, and military events known from biblical and extra-biblical texts. Military threats and attacks on the Israelite kingdoms and the response of those kingdoms to the threats are one example of short-term events. An example of long-term processes is the development of Israelite religion. Archaeological evidence pertaining to long-term processes enables us to reconstruct changes over time in many aspects of life, such as social and political systems, historical-geographical features like roads, administrative boundaries, economy and subsistence, arts and crafts, lifestyles, religion, faith, and ideology. Both the short-term events and the long-term processes stand as the foci of archaeological research relating to the Israelite monarchy and both can be closely related to biblical texts.

Short-Term Events: Archaeology of Warfare

Some of the major military events mentioned in the Bible in relation to the divided monarchy can be detected by archaeology with a great deal of certainty. A ninth-century example is the attacks by Hazael, king of Damascus, around 830 B.C.E. In the north, a severe destruction layer that put an end to the flourishing city of Reḥov in the Beth-shean Valley and an end to the royal enclosure at Jezreel may be related to this event. A conflagration that put an end to the greatness of the Philistine city of Gath (Tell eṣ-Ṣâfi) in the Shephelah fits the mention of the conquest of Gath by Hazael (2 Kgs 12:18). This is followed by all but the total disappearance of this city from later biblical references. The Tel Dan inscription mentions a battle against Jehoram, son of Ahab, king of Israel and Ahaziah, king of Judah (mentioned as *bytdwd*; though the kings' names were not well preserved and are largely reconstructed). In this case, as well as in Shalmaneser III's monolithic inscription describing Ahab's role in the battle of Qarqar, external inscriptions add new historical information that is unknown in, or differs from, the biblical narrative. They also add validity to the general historical framework of the ninth century as it is known to us from the biblical text, though at points these inscriptions may reveal the incompleteness of the biblical narrative and some distortions that occurred in the process of its transmission.

The local responses to the Assyrian threats have been detected by archaeological research. From the mid-ninth century onwards, the Israelites and their neighbors constructed massive fortification systems that were similar to those attested also in contemporary northern Syria. They include massive city walls with protruding towers, often with a second wall on the slope of the mound. Moats and earth or stone glacis were added in certain cases. City gates were massive and contained four or six guard chambers. An outer defense prevented direct approach to the gate structure. Such fortifications were intended to withstand the battering rams and other siege devices used by the Assyrian army.

The unique and sophisticated water systems found in Israelite cities were intended to provide water to the cities in time of siege. Such systems are unknown outside of Israel and their variety in Israelite cities reflects some degree of ingenuity, engineering skill, and the ability of the society and its leaders to carry out major public works. The best known is Hezekiah's tunnel in Jerusalem, with its 512-meter-long rock-cut tunnel designed to bring water from the Gihon spring to inside the city. Other systems led to the water table below the city (such as the Gibeon "pool" and the water system at Hazor) or to a spring or other water source (as at Megiddo, Beer-sheba, and the Gibeon tunnel).

The huge stable compounds at Megiddo, intended to hold military chariot horses, are another example of royal efforts of the state to sustain military power. Though some scholars would not agree with the identification of these structures as stables, several studies have shown that this identification is the most convincing one. About 450 horses could have been accommodated in these stables, which take up about forty percent of the area inside the forti-fied city of Megiddo. This underscores the high level of military organization and the priority given by the kingdom to maintain its military strength. The stables are dated by most scholars to the time of Ahab in the ninth century B.C.E., the same king whose chariots played such an important role in the battle of Qarqar mentioned above. The attribution of the stables to Jeroboam II in the eighth century as suggested by Finkelstein is less probable, though not impossible.

The Assyrian military attacks during the last third of the eighth cen-tury B.C.E. provide ample examples of the correlations between biblical texts, Assyrian written sources, and archaeology. Using a huge and well-organized military force equipped with sophisticated battering rams, the Assyrians managed to conquer, annex, or rule large parts of the ancient Near East. In 732 B.C.E., Tiglath-pileser III conquered the Galilee, and in 722 Samaria fell and the Northern Kingdom of Israel came to its end. Its population was slaughtered, or deported, or fled to Judah. A few years later, the Philistine cities of Ashdod, Ashkelon, Gaza, and Ekron surrendered to Assyria and in 701 B.C.E. Hezekiah, King of Judah, initiated a revolt against Assyria with the help of Egypt, the "broken reed" as denoted by Isaiah. Judah was attacked by Sennacherib, who conquered forty-six cities according to his inscriptions, including Lachish, the second-most-important city in the kingdom. Jerusa-lem alone was left unconquered.

Heavy destruction layers at many eighth-century sites caused by the conquests are evidence of the Assyrian success. The conquest of the Galilee and the Jezreel Valley in 732 B.C.E. by Tiglath-pileser III is attested by archae-ology in the form of destruction layers at all major excavated sites, including Dan, Hazor, Kinneret, Beth-shean, Tel Reḥov, Megiddo, Yoqneʿam, and Dor. The final conquest of the Northern Kingdom in 722 B.C.E. is attested at Samaria and Tirzah (Tell el-Farʿah), as well as at minor sites such as Khirbet el-Marjameh. Following the Assyrian conquest, many of these places were abandoned, in line with the biblical portrait and Assyrian records of mas-sacre and mass deportation of populations. I had the opportunity to excavate two such destruction layers. At Beth-shean, we uncovered an elaborate eighth-century dwelling that was burnt in 732 B.C.E. Many household pot-tery vessels and artifacts were found in the destruction layer and this was followed by the town's abandonment. In our excavations at Tel Reḥov, three miles to the south of Beth-shean, we detected a nine-meter-wide mudbrick city wall, which seems to have been constructed hastily during the eighth century. Perhaps it was intended to stand against the blows of the battering rams. We also discovered evidence of a massacre in the form of human skel-etons thrown in the destruction layer of two houses. At both of these sites, the Assyrian conquest was followed by a short period of squatter occupation which in turn was followed by abandonment or a long gap in occupation. At Tel Reḥov, graves that included Assyrian pottery may have belonged to Assyrian soldiers or officials who served at the local, yet still-unexcavated Assyrian fortress, like the ones discovered at Hazor and elsewhere.

Sennacherib's invasion of Judah in 701 B.C.E. is one of the best-documented events of the Iron Age. Biblical texts, Assyrian inscriptions, Assyrian monumental reliefs and archaeological evidence from Judah can be integrated into one comprehensive picture. In Judah, preparations for the Assyrian invasion included the fortification of Jerusalem and the hewing of Hezekiah's tunnel—both are mentioned in the biblical records. Jerusalem's seven-meter-wide and approximately three-kilometer-long stone city wall, parts of which were uncovered in the Jewish quarter of the Old City, was probably constructed by Hezekiah to defend the city against Sennacherib's battering rams. While constructing the wall, earlier buildings were dismantled, recalling Isaiah's words: "and you counted the houses of Jerusalem, and you broke down the houses to fortify the wall" (Isa 22:10).

The water projects of Hezekiah in Jerusalem are mentioned in several biblical texts: "The rest of the deeds of Hezekiah, and all his might, and how he made the pool and the conduit and brought water into the city, are they not written in the Book of the Chronicles of the Kings of Judah?" (2 Kgs 20:20); "You made a reservoir between the two walls for the water of the old pool" (Isa 22:10–11); "This same Hezekiah closed the upper outlet of the waters of Gihon and directed them down to the west side of the city of David" (2 Chr 32:30). Hezekiah's tunnel is indeed well known to us and the Siloam inscription found close to the end of the tunnel describes in a vivid, poetic Hebrew the moment when the two groups of workers who cut into the rock from both sides of the City of David met midway in the tunnel. Recently, two revisionist scholars attempted to date this inscription to the Hellenistic period, yet this is just one extreme example of absurd assumptions in historical studies of ancient Israel. Recent ^{14}C dating of the plaster on the tunnel's walls confirmed its date in the eighth century B.C.E., and the fact that it was cut by two groups of workers who met at a central point, just as described in the inscription, is confirmed by chisel marks on the walls of the tunnel. This tunnel is evidence of unusual ingenuity and engineering capability in eighth-century Jerusalem.

An important discovery related to the organization of Judah as it prepared for its revolt against Sennacherib are the thousands of jars of similar size (about forty-five liters in capacity), shape, and clay composition. Approximately one-tenth of these jars were stamped with a royal seal carrying the word *lmlk* "belonging to the king" and one of four place-names (Hebron,

Ziph, Sokoh, Mmsht). In fewer cases, one of the jar handles was stamped with the seal of an official, whose name along with his father's name are mentioned. About two thousand *lmlk* impressions are known today. They are found mainly in the "war zone," that is, in the areas of Jerusalem and the Shephelah where the battles against the Assyrians in 701 B.C.E. took place. The jars were probably utilized for storage and shipment of food supplies and indicate thorough preparations for the war by Hezekiah and his officials.

Sennacherib's invasion of Judah left behind a series of destroyed cities. Of these, the conquest of Lachish is best documented by biblical sources (2 Kgs 18:14, 17), Assyrian sources, and archaeological discoveries at Lachish itself. The Assyrian sources include detailed inscriptions as well as huge and detailed wall reliefs in the innermost room of Sennacherib's palace at Nineveh. The reliefs depict the city walls, siege ramparts, and various details of the Assyrian army, as well as the defeated Judeans who were executed or driven into exile with their families. The excavations at Lachish revealed the only known Assyrian siege rampart ever found, as well as remains of weapons and artifacts related to the war. The effort of the defenders can be surmised by their construction of an inner rampart, which they placed opposite the Assyrian one.

Virtually the only city in the ancient Near East that was saved from Assyrian conquest was Jerusalem. The Bible attributed this to a divine miracle (2 Kgs 19:35). In fact, the city was saved thanks to its tremendous fortifications and perhaps due to events in Assyria that forced Sennacherib to abandon his siege prematurely. The location of the Lachish siege relief in the most important room in Sennacherib's palace at Nineveh and its huge size perhaps points to the king's frustration over not being able to conquer Jerusalem. We might conjecture that the presentation of the conquest of Lachish in the heart of the Assyrian palace was a form of compensation for the Assyrian failure in Jerusalem and a propagandistic distortion, since Lachish was a small town when compared to other cities conquered by the Assyrians throughout the ancient Near East.

It would be interesting to imagine what would have happened had Sennacherib been successful in destroying Jerusalem. The eminent Israeli Assyriologist Hayim Tadmor proposed that the fate of Judah would probably be like that of the Northern Kingdom twenty years earlier: massacre and deportation would have brought an end to Judah as an independent state. In such an event, we may imagine that the incredible development and intellectual achievements of Judah in the seventh and early-sixth centuries would not have been realized. In such a case, perhaps the Bible would never have been written and Judaism would never have developed as it has, not to speak of Christianity and Islam!

The Babylonian conquests of Philistia and Judah between 605 and 586 B.C.E. were even more devastating than the Assyrian ones. Violent conflagrations have been identified at Ashkelon, Ekron, Timnah (Tel Batash), Jerusalem, Lachish, and the rest of Judah. In Jerusalem, one of the burnt houses on the eastern slopes of the City of David contained a collection of fifty-three seal impressions on clay bullae that sealed folded papyrus documents. As elsewhere in Judah, most of the names end with the suffix -*yahu*, and one is a person known from the book of Jeremiah, namely, Gemaryahu son of Shaphan, the scribe in the court of Jehoiakim, king of Judah (see Jer 36:10). In his office, Baruch son of Neryah, Jeremiah's assistant, read Jeremiah's prophecy against Jerusalem. Another bulla with the name of a person known from the book of Jeremiah was recently found above the foundations of the large building northwest of the Stepped Stone Structure in the City of David in Jerusalem. It mentions Jehochal, son of Shlamyahu (Jer 38:1), one of the four officials who charged Jeremiah with crimes, resulting in his imprisonment in a cistern full of clay during the days of Zedekiah shortly before the fall of Jerusalem. The Lachish letters, eighteen ostraca found in the city gate of Lachish, tell the story of the last days of Judah. In one famous line the writer records: "we are watching for the [fire] signals of Lachish . . . for we cannot see Azekah." This is considered by many to be a letter written during the last days before the fall of Lachish to the Babylonians and recalling Jer 34:7.

Following the Babylonian conquest, Jerusalem and most of the rest of Judah stood in ruins for several decades. Continuance of life during the Babylonian period can be attested only in the land of Benjamin north of Jerusalem. This is in accord with the biblical evidence related to Gedaliah son of Ahiqam and several references in the book of Jeremiah alluding to the continuance of the Judean population in this particular region.

LONG-TERM PROCESSES: THE CASE OF ISRAELITE RELIGION

This superficial survey indicates that the framework of the biblical narrative in regards to short-term historical events is fairly accurate and can either be corroborated by, or examined and corrected in light of, archaeological data. Yet, such short-term events and their archaeological record are just one aspect of the archaeological enterprise. Much of the research is dedicated to the reconstruction of long-term processes regarding various aspects of life. The social and economic aspects of ancient Israel and its neighbors during the Iron II period have become subjects of extensive research in recent years, resulting in a large number of studies referring to settlement history, agriculture, technology, urban planning and architecture, and many other aspects of life. Several recently published syntheses on some of these subjects (such as religion, social structure, and daily life in ancient Israel) are based on wide-scale, extensive field research, which has recovered much new data. In the present context it is impossible even to touch briefly on these issues. I will confine myself to just one aspect, namely, the religions of Israel and Judah. This subject has been discussed at length in several recent studies, among them the comprehensive books by Ziony Zevit, Rainer Albertz, and William G. Dever.

Each Iron Age territorial state had it own major god: Milkom in Ammon, Kemosh in Moab, Qaus in Edom, and Yahweh in Israel and Judah. Private names found on seals, seal impressions, and other written documents in Judah (mostly from the eighth century B.C.E. and later) include in many cases the theophoric ending -*yahu*, while in northern Israel the common ending is -*yo*. Both reflect belief in the god of Israel, Yahweh, the national god of both kingdoms. However, in northern Israel, where the older Canaanite legacy was stronger, we find also private names with Canaanite theophoric endings like Baal. Indeed, the population of the Northern Kingdom included many indigenous Canaanites, who inhabited the main northern valleys. In addition, Israel was heavily influenced by nearby Phoenicia.

An analysis of the biblical sources as well as the archaeological remains shows that Israelite religion passed through several stages of development. The worship of Yahweh alongside a consort named Asherah is known from the inscriptions at Kuntillet ʿAjrud, a fortified citadel-like structure in the eastern Sinai desert dated to about 800 B.C.E. This unusual and remote site, located on the main highway between Gaza and the Red Sea, seems to have been used as a roadside station, but was also a place of religious activity. It seems to have been utilized by people from both Israel and Judah, as can be detected by pottery types that represent both kingdoms. Ink inscriptions and paintings found on the white plaster of the walls, as well as on large pottery containers and a stone trough, contain dedications, prayers, and blessings. The most revealing is a dedication or prayer to Yahweh and "his Asherah." A similar combination of Yahweh and Asherah appears also on an inscription from a cave at Khirbet el-Kom (biblical Makedah?) in the Shephelah. This combination probably reflects a theology that is substantially different from the pure monotheistic religion as it is preserved for us in the Hebrew Bible. This evidence indicates a strong continuity with Canaanite religion, where El was the head of the pantheon and Asherah was his consort. While the worship of Asherah was condemned by the Jerusalem prophets, they probably represent the new theology that was emerging towards the end of the monarchy among the Jerusalem intellectual elite, while the popular religion embraced by the common folk was much more traditional, preserving indigenous ideas and beliefs rooted in Canaanite religion.

The stately citadel of Arad in the northern Negev guarded the desert border and the roads leading to Edom from the ninth century onwards. It contained the only Judean temple recovered so far. The temple comprised a broad hall with a niche, in which were two standing stones (*masseboth*), one larger than the other, with two incense altars at their front. In the court-yard in front of the hall there was a sacrificial altar. The two standing stones and related incense altars may signify the worship of Yahweh and his consort Asherah, as in the case of the inscriptions mentioned above. The excavator, Yohanan Aharoni, dated the temple at Arad to the tenth through seventh cen-turies and proposed that it was damaged during Hezekiah's religious reform and fell out of use during Josiah's religious reform in the late-seventh century. This was thought to be a prime example of archaeological fieldwork illus-trating famous biblical passages. But alas, a more recent analysis of the Arad stratigraphy and chronology has led Zeev Herzog to doubt these correlations; he now suggests that the temple existed prior to the time of Hezekiah and went out of use even before his time. This conclusion, which deconstructed Aharoni's biblical correlations, must be evaluated eventually against a detailed (yet unpublished) excavation report.

The only public, monumental temple excavated so far in northern Israel is the one discovered at Tel Dan. It was identified by its excavator, Avra-ham Biran, as the temple (or *byt bamot*) erected by Jeroboam I at the end of the tenth century B.C.E. and as one of two religious centers intended to counterbalance the Jerusalem temple (1 Kgs 12:28–31). Even if this precise foundation date of the temple at Tel Dan may be questioned, the existence of a major temple at Dan during the ninth and eighth centuries B.C.E. is beyond question. The temple enclosure features a podium built of ashlar stones that probably supported a shrine, which might have contained the "golden calf" mentioned in 1 Kgs 12:29. In a spacious courtyard at the front of the temple, there was a large sacrificial altar with four horns, the latter being an essential part of the altar in the Bible. Subsidiary rooms at the side of the enclosure were used for ritual and other cultic functions. A similar four-horned altar constructed of ashlar stones from Beer-sheba was in use sometime during the ninth and eighth centuries B.C.E. Later, perhaps during Hezekiah's time, it was dismantled and its stones used as building material. This indicates that similar ashlar altars were common to both Israel and Judah in the ninth and eighth centuries B.C.E. It is interesting to note that in both cases, the altars were constructed of well-cut stones, in contrast to the biblical law, which requires that an altar be built from unhewn stones.

The golden calves, which the Bible mentions as the main cult object at Dan and Bethel, can be compared to the cherubim in the Jerusalem Temple. They probably symbolized the pedestal of the unseen god of Israel, similar to Canaanite and Aramean depictions of the storm god standing on a bull. As noted in part 2, a young bull appears in a cultic site, the "Bull Site," of the twelfth century from northern Samaria. The tenth-century pottery altar (known as a "cult stand") from Taanach mentioned above shows a bull or a calf below a winged sun disk at the top of a four-tier depiction. At the lower tier there is a naked goddess. Some suggested that the scene shows a combination of the god of Israel (symbolized by the winged disk and the calf) and Asherah.

Evidence for local cult places and places of worship near city gates or in open areas inside the city has been found at several sites, such as Dan, Tel Reḥov, Megiddo, Samaria, and Lachish. The use of standing stones, or biblical *masseboth*, has been detected at several of these places, for example, the city gates of Dan and Bethsaida (a large Aramean [Geshurite?] city north of the Sea of Galilee). Like Asherah, the *masseboth* were opposed by the prophets as symbols of a foreign (Canaanite) cult; however their presence at these sites indicates that these standing stones were popular in both Israel and Judah.

Hundreds of clay figurines found in both Israel and Judah representing naked women are probably related to the popular cult of Asherah. In the Northern Kingdom, as well as in Philistia, the depictions are naturalistic, the sexual elements are emphasized and the artistic style is rooted in Canaanite art and probably inspired by contemporary Phoenician art. In Judah, the figurines that were popular during the eighth and seventh centuries were more stylized. While the molded head is naturalistic, the body is depicted as a schematic pillar, perhaps as the trunk of a tree, which symbolizes Asherah. It also has two hands usually supporting protruding breasts. Hundreds of fragments of such figurines were found in Jerusalem in houses dated from the eighth to early-sixth centuries B.C.E., indicating that while the prophets of Jerusalem preached against the worship of Asherah, her cult was popular in the city as well as elsewhere in Judah. Naked female figurines are also the main decorative motif on clay altars from the tenth to ninth centuries found at Tel Reḥov (fig. 9) and Pella. These altars often have four horns, like the similar stone altars found at several sites. Such altars were used for burning incense or for making small sacrifices in residential cult corners, and they should be seen as part of the popular religion of the time. In a few other cases, such altars were more elaborately decorated, like the two tenth-century pottery altars found at Taanach, which yielded rich iconography rooted in the Canaanite art.

This brief survey reveals that during most of the monarchic period, Israelite religion, though centered on the national god Yahweh, was based on Canaanite myths, beliefs, and cult practices, and a great goddess was worshipped alongside the main male god. A major change took place during the late-eighth and the seventh centuries B.C.E. in and around Jerusalem, with the

Fig. 9. Four-horned clay altar from Tel Reḥov (tenth
to ninth century). Photo courtesy of the Tel Reḥov
excavations.

centralization of cult at the temple of Jerusalem. The inscriptions and artifacts
related to cultic practices show that Israelite monotheism was a product of
a long and gradual process. Jerusalem during Josiah's reign is considered by
many as the time and place when Judahite religion consolidated and became
the foundation for further development into monotheistic Judaism as we
know it, a development that further crystallized during the exilic and post-
exilic periods.

Archaeology can supply only hints to the vigorous flourishing of religious, theological, and literary activities of the seventh century B.C.E. The
only biblical texts actually to have been found in excavations and that date to
this time are two copies of the priestly benediction (Num 6:24–25), one of the
most important Jewish prayers to this day. They were found by Gabriel Barkay
incised in miniature letters on small silver amulets, which were among the rich

finds in a burial cave in the Hinnom Valley of Jerusalem. These indicate that such texts were well known in Jerusalem towards the end of the monarchy. In addition, a Hebrew letter found at the coastal fort of Metsad Hashavyahu is based on first-hand knowledge of the social laws in Deut 24:12–13, which prohibits taking from the poor his last piece of clothing. Thus, the Torah laws were well known and utilized in practical life in the seventh century B.C.E.

Epilogue

I have limited myself in this brief survey to a few subjects, yet archaeology of the Iron II period has much more to offer relating to society, daily life, economy and technology, international relations, art, and many other issues relating to the kingdoms of Judah and Israel, as well as to their neighbors, the Philistines, Phoenicians, Arameans, Ammonites, Moabites, and Edomites. Much more has become known of the Assyrian and Babylonian presence in the country. The discoveries from recent years relating to these topics are manifold and sometimes breathtaking, like the seventh-century royal inscription found in the temple of Ekron (Tel Miqne), mentioning five generations of kings, as well as the name of the chief goddess of this late-Philistine city, (probably to be read as *Ptgyh*).

Part 6

So What? Implications for Scholars and Communities

A Short Summary: Bible and Archaeology

Israel Finkelstein

B iblical history and archaeology are two different disciplines. The Bible is not an historical record in the modern sense, but a sacred text that was written by authors who had strong theological and ideological convictions. Its "historical" parts" are wrapped in themes such as the relationship between the God of Israel and the People of Israel, the legitimacy of the Davidic dynasty, and the centralization of the cult in the Jerusalem Temple. Other topics that would have been of great interest to the modern historian are not dealt with at all. Moreover, since much of the text was set in writing at a relatively late date in the history of Israel—in the seventh through the fifth centuries B.C.E.—it does not provide us with a direct, real-time testimony to many of the events narrated in it, especially those describing the formative stages in the history of ancient Israel. Besides, even those ancient texts that recount events from a real-time perspective, such as the Assyrian records of the ninth through seventh centuries B.C.E., are not free of ideological inclinations. Therefore, one cannot judge the biblical text according to modern criteria for historical precision. In fact, every historical description is bound to be influenced by the realities of the time of its compilation. It is enough to remember how many contradictory interpretations we give to events that happen today in order to demonstrate how difficult it is to accept an ancient text as providing a full, reliable record of events.

Archaeology, on the other hand, provides us with an ostensibly "objective" testimony to what happened in the past. It unearths finds such as ceramic vessels, weapons, and ancient buildings that give us a real-time picture of the period under investigation. One can say that these finds were "eye witnesses" to what happened in the past. Beyond revealing the material culture of ancient peoples, archaeology can shed light on long-term social, economic, and demographic processes (as opposed to short-term events). Were we able to read and fully understand the complex story that archaeology offers us, we would obtain the ultimate tool for the study of the past. Yet, beyond the fact that archaeological interpretation too is not free from modern trends and biases, it would be fair to say that without the text, archaeology remains, in a way, mute. The sherds and walls can give us only a general knowledge about what happened in their time. Many essential questions remain open: Who won? Who showed bravery in battle? Who was a "believer" and who behaved as an "apostate?" Without texts, one cannot answer these quite specific and simple questions. Furthermore, being mute, archaeological finds can be interpreted in more than one way. Almost every find is subject to more than one historical reconstruction.

Therefore, in order to reach a reasonable reconstruction of the early history of Israel, one needs to make use of all three available sources, namely, the archaeological finds, the biblical text, and other ancient Near Eastern records. Admittedly, there is nothing new in this statement. This has been the goal of biblical archaeology from its early days in the 1920s. So what is new then in what I have attempted to set forth in these essays? If we look at ancient Israelite history from a general, systemic point of view, there are two important new elements.

First, traditional biblical archaeology has been dominated by the biblical story. In many cases, the written, modern histories of early Israel have simply repeated, but in modern terms, the biblical story. The text was put in the spotlight, while archaeology played only a minor role—as a decoration, or a tool for retrieving pieces of evidence that supported the generally accepted biblical narrative. It was not considered as an independent, powerful tool for historical research. One of the best examples of this approach is the interpretation that was given to the finds of Tell el-Kheleifeh at the head of the Gulf of Aqaba, where, as outlined previously, whole sets of strata and finds were actually invented in order to fit the biblical story.

The lesson is clear: archaeology must be studied independently of the biblical text. It should play the first violin in the orchestra constructing the daily realities of antiquity. Only then should one turn to the biblical sources in order to check whether the two types of evidence—the material culture and the text—accord with each other, and, if not, then to ask why, and search for the reasons: Why did the authors portray history in the way that they did? This applies first and foremost to the formative stages of the biblical history of Israel, where many centuries may separate the compilation of the text from the supposed events portrayed in them.

The second difference is more profound. Most scholars have studied early-Israelite history in a chronologically sequenced order, from early to late, and in line with the biblical text. Since the general chronological outline of the Israelite and Judahite monarchs are well known, scholars looked back and searched (and assumed that they had found) the period of the Judges in the eleventh to twelfth centuries B.C.E., the Conquest in the late-thirteenth century, the slavery in Egypt and the Exodus in the days of Ramesses II in the thirteenth century and, naturally, the period of the Patriarchs in the early-second millennium B.C.E. But this approach is extremely naïve; what should be done is the opposite. First one needs to establish a solid basis for one's research by identifying the period when the traditions were put down in writing. As I pointed out above, this opens the way to understanding the social, economic, and political realities of that time. This is also the point of departure—to verify if text and archaeology are harmonious, and, if not, to understand the meaning of the text from the point of view of the needs, ideology, and goals of the authors. This is what the great French historian of the Annales school Marc Bloch described many years ago as *histoire regressive*: starting from a secure point and then reconstructing history step by step further back and deeper into the past. In short, instead of looking at history from early to late, at least in our case, one should investigate it from late to early.

This means that the early chapters in Israelite history—the narratives of the Patriarchs, Exodus, Conquest, as well as the golden age of David and Solomon—cannot be understood as portraying straightforward historical realities. At the same time, it is inconceivable that the authors invented stories—that they made up history. The biblical history was written in order to serve an ideological platform, and as such, it must have been written in a way that would sound reliable to the reader and/or listener. It was probably based on a collection of tales, myths, traditions, and possibly shreds of ancient memories that were known to the people of Judah and Israel. Needless to say, the authors would have otherwise lost their credibility and failed to transmit their messages and achieve their goals. It follows that one cannot simply assume that Abraham, or Moses, never existed in the same way that one cannot contend that these are "flesh and blood" historical figures. The important point is to acknowledge that the stories as we read them today belong more to the world of the authors then to the world of the vague primeval history of Israel.

Moreover, much of the biblical description of early Israelite history was written in view of a certain ideology that prevailed in Judah or Yehud between the seventh and the fifth centuries B.C.E. The authors selected the materials and decided what was to go into the text and what should not according to their thinking. We are reading, then, a selective history. The Bible does not represent other groups in Judah, possibly even dominant majority groups, which in all likelihood had utterly different perspectives on the history of Israel. It certainly does not represent the world of the Northern Kingdom. One can only imagine how different the history of ancient Israel would have been had it been written by a northerner from Samaria or Bethel, or by a rival of the "Deuteronomistic camp" in Judah.

In addition, it is only logical to assume that many of the stories in the Bible—especially those that describe the "early" history of Israel—conceal many layers of tradition that gradually accumulated over centuries of oral transmission and then redaction until the text reached its final shape. Take the story of David and Solomon as an example. Archaeology can help us in identifying at least some of these layers: an early, possibly original layer of heroic stories about David and his mighty men, a group of Apiru who were active on the fringe of Judahite society; another layer within the same story, often providing a mirror picture of the same events, but told from the point of view of northerners, the supporters of Saul; another stratum that described David's conquests and court in terms of ninth-century B.C.E. realities; still another layer that served the needs of the Davidic kings in the late-eighth century B.C.E.; a horizon that may have portrayed the realities of the Assyrian century in the days of King Manasseh; and, lastly, a Josianic layer of the late-seventh century B.C.E. How else can one explain the contradictions in the text? How else can one explain the description of Solomon as a great, wise, and rich king and immediately thereafter his portrayal as an old, senile apostate?

In short, one cannot view the early history of Israel in black or white, as a yes or no scenario; such-and-such happened or it did not, so-and-so existed or he/she was a fiction. The picture is much more complex and in several cases can be summarized as follows: "such-and-such an event did not happen as described in the text, though the text may contain certain vague memories of the past and the reason for the text to be written in the way it was is . . . ."

As we have already seen, much of what has been outlined here is applicable even to chapters in the later history of Israel that took place closer to the time of authorship, and which are supported by extra-biblical sources contemporary to the events they record. Though the broader historical outlines in these cases are accurate, much of the content reflects the theology of the authors more than an exact chronicle of the events or their details. The treatment of the Northern Kingdom and the description of the Assyrian century in the history of Judah clearly illustrate this point. In the former case, the strong animosity the southern authors held for the north succeeded in concealing the economic and political greatness of Israel during the ninth and eighth centuries B.C.E. As I have indicated in the introductory chapter, in the case of the latter too, the theology of the authors did not comply with the more daily realities of the time. In both cases, the two sources—text and archaeology—view events from two utterly different perspectives: theology versus daily reality. Needless to say, both are legitimate, but a scholar needs to be conscious of on which side of the divide he or she operates.

PAST AND PRESENT

This is the point to ask, where do we, today's scholars who study the past, stand in relation to the ancient authors and their world? Since the Hebrew Bible is the founding document of Second Temple Judaism and through it, Christianity and the broader Judeo-Christian civilization—our civilization— we are all the beneficiaries, so to speak, of these highly sophisticated ancient authors. Regardless of whether we are believers or secular people, our education compels us to identify most immediately with the stories. We celebrate victories, mourn defeats and are angry at the people of Israel when they betray their covenant with the God of Israel. But can this be the point of departure for our work as scholars? Needless to say, the answer is negative. Scholars must draw a clear, solid line between these images and historical research. This implies that there is no reason, for instance, to accept the negative, venomous attitude of the southern authors toward the Northern Kingdom. For the individual who attempts to reconstruct Israel's history, cult transgressions and social misconducts as perceived by the seventh or fifth-century B.C.E. Jerusalem authors are only two pieces in a much larger mosaic of events and processes. Building activities, trade relations, and diplomatic maneuvers are no less interesting, and, frankly, no less important.

What I am trying to say is that faith and historical research should not be juxtaposed, harmonized, or compromised. When we sit to read the Hagadah at Passover, we do not deal with the question of whether or not archaeology supports the story of the Exodus. Rather, we praise the beauty of the story and its national and universal values. Liberation from slavery *as a concept* is at stake, not the location of Pithom. In fact, attempts to rationalize stories like this, as many scholars have tried to do in order to "save" the Bible's historicity, are not only sheer folly, but in themselves an act of infidelity. According to the Bible, the God of Israel stood behind Moses and there is no need to presume the actual occurrence of a high or low tide in this or that lake in order to make His acts faith-worthy.

Some people tell me that all this is fine, but poses a severe danger to the modern state of Israel, as if the fate of nations is decided only according to the depth of their roots in the ground. Is one to conclude that by eliminating fifty or one hundred years of historicity, a modern state can lose its historical legitimacy?

In the 1950s, biblical archaeology served as an important element in the development of the modern Israeli ethos. The Conquest of Canaan by Joshua and the Settlement of the Israelite tribes were conceived as old, heroic forerunners to the no-less-heroic modern return to Zion. And the Golden Age of David and Solomon was taken as a symbol of prosperity and greatness to be repeated in the here and now. All this cannot be evaluated against the background of our current times, but rather against the 1950s backdrop of the need to build a new nation and a new identity for people who came from all corners of the globe after centuries of repression. Now that Israeli society has matured and the state of Israel is a fact, is it really important to show that the walls of Jericho fell when the trumpets blew, or that King Solomon ruled from Jerusalem over a vast empire? And what if Solomon ruled from a small God-forsaken village in the southern highlands over an area equivalent in size to a small American city and its suburbs? Does this have any implication on my future as an Israeli? The answer is clearly a negative one. The strength of Israeli society is based, first and foremost, on its being an open, liberal, democratic society. There can be no doubt that an unfettered, dynamic research agenda in our own day is no less important than the glamor of the past.

As far as I can judge, it would be a fatal mistake to impose the new understanding of the past on the realities of the present and the hopes for the future. In any event, I should make it clear that there can be no doubt about the existence of the kingdoms of Israel and Judah in the Iron II period; there can be no doubt that Jerusalem was the capital of Judah, that the Temple of the God of Israel and the palace of the Davidic kings stood at Jerusalem's center; and that a significant part of the Hebrew Bible was put in writing there. That should be sufficient enough for one's sense of tradition and identity.

And there is much more than that. Biblical history—the great saga that forms the foundation of western civilization—emerged from a relatively small city with a relatively poor material culture and from a relatively small state that was located on the margin of the great civilizations of the ancient Near East. It emerged in a time of crisis and calamity. In a matter of a few decades Israel fell, Judah had become a vassal of Assyria and was transformed into a full-blown state, Sennacherib devastated its countryside, the Assyrians pulled out, Josiah, the king who is described as the most righteous in the lineage of David, was killed at Megiddo, Jerusalem fell to the Babylonians, and many Judahites were exiled, and some then came back. Just rehearsing this sequence of events should make it clear—or so I hope—that the "truth" of the biblical story is not necessarily in the parting of the Sea or in the trumpets of Jericho; not even in the splendor of Solomon. The truth and greatness in the biblical story lies in the realities, needs, motivations, difficulties, frustrations, hopes, and prayers of the people of Judah and Jerusalem in late-monarchic and early post-exilic times. It lies in the fact that in a short, stormy period of time, and out of a small, relatively isolated nation with a poor material culture, erupted an extraordinary creativity that produced the founding document of western civilization.

Concluding Summary: Archaeology's Message

Amihai Mazar

Archaeology, Historical Realities, and the General Public

In the beginning of the twentieth century, the radical biblical criticism of Julius Wellhausen and his students of the late-nineteenth century left a strong impression on European and Jewish intellectuals. In 1904, the famous Jewish publicist Asher Ginsburg, known as Achad Ha'am, published his essay "Moses." At this time, when archaeology was in its infancy, he wrote the following paragraph, which remains relevant to our subject even today:

> And so it is when learned scholars burrow in the dust of ancient books and manuscripts, in order to raise the great men of history from the grave in their true shapes; believing all the while that they are sacrificing their eyesight for the sake of "historical truth." It is borne in on me that these scholars have a tendency to overestimate the value of their discoveries, and will not appreciate the simple fact that not every archaeological truth is also an historical truth. Historical truth is that, and that alone, which reveals the forces that go to mould the social life of mankind. Every man who leaves a perceptible mark on that life, though he may be a purely imagery figure, is a real historical force; his existence is a historical truth . . . hence I do not grow enthusiastic when the drag-net of scholarship hauls up some new "truth" about a great man of the past; when it is proved by the most convincing evidence that some national hero . . . never existed . . . on such occasions I tell myself: all this is very fine and very good, and certainly this "truth" will erase or alter a paragraph of a chapter in the book of archaeology; but it will not make history erase the name of its hero. . . . because it's concern is only with the living hero whose image is graven in the hearts of men, who has become a force in human life. And what cares history whether this force was at one time a walking and talking biped, or whether it was never anything but a creature of the imagination . . . in either case, history is certain about his existence, because history feels his effect." (*Selected Essays by Ahad Ha'am* [Translated from the Hebrew by Leon Simon; Philadelphia: The Jewish Publication Society of America, 1912], 306–7.)

His basic idea was that the spirit and values embodied in the hero of the past is what matters rather than the question of whether or not he (or she) really existed. This line of thought still influences many even in the present day.

In 1999, Zeev Herzog from Tel Aviv University published in *Haaretz's* weekend magazine, an article whose title was rendered with huge letters on the front page: "Truth from the Holy Land: After 70 years of archaeological excavations in the Land of Israel it is clear that the biblical period did not exist." The title of the article itself was, "The Bible: No finds in the field," and the subtitles explain that "the Patriarchal stories, the Exodus, the Conquest, and the empires of David and Solomon are just folk stories. While scholars have known this for a long time, Israeli society prefers to repress it."

This article provoked quite a remarkable reaction in Israel. In one of the many letters to the editor, the great Israeli songwriter Naomi Shemer reacted in a fashion similar to that of Achad Ha'am ninety-five years earlier: it does not matter if the story really occurred or not, or if certain buildings that are mentioned in the Bible indeed existed or not; what matters is what these stories symbolize; their heritage persists even if they were not actual historical realities. Israel Levine and I edited, as a response to the article in *Haaretz*, a collection of essays on the subject that appeared in Hebrew. One of the papers, authored by Yair Zakovitz, a professor of biblical literature at the Hebrew University, was titled "Words, Stones, Memory and Identity." For him, the *words* of the Bible are those that shape our identity, not the stones. He goes on to conclude, "even if it will be proven that all that is written in the Bible is not historical, the foundation of my identity and my historical memory which is based on the Bible would not be shaken" (my translation). The Bible, in his words, "is the highest achievement of ancient Israel and of the Hebrew spirit and is the major factor in creating our [modern] identity and common memory. The Bible is the foundation stone of Jewish culture among all generations and so it will remain forever; its greatness cannot be measured by the scale of historical reliability."

In spite of being an archaeologist searching for the physical evidence of the past, I find myself in agreement with these words. The values, the theological ideas, and the intellectual messages of the Bible do not need archaeological confirmation. They stand on their own as some of the unique achievements of ancient Israel.

Archaeology's role is not to confirm the biblical narrative, but rather to attempt to determine the historical background to the formation of the stories in the Bible and whether those stories preserve valuable data on the ancient history of Israel—in other words, to determine their *Sitz im Leben*. Innovative current ideas like those of the extreme minimalists are increasingly being rejected as the archaeological exploration of the land of

Israel proceeds. Finkelstein and others suggest a more moderate approach, one that I would dub "reflective historiography," that is, the idea that many of the Bible's heroes are reflections of King Josiah and that their description in the biblical historiography was written with clear ideological motivation, intending to justify and glorify Josiah's political and ideological goals. This is an innovative, yet one-sided and narrow, view of the creative process of biblical historiography. In my view, it lacks sufficient proof and detaches the stories from their original settings. Israelite historiography appears rather to be the product of a much longer and more complex process of compilation, writing, editing, and copying of the biblical text that lasted for most of the eighth and seventh centuries B.C.E. In spite of the biblical authors' ideological and theological overcast, archaeology and ancient Near Eastern studies show that many of the stories are rooted in realities that precede the time of compilation by hundreds of years, some of them even rooted in the second and early-first millennia B.C.E. We can imagine the biblical authors as looking into the past through a telescope: the closer the authors were to the time of the events, the sharper the picture. The stories related to the emergence of Israel are at the far end of this view, but still they preserved ancient names, terms, geographical situations, and vague memories of certain events. Some of these events may be rooted in a time preceding the appearance of Israel on the stage of history. The conquest story of Hazor, for example, can be anchored in one of the most imposing events of the thirteenth century B.C.E., namely, the fall of the largest Canaanite city in the southern Levant. The memory of an event of such great historical significance could have been transmitted by the indigenous population for centuries until it was adopted into Israelite historiography much later. A story like the conquest of 'Ai can be explained as an old aetiology, itself rooted in an Iron Age I reality, preceding by centuries the time of writing. In such a way, archaeology can clarify the background to the formation of many stories in the books of Judges and Samuel, including those related to the United Monarchy. From the ninth century B.C.E. onward, biblical historiography can be corroborated or enriched by written sources outside the Bible as well as by archaeology. The biblical historical framework for this period appears to be more robust and dependable. Finally, when dealing with the late monarchy (late-seventh to early-sixth centuries B.C.E.), details of the biblical text can be corroborated as well by epigraphic finds; for example, the presence of names of certain people mentioned in the Bible on seals and seal impressions.

This does not mean that biblical stories are to be taken at face value as true history. Many of the stories must be explained as folk stories and traditions compiled, edited, and rewritten by later authors with exceptional literary talent and ideological and theological motivation. Yet, as archaeologists, we can dig into the remote inner layers of these stories, and uncover realities which the stories reflect. This can be done in many cases by linking the stories to archaeological evidence. At the same time, archaeology also has the ability to render improbable the historicity of some biblical stories, such as most of the conquest narrative. It is important to realize that historical memories may be long lasting, preserving echoes of past situations and events for many centuries through oral and written traditions.

Rather than "proving the Bible," current archaeological research in Israel is occupied mainly with increased understanding and reconstructing aspects of life in Israel and among its neighbors, including social structure, economy, technology, warfare, religious practices, and even cognitive issues. These are broad subjects for which we need to utilize the best research tools that archaeology has to offer, including the cooperation of a wide spectrum of sciences.

The current debate on the deconstruction of early Israelite history has generated great interest in the media, but the various views have left the public embarrassed and confused. Some have compared these views to a post-modern tendency in the historical research of Zionism in Israel by the so-called "New Historians" or "post-Zionist" historians who suggested alternative narratives for the history of Zionism, far removed from formal Zionist historiography. I am not convinced, however, that such parallels and designations are appropriate in this context and they should be avoided.

ARCHAEOLOGY AND ISRAELI SOCIETY

The evolution of Zionism during the first half of the twentieth century naturally created a need for national symbols that would relate the present to the past. Theodor Herzl called his novel, wherein he described the future Jewish state, *Altneuland* "old new land," a title that represents his basic idea of Zionism: the return of the scattered Jewish Diaspora to its old homeland. This idea has been a cornerstone in Zionist education ever since. In this framework, the "knowing of the Land," a free translation of the Hebrew term *yedi'ot ha'aretz* became an essential component of Zionist education, and archaeology was part of it.

This interest was stimulated by the activity of foreign and Jewish archaeologists. Although early on most of the archaeological exploration was carried out by European and American archaeologists, Jewish archaeological research began already at the turn of the twentieth century, and from 1925 Eleazar Sukenik was conducting archaeological research on behalf of the Hebrew University of Jerusalem, where in 1936 the Department of Archaeology was founded. The Israel Exploration Society has been active since the beginning of the twentieth century in research as well as in the popularization of the subject.

Archaeological activity developed immensely following the foundation of the State of Israel, and archaeology has held an important place in Israeli cultural and educational life. Sites like Masada and the Jewish catacombs at Beth-shearim became places of supreme national importance. It was a common saying in those days that archaeology in Israel was a national hobby. Many of the "founding fathers" of archaeology in Israel like, Benjamin Mazar, Yigael Yadin, Yohanan Aharoni, Avraham Biran, and others, were deeply motivated by Zionist education and indeed believed that in their work they revealed the ancient roots of the newly born nation-state in its homeland.

In fact, Yigael Yadin, the chief of staff of the Israel Defense Forces following the 1948 war of independence, studied with immense passon Jewish heroes like Joshua, conqueror of Hazor, the Zealots at Masada, the Essenes of Qumran, and Bar Kochba. Yadin knew how to publicize his discoveries in the media and in popular books, to the extent that they became part and parcel of Israeli culture, and well known worldwide.

Like every intellectual trend, earlier biblical archaeology must be understood against the background of the time and place. It is only natural that in those particular years and place, on the eve of, and just after, the foundation of the Jewish state, archaeology would play such a remarkable role in the enormous task of building Israeli identity.

Today, such tendencies have weakened to a large degree. Most current Israeli archaeologists consider themselves scholars, conducting research for its own sake (in university departments of archaeology), or in the service of public needs (in the framework of the Israel Antiquities Authority) without having any political or ideological agenda. Most of them are aware of the danger of mixing scholarship with modern ideologies and politics and the ideological use of archaeology is usually judged negatively. The interest of Israeli archaeologists lies in the entirety of the country's ancient history, from its most remote prehistory to the medieval period, and all its ancient cultures, ethnic groups, and religions receive serious professional attention. Scholarship, many claim, should be done for its own sake without any national or political motivation. This is correct and widely accepted by all scholars. Yet, let us recall that archaeological discoveries throughout the world are considered part of a nation's heritage and are therefore utilized in various forms of national education. The line between education of this sort and political or nationalistic exploitation of archaeology is at times gray. In Israel, we occasionally experience difficulties in restraining various ideologically motivated groups from adapting and exploiting archaeological discoveries in favor of their ideological agenda (on both the left and right of the ideological/political map). Yet, most professional archaeologists in Israel are well aware of this danger, and make every effort to avoid such uses of the past. They provide instead exegesis of the archaeological discoveries that is as objective as possible.

ARCHAEOLOGY'S HERITAGE AND ITS MESSAGES

What is the heritage or legacy that we archaeologists will leave behind for future generations? Clearly we seek to leave behind scholarly publications in the form of excavation reports and learned research books and papers; yet these mostly remain the domain of small scholarly circles. Popular writing, including summary presentations of our scholarly work, is important both for the general public and for scholars in related fields like biblical and religious studies, who do not have the expertise to fully assess the detailed archaeological studies. Popular or semi-popular books and magazines like *Near Eastern Archaeology* and *Biblical Archaeology Review* or the Hebrew-language *Qadmoniot* provide the broader public with the results of our research. The problem is that sometimes popular books and magazines, and, in particular, the general media, may distort or exaggerate archaeological findings and interpretations in the attempt to attract the public. Too often, the general media (and in particular TV programs) tends to emphasize the exceptional and the radical among new theories and views, and by doing so, it contributes to a distorted view of our profession on the part of the public. An example is the great publicity given to unacceptable views on chronology proposed by Emmanuel Velikowsky; or the attention paid to Emmanuel Anati and his impossible identification of Mount Sinai with Har Karkom, a mountain ridge in the southern Negev where he discovered evidence for ancient cult practices; but since his evidence comes from the fourth or third millennia B.C.E., it has nothing to do with Mount Sinai. The same is true of the often-rediscovered ark of Noah, or the holy ark of the covenant.

Archaeological research has an important message for Israelis—Jews and Arabs alike—and the general public outside Israel. The knowledge of the past and of our Jewish heritage is diminishing among wide circles of our community and it needs to be strengthened. The story that archaeology tells can be grasped visually and thereby more intimately through visits to sites and museums, participation in excavations, lectures, and responsible media programs. In such a way, archaeology can serve as an important educational tool providing a better understanding of the past.

Another important aspect of archaeology's educational role is the preservation and conservation of archaeological sites. Biblical sites in particular are in danger, since their proper conservation is difficult, if not often impossible, to maintain. In Israel, the sites of Tel Dan, Hazor, Megiddo, Beth-shean, Jerusalem, Tell Qasile, Lachish, Beer-sheba, and Arad have been well conserved, and some of them are now part of the national parks system of Israel. In 2006, UNESCO included three of these, Hazor, Megiddo, and Beer-sheba, in the World Heritage list, which gives them special status and worldwide publicity.

Biblical archaeology's heritage continues to be respected and studied. It has generated a considerable amount of interest among Jewish and Christian communities alike. The educational system in Israel includes selected chapters in archaeology as part of the study of the Bible or of the history of the land of Israel, though in my view these efforts are inadequate. All five universities in Israel teach archaeology either as a self-contained subject or as part of a broader program of Near Eastern and biblical studies. A good number of universities in America, Europe, and a few in the Far East (Japan and South Korea) provide programs in these fields, although in a wider variety of academic settings. In many theological seminaries and departments of religion or Jewish studies in the United States, biblical archaeology has become part of the standard curriculum, or part of a wider subject area referred to as "biblical backgrounds." Every year, hundreds of students and others participate in excavations in Israel and Jordan as volunteers, and many of these archaeological expeditions also conduct accredited educational programs or field schools. Thus, the message of biblical archaeology, complicated as it is, continues to be broadcast. It remains part and parcel of our Western education and heritage.

Glossary

Amarna-like society. A society in the highlands that resembles the one that had prevailed during the Amarna period (fourteenth century B.C.E.), involving a sparse sedentary population, a strong pastoral component, and groups of outlaws active on the margin of central authority.

Apiru. A term used in the second millennium B.C.E. to describe outlaws, uprooted people who were active in gangs on the margin of central authority, sometimes serving as mercenaries in the service of local petty rulers.

Collared-rim jar. The typical pithos (large storage jar) of the highlands of the Levant in the Iron I, having a collar-like ridge around its neck.

Four-room house. Typical house in the Levant in the Iron Age, having three longitudinal units (an open courtyard with two roofed aisles on its sides) and a broad room at the back.

Hoplite armor. Armor of heavy foot soldiers in the Greek world, starting in the seventh century and peaking in the fifth to fourth centuries B.C.E.

Low Chronology. A revised dating system for the Iron Age strata in the Levant, putting the Iron I/II transition in the late-tenth century B.C.E. (rather than ca. 1000 or 980 B.C.E. according to the biblically based, conventional dating system), and the end of the Iron IIA in the late-ninth century (rather than 925 B.C.E.).

Shasu. A term used in the second millennium B.C.E. to describe pastoral people similar to the bedouin of recent centuries.

Further Reading

There is an extensive body of literature on each of the topics discussed in these lectures. The following is just a small selection of books and articles.

General Reference Works: The Ancient Near East

Sasson, J. M., ed., *Civilizations of the Ancient Near East.* Volumes I–IV. New York: Scribners' Sons, 1995.

Meyers, E. M., ed., *The Oxford Encyclopedia of Archaeology in the Near East.* Oxford: Oxford University Press, 1997.

Freedman, D. N., ed., *The Anchor Bible Dictionary.* Volumes I–VI. New York: Doubleday, 1990.

General Introductions

General Introductions to Archaeology

Renfrew, C., and Bahn, P., *Archaeology, Theories, Methods and Practice.* London: Thames & Hudson, 1991.

Hodder, I., *Theory and Practice in Archaeology.* New York: Routledge, 1995.

Introductions to the Archaeology of the Land of Israel

Ben Tor, A., ed., *The Archaeology of Ancient Israel.* New Haven, Ct.: Yale University Press, 1992.

Levy, T. E., ed., *The Archaeology of Society in the Holy Land.* Leicester: Leicester University Press, 1995.

Mazar, A., *Archaeology of the Land of the Bible, 10000–586 BCE.* New York: Doubleday, 1990.

Sites

Stern, E., ed., *The New Encyclopedia of Archaeological Excavations in the Holy Land.* New York: Simon & Schuster, 1993.

History of Research

Silberman, N. A., *Digging for God and Country: Exploration, Archaeology, and the Secret Struggle for the Holy Land 1799–1917*. New York: Doubleday, 1990.

General books on the history and historical geography of Israel

Ultra-Conservative Approaches

Kitchen, K. A., *On the Reliability of the Old Testament*. Grand Rapids, Mich.: Eerdmans, 2003.

Hoffmeier, J. K., and Millard, A., eds., *The Future of Biblical Archaeology*. Grand Rapids, Mich.: Eerdmans, 2004.

Conservative Approaches

Aharoni, Y., *The Land of the Bible: A Historical Geography*. Trans. A. F. Rainey. 2nd ed. Philadelphia: Warminster, 1979.

Mazar, B., *The Early Biblical Period: Historical Studies*. Jerusalem: The Israel Exploration Society, 1986.

Mazar, B., ed., *The Patriarchs*. Volume II of *The World History of the Jewish People*. Jerusalem: Masada Press, 1971.

Mazar, B., ed., *The Judges*. Volume III of *The World History of the Jewish People*. Jerusalem: Masada Press, 1971.

Malamat, A., ed., *The Age of the Monarchies*. Volume IV of *The World History of the Jewish People*. Jerusalem: Masada Press, 1979.

Malamat, A., *History of Biblical Israel: Major Problems and Minor Issues*. Leiden: Brill, 2001.

Rainey, E. and Notley, R. S., *The Sacred Bridge: Carta's Atlas of the Biblical World*. Jerusalem: Carta, 2006.

Dever, W. G., *What Did the Biblical Writers Know and When Did They Know It?: What Archaeology and the Bible Can Tell Us about Ancient Israel*. Grand Rapids, Mich.: Eerdmans, 2001.

Shanks, H, ed., *Ancient Israel: From Abraham to the Roman Destruction of the Temple*. 2nd rev. ed. Washington: Biblical Archaeology Society, 1999.

Moderate-Critical Approaches

Ahlström, G., *The History of Ancient Palestine from the Palaeolithic Period to Alexander's Conquest*. Journal for the Study of the Old Testament. Supplement 146. Sheffield: JSOT Press, 1993.

Finkelstein, I., and Silberman, N. A., *The Bible Unearthed: Archaeology's New Vision of Ancient Israel and the Origin of Its Sacred Texts*. New York: Free Press, 2001.

Liverani, M., *Israel's History and the History of Israel*. London: Equinox, 2005.

Miller, J. M., and Hayes, J. H., *A History of Ancient Israel and Judah*. Second revised edition. Louisville, Ky.: Westminster John Knox, 2006.

Na'aman, N. *Ancient Israel's History and Historiography*. Winona Lake, Ind.: Eisenbrauns, 2006.

Revisionist Approaches

Davies, P. R., *In Search of "Ancient Israel."* Journal for the Study of the Old Testament. Supplement 148. Sheffield: JSOT Press, 1992.

Garbini, G., *Myth and History in the Bible*. Journal for the Study of the Old Testament. Supplement 362. London: Sheffield Academic, 2003.

Lemche, N. P., *The Israelites in History and Tradition*. Louisville, Ky.: Westminster John Knox Press, 1998.

Thompson, T. L., *The Bible in History: How Writers Create a Past*. London: J. Cape, 1999.

The Patriarchal, Exodus, Conquest, and Settlement Traditions

History and Archaeology

Mazar, A., "Remarks on Biblical Traditions and Archaeological Evidence Concerning Early Israel." Pages 85–98 in *Symbiosis, Symbolism and the Power of the Past: Canaan, ancient Israel, and their Neighbors from the Late Bronze Age through Roman Palaestina*. Edited by W. G. Dever and S. Gitin. Winona Lake, Ind.: Eisenbrauns, 2003.

The Patriarchs

Dever, W. G., and Clark, M. W., "The Patriarchal Traditions." Pages 70–148 in *A History of Ancient Israel and Judah*. Edited by J. M. Miller and J. H. Hayes. Louisville, Ky.: Westminster John Knox, 1977.

Thompson, T. L., *The Historicity of the Patriarchal Narratives*. Berlin: de Gruyter, 1975.

Van Seters, J., *Abraham in History and Tradition*. New Haven, Ct.: Yale University Press, 1975.

The Exodus

Frerichs, E. S., and Lesko, L. H., eds., *Exodus: The Egyptian Evidence*. Winona Lake, Ind.: Eisenbrauns, 1997.

Stiebing, W. H., *Out of the Desert?: Archaeology and the Exodus/Conquest Narratives*. Buffalo, N.Y.: Prometheus Books, 1989.

Hoffmeier, J. K., *Ancient Israel in Sinai: The Evidence for the Authenticity of the Wilderness Tradition*. Oxford: Oxford University Press, 2005.

Redford D. B., *Egypt, Canaan, and Israel in Ancient Times*. Princeton, N.J.: Princeton University Press, 1992.

The Conquest, the Settlement, and Israelite Origins

Alt, A., *Essays on Old Testament History and Religion.* Oxford: Blackwell, 1966.
Coote, F. M., and Whitelam, K. W., *The Emergence of Israel in Historical Perspective.* Social World of Biblical Antiquity 5. Sheffield: Almond, 1987.
Dever, W. G., *Who Were the Israelites and Where Did They Come From?* Grand Rapids, Mich.: Eerdmans, 2003.
Finkelstein, I., *The Archaeology of the Israelite Settlement.* Jerusalem: Israel Exploration Society, 1988.
Finkelstein, I., "The Great Transformations: The 'Conquest' of the Highlands Frontiers and the Rise of the Territorial States." Pages 349–67 in *The Archaeology of Society in the Holy Land.* Edited by T. E. Levy. Leicester: Leicester University Press, 1995.
Finkelstein, I., and Na'aman, N., eds., *From Nomadism to Monarchy: Archaeological and Historical Aspects of Early Israel.* Jerusalem: Yad Izhak Ben-Zvi, 1994.
Gottwald, N. K., *The Tribes of Yahweh: A Sociology of the Religion of Liberated Israel 1250–1050 B.C.E.* Maryknoll, N.Y.: Orbis, 1979.
Lemche, N. P. *Early Israel: Anthropological and Historical Studies on the Israelite Society before the Monarchy.* Trans. F. H. Cryer. Leiden: Brill, 1985.
Mendenhall, G. E., "The Hebrew Conquest of Palestine." *Biblical Archaeologist* 25 (1962): 66–87.
Oren, E. and Ahituv, S., eds., *The Origin of Early Israel: The Current Debate.* Beersheba: Ben-Gurion University of the Negev Press, 1998.
Stager, L. E., "The Archaeology of the Family in Ancient Israel." *Bulletin of the American Schools of Oriental Research* 260 (1985): 1–35.
Stager, L. E., "Forging an Identity." Pages 152–77 in *The Oxford History of the Biblical World.* Edited by Michael D. Coogan. Oxford: Oxford University Press, 1998.
Weippert, M., *The Settlement of the Israelite Tribes in Palestine,* London: SCM, 1971.

Archaeology of the Iron I Period: Beyond the Israelites

(See also the relevant chapters in the General Introduction to the Archaeology of the Land of Israel listed above.)

Bloch-Smith, E., and Alpert Nakhai, B., "A Landscape Comes to Life: The Iron I Period." *Near Eastern Archaeology* 62/2 (1999): 62–92.
Ward, W. A., and Joukowsky, M. S., eds., *The Crisis Years: The 12th Century B.C.* Dubuque, Iowa: Kendall/Hunt, 1992.
Gitin, S., Mazar, A., and Stern, E., eds., *Mediterranean Peoples in Transition: Thirteenth to Early Tenth Centuries BCE.* Jerusalem: Israel Exploration Society, 1998.
Killebrew, A. E., *Biblical Peoples and Ethnicity.* Atlanta, Ga.: Society of Biblical Literature, 2005.

The Philistines

Barako, T. J., "The Changing Perception of the Sea Peoples: Phenomenon: Invasion,

Migration or Cultural Diffusion?" Pages 163–71 in *Sea Routes . . . Interconnections in the Mediterranean, 16th–6th c. BC.* Edited by N. Chr. Stampolidis and V. Karageorghis. Athens: University of Crete and A. G. Leventis Foundation, 2003.

Dothan, T., *The Philistines and Their Material Culture.* New Haven, Ct.: Yale University Press, 1982.

Dothan, M., and Dothan, T., *Peoples of the Sea.* New York: Macmillan, 1992.

Dothan, T., "The Aegean and the Orient: Cultic Interactions." Pages 189–214 in *Symbiosis, Symbolism and the Power of the Past: Canaan, ancient Israel, and their Neighbors from the Late Bronze Age through Roman Palaestina.* Edited by W. G. Dever and S. Gitin. Winona Lake, Ind.: Eisenbrauns, 2003.

Mazar, A., "The Emergence of the Philistine Culture." *Israel Exploration Journal* 35 (1985): 95–107.

Oren, E., ed., *The Sea Peoples and Their World: A Reassessment.* Philadelphia: The University Museum, University of Pennsylvania, 2000.

Sanders, N. K., *The Sea Peoples,* London: Thames & Hudson, 1978.

Stager, L. E., "The Impact of the Sea Peoples (1185–1050 BCE)." Pages 332–48 in *The Archaeology of Society in the Holy Land.* Edited by T. E. Levy. Leicester: Leicester University Press, 1995.

Yasur-Landau, A., "The Many Faces of Colonization: 12th Century Aegean Settlements in Cyprus and the Levant." *Mediterranean Archaeology and Archaeometry* 3 (2003): 45–54.

TRANSJORDAN

Bienkowski, P., ed., *Early Edom and Moab: The Beginning of the Iron Age in Southern Jordan.* Sheffield: J. R. Collis and National Museums and Galleries on Merseyside, 1992.

Herr, L. G., "Tell al-ʿUmayri and the Reubenite Hypothesis." *Eretz Israel* 26 (1999): 64*–78*.

THE TENTH-CENTURY DEBATE:
DAVID, SOLOMON, THE UNITED MONARCHY

HISTORY AND ARCHAEOLOGY

(See also the relevant chapters in the General Introduction to the Archaeology of the Land of Israel listed above.)

Finkelstein, I., and Silberman, N. A., *David and Solomon: In Search of the Bibles Sacred Kings and the Roots of the Western Tradition.* New York: The Free Press, 2006.

Handy, L. K., ed. *The Age of Solomon.* Leiden: Brill, 1997.

Knauf, E. A., "King Solomon's Copper Supply." Pages 167–86 in *Phoenicia and the Bible.* Edited by E. Lipiński. Leuven: Peeters, 1991.

Na'aman, N., "Sources and Composition in the History of David." Pages 180–83 in *The Origins of the Ancient Israelite States*. Edited by V. Fritz and P. R. Davies. Journal for the Study of the Old Testament. Supplement 228. Sheffield: Sheffield Academic, 1996.

Stager, L. E., "The Patrimonial Kingdom of Solomon." Pages 63–74 in *Symbiosis, Symbolism, and the Power of the Past: Canaan, ancient Israel, and their Neighbors from the Late Bronze Age through Roman Palaestina*. Edited by W. G. Dever and S. Gitin. Winona Lake, Ind.: Eisenbrauns, 2003.

Yadin, Y., "Megiddo of the Kings of Israel." *Biblical Archaeologist* 33 (1970): 66–96.

THE CHRONOLOGICAL DEBATE:
THE TENTH CENTURY AND THE UNITED MONARCHY

Ben Tor, A., "Hazor and the Chronology of Northern Israel: A Reply to Israel Finkelstein." *Bulletin of the American Schools of Oriental Research* 317 (2000): 9–16.

Ben-Tor, A., and Ben-Ami, D., "Hazor and the Archaeology of the 10th Century B.C.E." *Israel Exploration Journal* 48 (1998): 1–37.

Fantalkin, A., and Finkelstein, I., "The Sheshonq I Campaign and the 8th Century Earthquake: More on the Archaeology and History of the South in the Iron I–Iron IIA." *Tel Aviv* 33 (2006): 18–42.

Finkelstein, I., "The Archaeology of the United Monarchy: An Alternative View." *Levant* 28 (1996): 177–88.

Finkelstein, I., "Hazor and the North in the Iron Age: A Low Chronology Perspective." *Bulletin of the American Schools of Oriental Research* 314 (1999): 55–70.

Gilboa, A., and Sharon, I., "An Archaeological Contribution to the Early Iron Age Chronological Debate: Alternative Chronologies for Phoenicia and Their Effects on the Levant, Cyprus and Greece." *Bulletin of the American Schools of Oriental Research* 332 (2003): 7–80.

Herzog, Z., and Singer-Avitz, L., "Redefining the Centre: The Emergence of State in Judah." *Tel Aviv* 31 (2004): 209–44.

Levy, T., and Higham, T., eds., *The Bible and Radiocarbon Dating: Archaeology, Text and Science*. London: Equinox, 2005.

Mazar. A., "Iron Age Chronology: A Reply to I. Finkelstein." *Levant* 29 (1997): 157–67.

Sharon, I., Gilboa, A., Jull, A. J. T., and Boaretto, E., "Report on the First Stage of the Iron Age Dating Project in Israel: Supporting the Low Chronology," *Radiocarbon* 49.1(2007): 1–46.

JERUSALEM

Vaughn, A. G., and Killebrew, A. E., eds., *Jerusalem in Bible and Archaeology*. Atlanta: Society of Biblical Literature, 2003.

Finkelstein, I., "The Rise of Jerusalem and Judah: The Missing Link." *Levant* 33 (2001): 105–15.

Mazar, A., "Jerusalem in the 10th Century BCE: The Glass Half Full." Pages 255–72 in *Ancient Israel and Its Near Eastern Context: Essays in Honor of Nadav*

Na'aman. Edited by Y. Amit, E. Ben-Zvi, I. Finkelstein, and O. Lipschits. Winona Lake, Ind.: Eisenbrauns, 2006.

THE NEGEV

Cohen R., and Cohen-Amin, R., *The Iron Age and the Persian Period.* Volume II of *Ancient Settlement of the Negev Highlands.* IAA Reports 20; Jerusalem: The Israel Antiquities Authority, 2004. (Hebrew with English summary.)

ISRAEL'S NEIGHBORS

Levy, T. E., et. al., "Reassessing the Chronology of Biblical Edom: New Excavations and ¹⁴C dates from Khirbet en-Nahas (Jordan)." *Antiquity* 78 (2004): 865–79.
Maeir, A. M., and Ehrlich, C. S., "Excavating Philistine Gath." *Biblical Archaeology Review* 27/6 (2001): 22–31.

NORTHERN ISRAEL AND JUDAH IN THE IRON AGE II

GENERAL SURVEYS OF THE IRON AGE II PERIOD

(See also the relevant chapters in the General Introduction to the Archaeology of the Land of Israel listed above.)

Dever, W. G., "Social Structure in Palestine in the Iron II Period on the Eve of Destruction." Pages 416–31 in *The Archaeology of Society in the Holy Land.* Edited by T. E. Levy. Leicester: Leicester University Press, 1995.
Herr, L. G., "Archaeological Sources for the History of Palestine in the Iron Age II Period: Emerging Nations." *Biblical Archaeologist* 60 (1997): 151–83.
Kenyon, K., *Royal Cities of the Old Testament.* New York: Schoken, 1971.
Isserlin. B. S. J., *The Israelites.* New York: Thames and Hudson, 1998.

ARCHITECTURE AND TOWN PLANNING

Kempinsky, A., and Reich, R., eds., *The Architecture of Ancient Israel.* Jerusalem: The Israel Exploration Society, 1992.
Herzog, Z., *Archaeology of the City.* Tel Aviv: Tel Aviv University, 1997.

DAILY LIFE

King, P. J., and Stager, L. E., *Life in Biblical Israel.* Louisville, Ky.: Westminster John Knox Press, 2001.

SOCIETY

Halpern, B., "Jerusalem and the Lineages in the Seventh Century BCE: Kinship and the Rise of Individual Moral Liability." Pages 11–107 in *Law and Ideology in Monarchic Israel*. Edited by B. Halpern and D. W. Hobson. Journal for the Study of the Old Testament. Supplement 124. Sheffield: Sheffield Academic, 1991.

McNutt, P., *Reconstructing the Society of Ancient Israel*. Louisville, Ky.: Westminster John Knox, 1999.

Faust, A., "The Rural Community in Ancient Israel During the Iron Age II." *Bulletin of the American Schools of Oriental Research* 317 (2000): 17–39.

RELIGION

Albertz, R., *A History of Israelite Religion in the Old Testament Period*. Louisville, Ky.: Westminster John Knox, 1994.

Miller, P. D., *Israelite Religion and Biblical Theology: Collected Essays*. Journal for the Study of the Old Testament. Supplement 267. Sheffield: Academic Press, 2000.

Smith, M. S., *The Early History of God: Yahweh and the Other Deities in Ancient Israel*. San Francisco: Harper & Row, 1990.

Zevit, Z., *The Religions of Ancient Israel: A Synthesis of Parallactic Approaches*. London: Continuum, 2001.

HISTORY OF THE BIBLICAL TEXT

Freedman, R. E., *Who Wrote the Bible?* San Francisco: HarperSanFrancisco, 1997.

Schniedewind, W., *How the Bible Became a Book: The Textualization of Ancient Israel*. Cambridge: Cambridge University Press, 2004.

Carr, D., *Writing on the Tablet of the Heart*. Oxford: Oxford University Press, 2004.

THE OMRIDE STATE

Biran, A. ,and Naveh, J., "The Tel Dan Inscription: A New Fragment." *Israel Exploration Journal* 45 (1985): 1–18.

Finkelstein, I., "State Formation in Israel and Judah: A Contrast in Context, A Contrast in Trajectory." *Near Eastern Archaeology* 62 (1999): 35–52.

Lemaire, A, "The Tel Dan Stela as a Piece of Royal Historiography." *Journal for the Study of the Old Testament* 81 (1998): 3–14.

Ussishkin, D., "Jezreel, Samaria and Megiddo; Royal Centres of Omri and Ahab." *Vetus Testamentum Supplements* 66 (1997): 351–64.

Williamson, H. G. M., "Tel Jezreel and the Dynasty of Omri." *Palestine Exploration Quarterly* 128 (1996): 41–51.

Judah in the Eighth–Seventh Centuries b.c.e.

Broshi, M., "The Expansion of Jerusalem in the Reigns of Hezekiah and Manasseh." *Israel Exploration Journal* 24 (1974): 21–26.

Finkelstein, I. and Silberman, N. A., "Temple and Dynasty: Hezekiah, the Remaking of Judah and the Rise of the Pan-Israelite Ideology." *Journal for the Study of the Old Testament* 30.3 (2006): 259–85.

Jamieson-Drake, D. W., *Scribes and Schools in Monarchic Judah: A Socio-Archaeological Approach.* Journal for the Study of the Old Testament. Supplement 109. Sheffield: Sheffield Academic, 1991.

Sennacherib's Invasion

Na'aman, N., "Hezekiah's Fortified Cities and the *LMLK* Stamps." *Bulletin of the American Schools of Oriental Research* 261 (1986): 5–21

Ussishkin, D., *The Conquest of Lachish By Sennacherib.* Tel Aviv: Tel Aviv University, 1982.

The Implications for Scholars and Communities

Shavit, Y., "Archaeology, Political Culture, and Culture in Israel." Pages 48–61 in *The Archaeology of Israel: Constructing the Past, Interpreting the Present.* Edited by N. A. Silberman and D. Small. Journal for the Study of the Old Testament. Supplement 237. Sheffield: Sheffield Academic, 1997.

Long, B. O., *Planting and Reaping Albright: Politics, Ideology, and Interpreting the Bible: Politics, Ideology, and Interpreting the Bible.* University Park, Pa.: Pennsylvania State University Press, 1997.

Popular papers on many issues discussed in these lectures can be found in the journals *Near Eastern Archaeology* (formerly the *Biblical Archaeologist*) and *Biblical Archaeology Review*.

INDEX

Index of Biblical Passages